Somebody to Love?

GRACE SLICK

Somebody to Love?

A
Rock-and-Roll
Memoir

with Andrea Cagan

WARNER BOOKS

A Time Warner Company

Warner Books, Inc., 1271 Avenue of the Americas, New York, NY 10020
Visit our Web site at http://warnerbooks.com

 A Time Warner Company

Printed in the United States of America
First Printing: September 1998
10 9 8 7 6 5 4 3 2 1

Library of Congress Cataloging-in-Publication Data

Slick, Grace.
    Somebody to love? : a rock-and-roll memoir / Grace Slick with
Andrea Cagan.
        p.   cm.
    ISBN 0-446-52302-X
    1. Slick, Grace.   2. Rock musicians—United States—Biography.
I. Cagan, Andrea.   II. Title.
ML420.S6625A3   1998
782.42166'092—dc21
    [B]   98-14758
                                                                   CIP
                                                                    MN

Copyright Acknowledgments

The author and publisher gratefully acknowledge permission to reprint the following material:

Lyrics from "Philadelphia Freedom," by Elton John and Bernie Taupin. Copyright © 1975 Big Pig Music Ltd. All Rights for U.S. administered by Warner/Chappell Music, Inc. Canadian Rights administered by Chappell Music Canada Ltd. All Rights Reserved. Used by Permission. Warner Bros. Publications U.S., Inc., Miami, FL 33014

Lyrics from "Somebody to Love," by Darby Slick. Copyright © Irving Music. Used by Permission.

Lyrics from "White Rabbit," by Grace Slick. Copyright © Irving Music. Used by Permission.

Lyrics from "Lather," by Grace Slick. Copyright © Icebag Corp. Used by Permission.

Lyrics from "Triad," by David Crosby. Copyright © Stay Straight. Used by Permission.

Lyrics from "Ride the Tiger," by Paul Kantner. Copyright © Ronin Music. Used by Permission.

Lyrics from "Comin' Back to Me," by Marty Balin. Copyright © Icebag Corp. Used by Permission.

Lyrics from "Third Week in the Chelsea," by Jorma Kaukonen. Copyright © Icebag Corp. Used by Permission.

Lyrics from "Starship," by Paul Kantner, Grace Slick, Marty Balin, and Gary Blackman. Copyright © God Tunes. Used by Permission.

Lyrics from "Manhole," by Grace Slick. Copyright © Mole Music. Used by Permission.

Lyrics from "Do It the Hard Way," by Grace Slick. Copyright © Ronin Music. Used by Permission.

Lyrics from "Hyperdrive," by Grace Slick. Copyright © Ronin Music. Used by Permission.

Lyrics from "Panda," by Grace Slick. Copyright © Helmets Without Heads. Used by Permission.

Book design by L&G McRee

Love to All

THANK YOU TO ALL WHO HELPED ME WITH THIS BOOK

Skip Johnson, my friend always

China Kantner, for being exactly who she is

Mom and Dad, for giving me so much more than existence

Chris Wing, for seeing with a child's eyes

Paul Kantner, for humor and invaluable help with my arbitrary memory

Andrea Cagan, for her friendship, her open heart, and her open mind

Brian Rohan, for introducing me to my agent

Maureen Regan, my agent, for talking me into doing this book and getting the "big bucks," respectively—and for her boundless energy in both personal and business situations

Rick Horgan, my editor, for his suggestions and for letting me play

The Great Society, Airplane, and Starship groups and all associates, for their talent and support

Sister Pat Monahan, for Bucky and for her ability to listen

Vincent Marino, for damn near unconditional love

Ron Neiman, for beautifying the outside and putting up with the inside of my head

Justin Davis, for his unique self and his photograph

And of course, to all the people who've followed our music through the years

AUTHOR'S NOTE

In writing this book, my cowriter, Andrea, and I *first* attempted to proceed by having her ask me questions, after which she'd go to her computer, armed with notes, and construct a scenario around a sentence or paragraph taken from our conversations. The results were sounding disjointed, so we tried a different tack.

The second, ultimately successful method involved Andrea's giving me a foundation for each chapter by providing a list of topics she'd heard me discuss, at which point I'd write down my recollection or interpretation of that aspect of my life. Andrea (being the pro) then organized my thoughts and my horrendous punctuation. I can construct an interesting scene and create plausible dialogue, but distinguishing between colons and semicolons has always struck me as something akin to gastrointestinal surgery.
Yup, these are my words, with the help of the runway, the mechanic, and the control tower.

By the way, several of the names in this story have been changed to protect the guilty.

PART

One

1

The Beautiful Blonde
from Bashful Bend

It's Chicago, 1973. Jefferson Airplane is tuning up and I'm standing onstage getting ready to sing. Some guy in the audience stands up and shouts, "Hey, Gracie—take off your chastity belt."

I look directly at him and say, "Hey—I don't even wear underpants." I pull my skirt up over my head for a beaver shot, and the audience explodes with laughter. I can hear the guys in the band behind me muttering, "Oh, Jesus."

My response to that particular heckle was actually pleasant compared to what I did in Germany, four or five years later, when I was so drunk, I went up to a guy sitting in the front row and picked his nose. It was the night before I left the band for the first time. To be more accurate, I fired myself. Fed up for a variety of reasons I'll discuss later, having ingested the entire contents of the minibar in my hotel room before I arrived at the venue for the show, I stuck my fingers in this guy's nostrils just because I thought they'd probably fit. Luckily, the majority of that particular German audience had never seen us before, so they must have figured we were some kind of punk band and just let it go.

Why did Grace Wing, a well-educated, contented girl who grew up in a *Leave It to Beaver* household, ultimately embrace such a maverick persona?

Well, sarcasm was always a family trait, but the *real* reason for my tendency toward raucous behavior can best be explained by a 1949 film that I watched when I was a young girl. I recently saw a rerun, and it was all right up there on the screen: a combination of humor and fantasy that was especially appealing to a young child looking for a Technicolor reality.

TV Guide listing in May 1997:

> *11:40 (DIS) movie, Beautiful Blonde from Bashful Bend—comedy (1949) 1:35 Betty Grable.*

Love the title.

When I was between the ages of five and nine, the soldiers of the Second World War wanted to *have* Betty Grable, but I wanted to *be* Betty Grable. She was the epitome of an alluring woman; she had it all as far as I was concerned.

My mother told me, "She's got caps on her teeth, bleached blonde hair, and no talent." Mom, being a natural blonde with a mouth full of perfectly straight teeth, was feeling some resentment. But Miss Grable could have been head-to-toe Styrofoam for all I cared. Whatever it was, it worked for me. When I saw that movie, I figured I had all the information I needed to ride through life like an armored blonde goddess.

The opening shot of *The Beautiful Blonde from Bashful Bend* takes place in 1895 in a small western town. Betty's in jail, still in the fabulous outfit she was wearing for her evening's saloon singing. She's only slightly put out by being in the slammer, and a friend tells her, "Don't worry, you'll be out in minutes. Nobody liked the guy you shot, anyway."

After a rousing evening of performing for assorted drunken cowboys in a saloon and shooting a rabble-rouser, she shows up for her trial the next morning, where she speaks out of order and then winds up shooting the judge in the ass.

A comedy.

The point is, what nine-year-old Grace saw was a woman who looked like a princess, behaving in a primarily offensive, often masculine way and producing slapstick results. No heavy feminist stuff, no serious reprimands. Just a series of entertaining events, showcasing the character's comedic qualities and instinct for following her whims.

In scene two, Betty's character, as a little girl, is being coached in sharpshooting by her grandfather.

"Can I go play with my dolls now?" she asks.

"Young lady, the frontier is a wild place," says her grandfather. "Nobody's gonna take care of you; you gotta take care of yourself—and nobody argues with a gun. You get good enough with that piece, you won't find no trouble you can't get out of."

Little Betty blows ten bottles off the wall from twenty paces, and says, "Can I go play with my dolls *now?*"

"Okay," says Gramps, mumbling under his breath, "Boy, she's an amazing shot."

In the following scenes, Betty's adult character continuously lets fly with sarcastic remarks, takes no guff from children and adults alike, and lets her various suitors know she's charmed by their attention but not available. A class A gunfighter, she hikes up her skirts and plows into the fray with John Wayne–style resolve. When she falls in love with Cesar Romero, *she* has to save *him*—both from winding up on the losing end of a gunfight and from his own confused thinking.

Significantly, she takes it all on with no whining or lobbying against sexist attitudes. She just tackles one problem at a time, always with a sense of humor, always self-possessed, always unruffled. At the end of the film, when she discovers that Romero has a woman on the side, she dumps him with a few well-chosen remarks and shoots the same judge in the ass again—this time hitting *both* cheeks.

"Feminist comedy," practically an oxymoron, had a couple of good years after WWII. Chalk it up to the forced female autonomy that occurred during wartime, when Rosie the Riveter went to work in the factories, constructing the Allies' war machines while taking charge of the finances, the home, and the children. Those movies gave little girls in the audience the green light for self-reliant, admittedly-leaning-toward-violent behavior. No preaching, no bra burning, just facing and enjoying the humor of life as it was, wherever you were, whatever was going on.

All those images on celluloid filled out a picture of how *I* wanted to be.

Even though the fifties seemed to regress into the pocket of a fluffy Doris Day apron, I clearly was influenced by the do-it-yourself heroines I'd watched as a child. They took it all on without viewing "it" as something that needed a great deal of support to handle. Consequently, in the early sixties, when women started telling me I should join "the Cause," that we should stand up for each other, march in D.C. and so forth, I thought that was about as interesting as joining the Daughters of the American Revolution. It seemed like a new slant on an old Tupperware party.

By the time I was old enough to consider how I wanted to live my life, I'd read about and heard of Golda Meir; Indira Gandhi; Babe Zaharias; Clare Boothe Luce; Eleanor Roosevelt; Marie Curie; Cassandra of Troy; Cleopatra; Elizabeth Taylor; Melina Mercouri; Anna Pavlova; Moira Shearer; Isadora Duncan; Maria Tallchief; Mary, Queen of Scots; Queen Isabella and Queen Victoria; Mary Shelley; Louisa May Alcott; Betsy Ross; Susan B. Anthony; Marian Anderson; Ella Fitzgerald; Carmen Miranda; Tokyo Rose; Sarah Bernhardt; Georgia O'Keeffe; Gertrude Stein; Annie Oakley; Amelia Earhart; Joan of Arc; Mother Teresa and Guru Ma; Julia Child; Pamela Harriman; Catherine the Great; Evita Perón; and Snow White.

The above-listed women collectively represented every attitude and occupation, so I figured my field of possibilities was wide open. I assumed that women who lived for the home front—housewives, homemakers, whatever the euphemism was—*chose* to do that; otherwise, they'd be doing something else. I couldn't imagine anybody doing something they didn't *want* to do.

Apart from rectal examinations and dental visits, why do something you don't like?

Financial circumstances might have demanded certain unpleasant activities, but if you did decide to specialize in the homemaking arts, I thought it should be because you were fulfilling a dream, not bowing to societal pressure.

At the time, that wasn't the accepted way of thinking, but since adults had made the Betty Grable films, I figured *some* people *somewhere* knew it was possible to experience life on a grand scale. They knew you didn't have to acquiesce, didn't have to be drab.

For years, I've followed the Grable credo: say what you mean, mean what you say, and throw a joke and a song in the mix now and then.

2

I Love L.A.

I"If I didn't get straight A's on my report card, my mother would beat on my rear end about twenty times with the wooden side of a hairbrush. We wore so many petticoats under our dresses in those days, the spankings didn't hurt as much as she thought they did. I'd try not to laugh out loud when she'd go at it so hard, all the hairpins would come flying out of her head in every direction, ruining that big doughnut-shaped hairdo that was stylish then. By the time she got through running after me, tripping on the hem of her long dress, and working on my butt, she looked like *she* was the one who'd been punished."

That wasn't me speaking; those were my mother's words. For my grandmother, societal pressure had been everything and my mother received the brunt of her Victorian propriety. When I was growing up, the pressure to conform wasn't exactly imposed; usually it was implied. But God only knows what kind of absolute discipline was acted out on my grandmother, because she never mentioned it. The stories she told me were usually wonderful lies about fantastic adventures she'd enjoyed as a young girl

I called my grandmother Lady Sue, not as a result of any nobility. It was just logic; I liked nicknames, she was a lady and her name was Sue. Lady Sue used to sit in a big chair by my bedroom window and sew costumes for me, because she knew my world was largely inhabited by colorful characters from the children's classics: Robin Hood, Alice in Wonderland, Snow White, Peter Pan, and certain cartoon heroes like Red Ryder, Prince Valiant, and Li'l Abner. I *became* those people, man or woman, it didn't matter. Put on the outfit and the twentieth century disappears. Go back in time, switch gender, change my accent, change my age—no problem.

I'd sit by my grandmother's side, both of us squeezed into the big chair. Her hands moving quickly with the needle and thread, she'd just start talking, never looking up from her work, and as she told each story, the costume for it was materializing.

Beautiful.

One day, when she was making a short skirt for me to wear to the ice skating rink, she began, "When I was about your age, I was asked to be the star of a number in the Ice Follies. You see, I could skate so fast, it was like watching a blurred image circling the rink. So, to make it even more spectacular, I attached tiny electric light bulbs to the top of the toes of my skates. What the audience saw was a fifty-mile-an-hour rainbow of colors streaking around the darkened arena."

Of course, when she was a little girl, they couldn't do that with electric lights. My forward-thinking grandmother. She and I both knew she was making up stories as she went along, but together, we entered altered states with amused conviction. My mother would walk into the room from time to time and smile at what looked to her like two children thoroughly lost in make-believe. She couldn't join in—it was a small club, and she was too pragmatic for the existing members.

My mother, Virginia, was a twentieth-century woman, modern, sophisticated, and elegant. Her land of enchantment was "right now." No going back, no sci-fi. She wasn't tedious about it, though. She had her own way of "dressing up," and she was good at it. So good, I often viewed her persona as some elevated, barely attainable level of existence.

In the early thirties, my mother had taken a shot at Hollywood, becoming an understudy for Marion Davies (newspaper mogul William Randolph Hearst's paramour). She also did some nightclub work as a band singer, performing at the old Pantages Theater on Sunset Boulevard. But when it came time to be the wife of a young investment banker, her less than pristine entertainer's life had to stop. Maybe, if she'd made it to the Betty Grable stage, I wouldn't be here at all. She'd probably be on her fifth husband and her unfortunate daughter would be writing a nasty little book about her.

My parents both graduated from the University of Washington, Seattle. Soon after they were married, my father was transferred from the San Francisco–based investment firm of Weeden and Company to the Chicago office. Then, on October 30, 1939, at Chicago Hope Hospital, Virginia Wing gave birth to Grace Barnett Wing at 7:47 A.M. Well, not really. I don't know my actual time of birth or the name of the hospital, because they weren't written on my birth certificate. Back then, record keepers weren't as anal-

Infanta: me at three. (Ivan Wing)

compulsive as they are today, so I've always made up my own stats when it was time to fill in the blanks.

After my mother had taken lots of legal drugs (they weren't into natural childbirth in those days), with no perceptible complications, she and my father, Ivan, took their firstborn back home to 1731 Rice Street, Highland Park, Illinois. (That address *is* on the birth certificate.) We lived in an old, dark wood-shingled house surrounded by trees, flowers, squirrels, and birds. My mom and dad were the prototypical *Leave It to Beaver*–type parents, as yet unsuspecting of the iconoclastic behavior that would shortly issue from their fat blonde daughter. Yup, I was blonde at birth and stayed that way until puberty.

My only memories of that time come from what my parents told me, or from the pictures in my father's photo albums. Whether or not we're *supposed* to remember what those big faces were saying about us when they were hovering over our cribs, I don't know, but a train ride is one of the first things I can remember, unaided by photographs.

When I was three years old, my father was once again transferred to another office, this time in Los Angeles. While my parents stayed behind in Chicago to take care of packing up our belongings, my mother's youngest sister accompanied me for the three-day trip on one of the old Pullman sleeper trains. Navy blue–uniformed porters set up a small hammock directly over my aunt's berth by the window. That was my bed. My most vivid memories are of the constant train rhythms, a dance where you don't have to move, it moves you. The hammock's swinging, trees and buildings parading past the window, the clacking of the wheels as they hit the small splits in the rail, the diesel smell that overpowered the fragrance of a single flower in a white vase on a white tablecloth in the dining car—these are all clear pictures and sensations I have in my head of the train working its way west. But I don't remember how my aunt looked or what she said. My memory is only of the machinery.

All of my mother's relatives lived in Los Angeles: three sisters, their husbands and children, one brother, and my grandmother. Suddenly, I had a huge family. "I love L.A.," croons songwriter/singer Randy Newman.

So do I.

Our big family would get together at my uncle Fred's Malibu home, where various sisters, aunts, children, assorted family friends and dogs wandered in and out of the beach house talking, laughing, and eating. The country was at war in Europe and Asia then, but I was aware of it only through the adults' conversations. And even then, the impact on me was minimal: squeeze the red dot in the margarine to make the white cube look yellow like butter, pull the shades down for blackouts, and cover your ears during air raid sirens. It all seemed like a game. I was too young to understand and lucky enough to be unaffected.

My uncle Fred, a writer, sometimes took me to his office at the Farmer's Market, where I loved the carnival-like atmosphere. Colored booths and outdoor shops were decorated with Mexican hats and dolls, and garlands of red peppers and postcards were strung across restaurants serving food to laughing bronze-colored people in big sunglasses. Another uncle, Daniel, was a cinematographer at MGM. He introduced me to Dore Schary, who was then the head of the studio, but I wasn't as impressed with the production end of the business as I was with the "artists." I thought films were the ultimate art form, a medium that included all of the other arts—music, dancing, set decoration, photography, costume design, acting, and writing. It was *moving* art, not something that was tucked away in a palace where only a privileged few could appreciate it, but an accessible and constantly changing experience for everyone.

On the first day of preschool in L.A., I inadvertently marked my territory (like a good dog does) by being too polite. The teacher was speaking and I had to go to the bathroom, but I didn't want to disrupt the class by butting in with a request to leave the room. I thought I could hold it, but just before she finished her speech, I raced from the room, trailing a yellow stream behind me.

Welcome to higher learning.

That was my first taste of embarrassing myself in public. I must have enjoyed something about it because I've been getting myself into embarrassing situations ever since. Sometimes they're inadvertent, usually they're planned, or at least they seem like a good idea at the time.

3

Geisha Grace

In 1945, reality kicked in again. Another transfer for my father, this time to the main office in San Francisco.

We moved into a small stucco row house, 1017 Portola Drive, a busy extension of Market Street, one of the city's main thoroughfares. Directly across the street was Saint Brendan's Catholic school, and I felt sorry for those kids, all having to dress the same, constantly being watched by those strange, gray-faced women in the long black outfits. I was glad my parents didn't belong to any weird organization that required such rigid, ritualized behavior. It was much later that I learned how each person imposes some version of rigidity on themselves anyway, with or without the help of organized religion.

I went to kindergarten at Miraloma, an old World War I army barracks with cloakrooms and coal-burning stoves. We lived directly below Mount Davidson, which was covered by forest and crowned with a gigantic cement cross, and I instantly became Robin Hood on that hillside. I'd drop the twentieth century and all its prefab buildings and drab clothing, and go back to a time when everything was handmade—when artisans spent long hours creating the houses, the bridges, the clothes, and the books. No assembly-line products, no carbon monoxide, no atom bomb, no DDT. I followed my imagination to the Renaissance, to the grass banks of the River Thames, to the turn-of-the-century Wild West, to the court of Priam of Troy, to the steps of Notre Dame, to the palace of Ramses, to Jerusalem, Kenya, Oslo, Saint Petersburg—anywhere but where I was. Anywhere I could invent myself all over again.

One of those places for invention *was* here and now, however—the De Young Museum in Golden Gate Park. Located across from the band shell and the aquarium, it was a grand and beautiful neoclassical building filled with antiquities, the four-structure enclosure spreading out from the Japanese tea gardens to the tree-lined streets. Every time I walked up the steps to the museum, I knew I was about to be surrounded by handmade beauty: paintings, sculpture, suits of armor, displays of antique clothing, and the elegant exterior of the building itself.

A quiet appreciation of the museum's contents instilled itself in everyone who entered—children and adults alike. Some people who'd been loud and hurried outside became quiet and reverent as soon as they entered the main hall. Because of its size, there was a noticeable echo and a nice residual sound from the clicking of high heels on the marble floor. Red velvet cords looped through brass poles, which were placed four feet in front of the paintings as a reminder to "look but don't touch." They were right to rope off the exhibits. I would have loved to have touched those paintings, to have felt the ridges of the brush strokes. I moved in as closely as I could to see the manner in which the artist had layered the paint.

Just below the museum was the band shell, where I used to watch orchestras play. I loved to see the forties musicians with their chairs, sheet music, dark suits or long dresses, and, of course, the conductor. As an adult, I played that same stage many times, but we had amplifiers, no written music, jeans and T-shirts—and *no* conductor. Instead, we had a wild assortment of individuals wandering around onstage "shit-dancing" (a term my daughter uses to describe the way white people move awkwardly to rock music), smoking dope, handing out flyers, and interacting in their own way to whatever was going on. Little did I know then, as I watched the rigidity of the forties performances, that I'd be a part of loosening up the band shell ritual. Today, there are still "respectable" orchestras playing there, but the rock bands broke the tradition of formality generally associated with Sunday concerts in the park.

On one side of the De Young Museum was a Japanese tea garden. It offered an excellent duplicate of the seemingly free-form arrangements of plants, rocks, steps, and flowers that typify the Japanese style of specific placement, which ironically gives the illusion of impressive spontaneous growth. Even during the time we were at war in the Pacific, the tea gardens continued to employ delicate-looking, young Oriental girls dressed in the elaborate costumes of Japan's Meiji era. The girls served tea and cakes to a steady stream of tourists and locals who, for at least a half hour, were able to suspend knowledge of the carnage that was taking place half a world away.

The weekly art classes I joined in 1946 met right there at the tea gardens. About ten elderly women and seven-year-old Grace would bring paper and pencils and, for an hour and a half, struggle to capture the beauty of the place. Each of us was hampered by a lack of artistic ability, but we'd all compliment each other, primarily for persistence. If I finished or gave up before the allotted time, I'd drift into a reverie and "become" a fifteen-year-old geisha girl, serenely waiting to be the performer in some elaborate ancient ceremony.

At seven years of age, I not only imagined myself as various characters, but I rummaged around in our closets and my mother's sewing boxes for actual costume and prop possibilities. On one dress-up occasion, I managed to make my parents run for the camera and, if only for a moment, reconsider their Republican political choices.

I cut out a rectangle from a black piece of paper and stuck it on my upper lip—Adolf Hitler. I put on my father's coat and hat, which, with the mustache, softened Hitler into the then current presidential Republican candidate, Thomas E. Dewey. Finally, I stuck my hand into the coat between the second and third button for the Napoleon look, completing my impromptu triad of conservative power freaks. My parents still voted for Dewey, unswayed by their incipient liberal daughter, who was simply filling time until Mort Sahl and Lenny Bruce would really have them in the aisles.

Since my favorite cartoon character was Red Ryder, on my eighth birthday, I got a blue fat-tired Schwinn bicycle, a cowboy hat and boots, two pearl-handled thirty-eights with a double holster, a plaid flannel shirt, and a pair of Levis. So I *was* Red Ryder for at least six months. Then, at Christmastime, I turned my parents' hearts to mush by "becoming" the Virgin Mary, complete with white cardboard halos for me and my doll named Jesus, a white sheet draped over my head and down my body, some Kleenex swaddling diapers for Jesus, and a nauseatingly benign smile plastered on my face for the duration of the performance. You would think with all this carrying-on that I would have become an actress, but the idea of having to say someone else's lines has always bothered me, right up through the writing of this book.

Don't put *your* words in *my* mouth.

Fear of forgetting lines added to my distaste for the acting profession. If someone gave me a situation and let me make up the dialogue as I went along, I would have loved it. But movies cost too much to rely on that much freedom of expression.

At my school's fourth-grade talent show, I decided to die. The decision was inspired by Edvard Grieg's *Peer Gynt Suite* (one of the three albums that composed my parents' record collection), which had a particular cut I liked, an instrumental piece called "Asa's Death." I purloined one of my mother's old gray curtains, wrapped myself in it, and did an unintentionally funny four-minute dying scene, writhing around on the floor to the accompaniment of the dolorous music. "It looked," my mother said, "like a send-up of Isadora Duncan." But she was kind enough to keep that criticism to herself until I was old enough (thirty-five) to appreciate the humor.

In hindsight, the most appropriate getup of all was the *Alice in Wonderland* costume Lady Sue made for me to wear in my school's Halloween parade. I was about the right age, eight, and at that time, I had long blonde hair, so apart from being a bit too chubby, it was probably the closest I came to actually looking like the character I'd chosen to inhabit for the day. That was my second-favorite Halloween costume, the very best being an accident of nature and my own stupidity.

As I was walking to school one morning, I noticed some beautiful, bright red and gold fall leaves. I gathered up an armful to take to my sixth-grade teacher, running all the way to school to get there early and surprise her with my lovely gift. She was surprised, all right. And she forgot to thank me. The instant I walked into the room, she said, "Grace, put the leaves in the garbage very slowly, and then go home and tell your mother to take you to the doctor."

It was poison oak and I had third-degree burns all over my arms and face. By the time Halloween rolled around, the red raw skin had progressed to a disgusting crust of scabs, and the oozing sores prevented me from going out with my friends for trick or treat. But my disappointment was fully redeemed by the horrified expressions on the little kids whom I greeted in all my ghoulish splendor, holding a plate of dyed-red scrambled eggs for their "treat."

No one had a better Halloween outfit that year.

4

1798 or 1998?

My childhood desire to wear costumes and travel back in time had nothing to do with being unloved. It wasn't about having a dysfunctional family or abandonment issues or domestic violence or obsessive/compulsive disorder or "de Nile" or "adickshun" or . . . yawn. It had to do with aesthetics. The way things looked to me, the way they sounded, the way they felt.

To understand what I mean, I'd like you to place yourself in two different settings—the first, a bedroom in the year 1798.

It's 8:00 A.M. You're lying on your back in bed. Everything you see in the room is handmade, including the big wooden crossbeams supporting the troweled ceiling. The bed and the dresser have been carved by an artisan and rubbed to a warm finish with stains and waxes. Your nightgown or nightshirt, the wrought-iron chandelier, the honey-colored candles that you extinguish with a brass candlesnuffer, the ceramic bowl and water pitcher on the dresser, the leaded glass windows framed by crown moldings and covered by homespun curtains—each is the result of an individual's imagination and ability to realize the final artifact.

Your dog, who's been sleeping on a cushion in the recessed window seat, slowly wakes up, stretches, looks out the window, and listens to the soft clicking of the horse and carriage passing by on the cobblestone street. He goes over to the solid oak door with the hammered brass handle and barks. He's letting you know that it's time to take a morning walk on the three-hundred-year-old brick path, lined with trees, flowers, and the occasional deer or rabbit scampering in the bushes where birds are chirping at the sunrise. The path leads to the center of town, where a few red-cheeked merchants are rolling out their wheelbarrows full of produce from the local farms, to display around the town square.

You and your dog pause under a carved wooden sign, hanging by wrought-iron hooks from a seven-foot-high horizontal post, that says BAKE SHOPPE. The smell of warm biscuits circles through the air, beckoning two or three people to join you for breakfast and to listen to the town crier. He literally sings the morning news, and accompanying him are two musicians in Robin Hood-like attire— one playing the lute, the other playing a pennywhistle— hoping to catch a few nickels for their impromptu performance. When the old church clock chimes nine times, everyone moves on to the business of making something by hand, from scratch, so they can trade it or sell it in the marketplace for something else they need.

The day ends with a late dinner by candlelight and congenial conversation with friends over a couple of mugs of mulled wine. While you and the dog enjoy the warmth of the big stone fireplace, you read a few pages of an essay on freedom by Thomas Jefferson. Then you both climb the Dutch-tiled stairs. The distant sound of the grandfather clock in the hallway—eleven chimes—confirms it's time to retire. The last thing you see before you drop off to sleep is the view through the bedroom window: bright stars shining through a clear atmosphere, unclouded by smog or artificial lights of any kind.

OR

The year is 1998.

It's 8:00 A.M. Again, you're lying on your back in bed, waking up. Everything you see has been mass-produced; not one human being touched anything in the room before it hit the retail store or the construction company warehouse. The ceiling is wall-to-wall twenty-year-old, white, asbestos-insulated cardboard tiles. The dresser amounts to four plywood drawers you were forced to assemble from twenty-seven separate pieces that came in a box marked IKEA, which spits Styrofoam balls. You can switch the seventy-five-watt track floodlights on and off by pushing a button on a plastic panel on your metal headboard, which features rows of electronic remote units. They've been specially designed to keep you either immobile or comatose after your rigorous workout in a fluorescent-lit room filled with fake bicycles, digital readouts of your progress, gym instructors lurking behind overdeveloped muscles that look like tumors, people in eye-blinding synthetic glow-in-the-dark spinning suits, and seventy-five-year-old pensioners who've been ordered by doctors to engage in repetitive contortions because of heart problems caused by eating gigantic amounts of animal fat. Young girls are working out there, too, with fake lips, boobs, hair, and noses, talking about liposuction, and there are mirrors everywhere to remind you of your imperfections. In the corner is an isolation booth full of dry heat and infrared light bulbs to ease your pain and send your aching and tortured body back through streets redolent of carbon monoxide.

The sounds of screaming ambulance sirens accompany you to your fourth-floor apartment in a twenty-story block of cement. There, you've installed a bunch of big black plastic boxes with knobs all over them that are capable of playing 130 decibels of music written by an angry fifteen-year-old with a third-grade education (who makes more money in four minutes than you make all year, and who gets paid to yell at you through speakers loud enough to break glass). It's comforting to know that you won't miss a note of the three-chord drivel that you paid seventeen dollars per CD to enjoy with your hearing-impaired dog who eats from his plastic bowl with cutesy paw prints on it stamped by a machine that has cranked out eighty million of the exact same doggy bowl worldwide.

When Fido finishes eating the suspicious ingredients in Barkos, he goes over to the solid metal door, which is secured with seven dead bolts to keep everyone out who might want your stereo or your life, and he barks. He's letting you know it's time for a walk—a stroll that will include his taking a shit on a street populated with more dogs attached by leashes to more humans wearing fanny packs full of credit cards. You and your fellow dog walkers will sweep the shit into bags, tie the dogs to parking meters, and enter stores in search of even more plastic life accessories.

Before you're through, you'll purchase one of those gizmos that makes fake ocean noises, hoping to soothe enough of your stress-riddled, buffed-out body to make it through the rest of the day and start your wonderful waking life all over again in twenty-four hours.

Let's get real now: plumbing differences aside, which of those two settings seems the most conducive to a life of abject inanity?

As a child, with few responsibilities compelling me to accept the twentieth century's plasticized, cookie-cutter lifestyle, I chose the 1798 spin on reality. Aided by an imagination that was always ready to shift centuries, I simply ignored most of the mediocrity that prevailed. The persistent rejection of anything modern is usually only found in elderly people—you know, the type who begin every sentence with, "In the good old days . . ." My entire life, though, has been an exercise in counterprogramming. You say "White," I say "Black." It's only recently that I've started to bend a little. I'm more accepting of nonbiodegradable packing-crate decor and polysynth sweatpants now, in my "old fart" years, than when I was seven years old.

5

Grouser

Aside from my lack of appreciation for synthetic materials and assembly-line furniture, as a kid I was pretty easy to please. I was only an average student, but I liked school. My favorite subjects were English, ancient history, art, geometry, composition, and Latin. I slid through algebra with a D (the only reason I didn't get an F was because I had perfect attendance). I slept through American history and science. And I considered economics useless. Boy, was that a mistake: only later did I realize that "artists" need to know business games and numbers. It's unfair, really, because business types never have to learn to draw, sing, dance, or write lyrics.

I played war games with the boys and jump rope with the girls, I went to Western movies with my father and shopped for clothes with my mother. Whatever anyone wanted to do sounded interesting to me. I didn't develop the "Fuck you, I do what I want" attitude until I was long gone from my parents' control. As a kid, the only time I balked was when I was told *not* to do something.

WHY NOT.

One evening, I was sitting in the living room, sort of absentmindedly fiddling with the ashtray on the coffee table. My father, who was sitting across the room, said, "Don't touch the ashtray."

"Why not? There's nothing in it," I said.

"Because it's not a toy," he answered.

I placed my index finger about a quarter of an inch away from the inside of the ashtray so he'd have to stand up and come over to my side of the room to determine whether I was contradicting his order. Since I wasn't, he simply gave me a disgusted look and returned to his chair. But after I got him out of his chair again, he said, "That's not funny." And he proceeded to challenge me in a contest of wills. I was sitting in a rocking chair, so the following exchange had a rhythm all its own.

My father said, "Are you going to do that again?" And he pushed my forehead with the tips of his fingers.

I said, "Yup."

He said, "Are you going to do that again?"

I said, "Yup."

Each time I spoke, he pushed my forehead so that the rocker, with me in it, went backward. This went on for about fifteen minutes, until my mother broke the seriousness of the game by laughing out loud at both of us. "Boy, you guys are stubborn."

Truce.

Most people who write autobiographies have some crucial whining to do about parental aberrations, but not me. When I got punished, it didn't surprise me a bit. Usually I was sent to my room as a penalty for misbehavior, but it happened so rarely that I don't recall any specific incidents that were horrible enough to mar my outlook on life. What can I say? I simply *knew* when I'd done something wrong. When you're a kid, you don't break rules and then sit around wondering why you're being reprimanded.

If you can't do the time, don't do the crime.

I understood that, so I almost never complained. What was there to complain about? I was either too stupid or too happy (or some of both) to recognize opportunities for grumbling, so my parents sarcastically nicknamed me Grouser, which means "one who complains." I didn't know what the word meant at the time, but since they always said it in a friendly fashion, I just accepted it. I called my father Lid because he always wore a hat. My uncle called my aunt Slats because of her long, skinny legs. I called my daughter the Goon because of the funny expressions she'd get on her face as a baby. The whole family is saddled with silly nicknames.

Occasionally, my parents wanted to go to a party or just be alone for a while, so they'd hire a young, quiet schoolgirl, Elva, to baby-sit. With her brown hair in a bun and wearing glasses, she'd show up with an armful of homework and several novels. I amused myself by doing the usual Jekyll and Hyde routine with costumes, or I annoyed her by drawing her face. Being watched is uncomfortable for someone who's shy (which she was), so in order to get the angles and colors right, I had to keep looking at her—up close. She suffered in silence, and, ever the polite girl, she always complimented me on the finished portrait.

Usually, though, I went out *with* my mother and father because their idea of a night on the town was to go to dinner at a five-star restaurant. One evening in December 1948, I can remember the three of us riding in our old 1938 black Buick on the way to the Tonga Room in the Fairmont Hotel, when my father said, "We have something special to tell you, but we'll wait until we get there."

Suspense.

When we arrived, my parents asked me to sit at a table with them instead of whirling around by myself on the carousel that was in one of the lounges. "We have good news," they said. "You're going to have a little sister or brother pretty soon." My parents hadn't planned the pregnancy, but it sounded all right to me. As it turned out, I didn't hear the phrase "sibling rivalry" until years later, when I was too old to be affected by it, so the usual inherent jealousies didn't get much of a workout.

My brother, Chris, was born the following September, 1949, at Saint Mary's Hospital in San Francisco. All I knew was that Mom and her big stomach and her small suitcase went off to the hospital, and a couple of days later, she came home with a tiny, crying boy. Newborns are usually kind of funny-looking, and Chris was no exception. His skin was dark pink and he had a shock of bright red hair that stood straight up in a point at the top of his head. In those months after he arrived, I'd watch my mother tend to him; I'd observe the constant feeding, lifting, rocking, covering, singing, and diapering. It looked like a lot of work for an indiscernible reward, and it was clear to me right then that occupations such as nurse or schoolteacher wouldn't be high on my list, nor would having lots of children.

The nine-year age difference between Chris and me made the business of hanging out together a bit problematic. He usually didn't want to do what I wanted to do and vice versa. I baby-sat for him once in a while, but by the time he was eight, I was already away at college in New

York. Today, I see him once in a while, but since I live in L.A. and he lives in Palo Alto, our relationship is sporadic.

Blood doesn't necessarily bind.

Maybe it was because my parents hadn't expected another child, that I wasn't raised like most girls. It's not that they gave me knee pads and a football helmet, but they were unusually open concerning guidance for a female child. Considering their conservative upbringing, I would say they were lenient about my obvious disinterest in the homemaking arts. If I seemed to have an affinity for something, they encouraged me. But that comes later.

When I watched my mother cook, the routine consisted of chopping, turning stoves and ovens off and on, shuffling pans around, cleaning up messes, setting the table, and washing dishes. Not terribly exciting. When I asked her if she actually liked cooking, she said, "It's something that needs to be done, like brushing your teeth."

Ballet, on the other hand, was enchanting, beautiful, graceful, and people clapped when you finished, so I *did* ask for ballet lessons. Stretch, point, turn and bend, memorize positions, plié at the practice bar, costume fittings, and at long last, the day of the performance. We were performing *The Nutcracker Suite,* and I had my part down at the dress rehearsal. But when it came time to step onstage, it occurred to me that there were more interesting moves that could be executed in the Sugar Plum Fairy's role, so I proceeded to do my own version of the piece. When the show was over, the instructor approached my mother. "Maybe Grace has talents in other areas," she suggested. Not only was I too short and fat to be a ballet dancer, it was also becoming apparent that taking direction was *not* my forte.

6

Toodles

My initial training in the sexual arts left a lot to be desired. Literally. Since my parents *never* wandered around without clothes, I had no idea what their bodies looked like, much less anyone else's. They usually went to sleep a couple of hours after me, and my father always turned off *all* the lights in the house.

I was lying in bed at about 3:00 A.M. one night, thinking about nothing in particular, when my father got up to go to the bathroom. He had to pass by my room to get there, and since my door was open and he was wearing only his pajama top, I got a shadowy glimpse of his privates. I wasn't aware of the one penis/two balls setup, and it looked to me like he had a crotch full of swaying thumbs. I suppose the darkness added to the genital mystery.

I told one of my older girlfriends—she was nine—about it the next day, and she looked at me as if I had the brains of a matzo ball. "Oh, of course. Those are 'toodles,'" she said. She wore that condescending look, as if it was one of those Latin medical terms only doctors use.

A real sophisticate.

So I started off with an inaccurate vision of men being all thumbs, in a manner of speaking, and the first name I heard for a man's apparatus would have been better suited to a breakfast cereal:

TOODLES
Breakfast of Sluts

My second sexually explicit event—apart from those times when I benignly stared at the nude statues in the museum—was a watering-can tryst. Another girlfriend, Jessie—who was my age, seven—gave me a questionable lesson in copulation. She was either operating from a vague natural instinct of this-fits-in-here-nicely, or she'd seen some unusual behavior that she was mimicking. We were in her parents' basement, looking at the standard clutter that lives in such places, when she took a watering can down from a shelf and filled it with water. I thought we were going to spray the petunias, but she said, "Let's play doctor." She pulled down her pants and said, "Now you put this [the slender nozzle on the watering can] in here." She pointed to her crotch.

I'd never really checked out even my own crotch thoroughly, so I didn't know there was a *hole* into which the spout would fit. After I aimed it in her general direction and squirted water all over her thighs, she said, "No-o-o-o, let me show you." Now it was my turn to be the patient. Sure enough, the watering can not only found its mark, but a kind

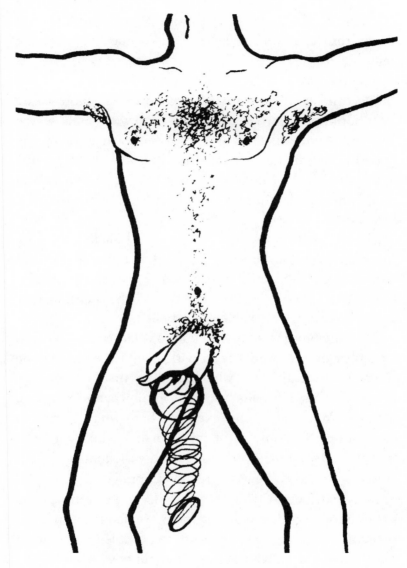

"Toodles" (Grace Slick)

of pleasant, albeit messy, stream of water went in, then slowly turned around and came out of me—all over the cement floor.

Thanks, Doc.

My third childhood sexual encounter had more to do with not knowing when to shut up than with direct sexual activity. A boy called Frank Funk (I'm not making up the name) kissed my hand on a whim after we'd been playing with my next-door neighbor's rabbits. I was honored and said, "Oh, Frank, that's so sweet and old-fashioned. You kissed my hand!"

He was obviously embarrassed that I'd made such a big thing out of it, so he said, "No, I didn't. I spit on it." I looked at my hand and I didn't see any spit, so the conclusion seemed to be: Don't bring too much attention to a young boy's romantic behavior or he'll balk.

Over my lifetime—for God knows what reason—I dated a number of guys who'd been with my girlfriend, Darlene Ermacoff. I was thirteen when I had my first taste of Darlene's leftovers. His name was Nelson Smith, and I suppose it still is. You reading this, Nellie? That's what his friends called him. Not only my family but my whole circle of friends seemed to be overly fond of silly nicknames. Like a bunch of rap stars, we wore them with pride.

I invited Nelson over to watch TV one evening, and since the set was in the dining room, we had to sit in these two stiff-backed chairs. I was so preoccupied with *him*, I have no idea what we watched; it could have been *Howdy Doody* for all I cared. All I remember is that it took him a tantalizing two and a half hours to get from the position of simply having his arm around my shoulders to dropping his hand and lightly caressing my breast. We kissed a couple of times and since I'd hadn't yet heard of "hard-ons," I didn't realize what kind of pain a two-and-a-half-hour erection was probably causing him.

Teenagers' sexual advances—or lack thereof—are fraught with such intensity it's amazing they don't regularly culminate in a big blast of hormone-driven shrapnel.

7

Fat

In the early fifties, my father got a pay raise, so we moved from our small, rented San Francisco house to a larger, two-story home in the suburbs. Palo Alto, home of Stanford University, was a college town that provided a safe and proper environment for bringing up well-adjusted (?) children. Suddenly, we were right in the middle of the WASP caricature of family life, complete with two children, a two-story house, a two-car garage, and the promise of many more "well-adjustments" on the horizon.

I didn't mind our move as much as I minded my parents selling our old black 1938 Buick, my fat friend that lived in the garage. They just went and *sold* it—the car that had faithfully transported us since I was born. Although crying was something I rarely indulged in (I usually got either quietly annoyed or verbally abusive), tears flowed for my intimate four-tired friend. I was sure that cars had feelings. It just seemed such a betrayal that a 1949 two-tone gray Oldsmobile was now usurping the Buick's position as a member of the family.

Fat blonde doing a Sharon Stone exhibition: me at nine. (Ivan Wing)

Still, Palo Alto was interesting enough—not exactly Barnum and Bailey, but for a ten-year-old, it was at least accommodating. Unlike in hilly San Francisco, the roads here were flat and you could ride a bicycle all day and not get tired. And was it peaceful. For the first time, I could pretty much go anywhere I wanted and my mother didn't have to worry.

I was rarely alone, though. I met two girls several days after we moved in who would be my pals for the next couple of years. They were into a more athletic style of play than I ordinarily favored, but since neither suggested going to a museum and I wanted to have friends, I took up handstands, cartwheels, hide and seek, swimming, and roller skating. Unconsciously, I was beginning to learn about social groups and the hierarchies that inevitably sprung from them. There were the cool guys and the nerds, and I quickly realized that I was going to have to shed the nerd cocoon if I wanted to be part of the pack.

It was time to start letting go of individuality. Lose the art books, get into Marvel Man comics, take off the saddle shoes and get some flats, never mind Chopin, check out Chuck Berry, adults are a drag, kids rule. Are you too fat? Is your hair the right style? Here it comes: the big teenage mold. The big question was: DO I FIT IN?

And then there were *boys*. In 1950, when I was ten, Jerry Slick, one of my neighbors, was in my sixth-grade class. I thought he was a dufus with his round face and glasses, but then, in 1961, I married him.

So much for the judgments of a ten-year-old.

Now Red Hendricks—*he* was another story. He was cool and dangerous, a member of the "fighting Irish," with a knocked-out front tooth, a greased-up fifties pompadour, and a heavy attitude under a black leather jacket. Too bad I was a fat dufus myself. He wasn't interested.

I remember another kid, named Ricky Belli (his dad was Melvin Belli, one of San Francisco's flashiest lawyers), who lived down the street. He and my friend Susan used to make out in his garage. Did they go all the way? She said no, he said yes. But no one pulled *me* into any garage fun. There were no debates about whether *I* had gone all the way. No one raced after *me* when the kissing games began.

Something was wrong with my picture: braces and fat, for starters.

I arrived on the first day of class at Jordan Junior High School, wearing the wrong clothes and the wrong hairdo, with the wrong binder and a complete lack of teenage skills. But I *did* notice the girl with the blonde hair, big smile, big boobs, long legs, and cool outfit. She's the one, I thought. It was Darlene Ermacoff. I knew she'd graduated from one of the other grammar schools closer to the center of town, where the kids were more sophisticated. Her boyfriend, Johnny Schwartz, was good-looking, dark haired, and slender with a great smile, and his father, "Marchie" Schwartz, was the Stanford football coach. When I watched Darlene and Johnny strolling by, I knew I was looking at high school royalty—the king and queen of the prom. So I got the clothes, the shoes, the binder, and the hang of the way to talk. And since I was blonde, I figured as soon as puberty kicked in, Darlene and I would be neck and neck in the Barbie doll marathon.

But something went wrong. At thirteen years old, my hair turned fuzzy dark brown, the large boobs never materialized, and after the weight dropped off, I was nothing more than a skinny, sarcastic, dark-haired basketball cheerleader. What I didn't appreciate at the time was the wonderful workout a woman's imagination gets when she can't rely on her looks to make it all happen. She has to be ready for contingencies, and she knows that any acceptance she *does*

Smiling through the transition: me at thirteen. (Ivan Wing)

get is a compliment to her creative ability, not her genetic code.

But that "silver lining" didn't mean shit in high school.

Darlene was one of those girls who had it all: good code, good humor, *and* a good mind. We became friends, anyway, and a couple of months ago when she was staying at my house for a few days, I asked her why she'd stooped to hang out with my nerdy self. We were laughing about the phases, the years, the mistakes, the boys/men, the death-defying drug use, the whole diary, and she said she'd thought that *I* was the pretty one, the clever one, and so forth. If only I'd known that in 1952. I don't remember feeling like a *total* loss back then, but until I was about twenty-four and saw myself as a social steamroller, there was always this intangible next step that needed to be taken to feel like I had the situation locked.

A step I could never quite manage.

So having become at least a second-string member of the ruling social class at junior high, I let the family flag of sarcasm fly in all directions. I figured my mouth was all I had, that my sarcasm was my way *in* with the popular girls. And everything seemed to be going relatively well, until the night of my fourteenth birthday. I was at home, celebrating with my family, when my girlfriends called me up. I ran to the phone excited, figuring they wanted to wish me a happy birthday. Instead, they told me that my lack of consideration for other people's feelings—aka sarcasm—had led them to the decision to drop me from the group.

No friends?

Tears. My mother had a diamond ring I'd always loved, and when she saw my sadness, she gave me the ring in an attempt to snap me out of it. Diamonds as a substitute for friends? The ring did nothing to cheer me up, and I realized that this bauble I'd coveted for so many years was now nothing more than metal and minerals.

Did I learn anything from the experience? Not really. People are only occasionally more important than metal, minerals, black humor, and cars.

Stubborn.

8

Blue Balls

Nineteen fifty-five. I was a fifteen-year-old sophomore at Palo Alto Senior High School, and I joined a girls' club to get in the swing of things. On initiation day, I was blind-folded by the other girls and told to take my blouse off and put it on backward. Oh, shit, they'll see the Kleenex stuffed in my bra. But nobody said anything. Were they too polite or was the bra too dense to see through? I'll never know.

Girl-ask-boy dance. Okay. I went straight to the top by asking the school's star quarterback to be my date. He was older and he didn't know who the hell I was, but he said yes. Polite, I guess. I bought a pink, flower-covered, wedding cake–like monstrosity of a dress and went with Mr. Hotshot to a pre-dance party thrown by a senior cheerleader. She opened the door in a red, body-hugging floor-length number with four-inch dangling earrings, which made me look like an exploding cotton candy machine. After the evening, when I asked my mother what she thought of my "catch-of-the-century" date, she remarked, "He's not very bright, is he?"

No, but were brains really the point?

I was a flat-chested fifteen-year-old sophomore trying to impress myself and my friends by pulling in the school jock. This was not about brain surgery. On a Friday night, a few hours before another dance, I ripped off a fifth of bourbon from my dad's basement stash, and my friend Judy and I polished off the whole bottle. She passed out; I thought I was Betty Grable and went to the party with a Catholic boy who smelled like fish. (That's all I can remember about him.) I sprayed perfume in my mouth so nobody would notice my breath, but of course, it didn't work. I danced like a puppet, thought I was Ginger Rogers, stayed up all night, and threw up all the next morning.

Did I learn anything from the experience? Not really. I figured it was all in how you weighed it: how much fun you had balanced against how much you had to suffer through in the morning. I loved getting high, so I paid the price.

You want a Rolls Royce? You gotta pay for it.

During school breaks, we'd all pile into someone's car and go to a drive-in for burgers, gossip, and boy watching. I gravitated toward Judy Levitas. At age sixteen, Judy had her own car, and instead of going to public school like the rest of us, she went to Castilleja, a private school for girls. She wasn't as judgmental or as enslaved to teen peer-pressure rituals as most of the girls I knew, and I liked her easy-going way of looking at things. Judy, who had very understanding parents, often had a bunch of kids over to her house on the weekends to party and swim in her pool. She gathered boys from Catholic school, boys from Palo Alto, boys from Stanford, and boys who'd dropped out of school to work on cars, along with girls from many different backgrounds and locations—a good mix.

It was at one of Judy's parties that I met my first love, Alan McKenna, a Catholic school boy. He seemed to be holding court on the other side of the pool, and although I couldn't hear what he was saying, I guessed from all the giggling women around him that he had a personality to go with his good looks. When I got closer, his green eyes surrounded by thick dark eyelashes nailed me to the air. I was hooked and we became a steady couple.

Alan and I used to do some serious necking, sprawled out on the backseat of my parents' brand-new 1955 Oldsmobile. He knew how to make me laugh and he inadvertently gave me my first string of orgasms, although not by penetration. In the missionary position, when he had his clothes on and got hard, his penis was in the perfect position to massage my clitoris, so with both of us fully dressed, I was getting off every time. But he was getting "blue balls."

"What," I asked, "are blue balls?"

He explained that a prolonged erection without release gets to be painful. Since none of the so-called nice girls went "all the way," and for many of the Catholic guys, masturbation was considered a sin, there were a lot of Pope-restricted teenage boys running around with bad cases of blue balls. Now that *might* have produced a sufficiently large guilt trip to sway me into having some real sex—but I didn't go for it. In hindsight, screwing Alan McKenna, somebody I liked, would have been a better choice than the one I made. But I was dumb enough to do it the first time with somebody who didn't mean that much to me—when I was drunk.

It was after Alan and I broke up. I'd switched to Castilleja private school because Judy Levitas went there, and I went to my graduation dance with a blond boy from

Carmel. I generally liked my guys to be dark, smart, and dangerous (I still do), and David, who was healthy, blond, tan, and conservative, wasn't really my type. But he knew a friend of mine, so we double-dated for the graduation party, which was held at a local country club. At the end of the evening, we ripped off some clothes from the club's golf shop and then took off for David's place in Carmel. His parents were away, so after we loaded up with lots of liquor, we took off for different bedrooms with our respective partners. It turned out that each woman in the house (both my girlfriend and me) got poked that night for the first time.

Fortunately, I never compared my future lovers to my first experience, which most people say is the most exciting, because I was too loaded to remember it, so essentially, it didn't exist. When I ran into David, the Carmel boy, a couple of years ago in a department store (he was selling furniture), I didn't even recognize him. People often spot me; because I was onstage for so many years, they feel like they know me. But I don't necessarily know them. So when I heard someone say my name, I just smiled politely.

"Grace, you don't recognize me, do you?" he asked.

No, I didn't, but I looked a little closer.

"It's me. David."

When he said his name, I laughed because he looked as old and lumpy as I did. You get sort of used to looking at yourself in the mirror, but when you haven't seen someone for about thirty-five years, it's shocking. Like those computer gizmos that can automatically age your face, I sometimes get a time-warp feeling of racing mortality when I run into old friends.

No reunion parties for Grace.

9

What to Do with
a Finger Bowl

In 1957, while I was at Castilleja High School, I met another one of those icon girls, Sue Good. She was a year ahead of me and was one of the main reasons I decided to go to Finch College in New York. Sue had the disciplined ballet-trained body, the ingratiating personality, the requisite blonde hair, and the good report cards. When I found out that Finch was her choice for higher learning, I thought it would probably be a good idea for me, too. I was still plodding behind the blonde Barbie dolls.

The truth is that I didn't particularly want to go to college, but I *did* want to live in New York City for a while. Asking my parents for twenty thousand dollars to hang out and play in a city three thousand miles from home was a request that definitely wouldn't work, so I presented Finch as a more appropriate option. They went for it.

Although it didn't bill itself as such, Finch was a finishing school for girls from wealthy or prominent families, who went there (if they didn't have the grades to get into

Vassar) to learn the basics of how to get and keep a Yale or Harvard man. Not that I was interested in that. My freshman class was made up of women like Sandy Seagram (yup, the booze family), three or four Oklahoma oil heiresses, my roommate, whose father was an Estée Lauder CEO, Cece Shane, who was a rich girl from Beverly Hills, and several more up-and-coming socialite types.

One of the first boys I dated in college was a Princeton boy, Andrew Mathison. No group of people is better at polite disdain and unwarranted contempt than the wealthy old East Coast WASPs. In fact, they're so proud of their lineage as the "earliest settlers," they refuse to acknowledge that most of the Plymouth Rockers were actually a bunch of malcontents and thugs who sailed over here to escape ridicule and prison back in Europe. My mother was eligible for the DAR, because somebody or other in her bloodline had made the *Mayflower* boat trip. But she considered the DAR a pretentious group of effete snobs who didn't have the courage to go farther west than Connecticut.

Ouch.

Even in the face of that sound information, I managed to go out with Andrew, who came from one of those East Coast genetically incorrect blue-blood families. He was an intelligent boy with buckteeth and a good sense of humor, but I wasn't aware of his lofty ancestry until the seventies, when a woman who was doing some biographical material on me reported that his "people" refused to talk to her about our relationship. His family probably didn't want it known that their bucktoothed scion had banged a rock-and-roll slut. Buckteeth aren't bad in and of themselves, but why, with all that money, didn't his parents slap some braces on their rodent-toothed kid? I'm very grateful to *my* parents for having my teeth fixed. Otherwise, I would have been the poster child for my own song, "White Rabbit."

Jimmy Gaither, another Princeton boy whose parents had political and diplomatic affiliations and a fancy four-floor town house on the East Side, was Sue Good's boyfriend and, later, became her husband. The two of them, along with Andrew "Bugs Bunny" Mathison and I, went on a double date one time and made the mistake of staying out all night. No sex, no drugs, just some romping around in the snow in Central Park. But the Finch social police declared our night-time activities to be a scandalous travesty of the "nice girl" code. They found it necessary to call a closed meeting of teachers and housemothers to vote on our possible expulsion from that immaculate school of etiquette. I still remember the hours of fear, awaiting their verdict.

Thanks to Sue's cherubic persona, the faculty admonished us for our scandalous behavior, but we were allowed to stay in school so that we could continue the strenuous curriculum of studying the social graces. No pun intended. We learned things like:

1. *Which fork to use with which course in a seven-course meal. 101*
2. *What to do with a finger bowl. Don't drink it. 102*
3. *Sit properly, legs crossed at the ankle, never at the knee. 103*
4. *Find out, in the most subtle manner possible, the extent of your escort's liquid assets. 104 (This was everyone's major.)*

Along with the above meaty courses, some English, history, and drama were thrown in so we could conduct ourselves properly at a formal dinner *and* string a couple of sentences together without making any glaring grammatical errors. And they wanted us to be able to speak to each other, hoping that we would develop those cherished and fondly remembered friendships that college life is so famous for. But today, I don't even know if any of those "fond friends" are alive or dead, except one person—Celeste Shane, better known as Cece.

In the beginning of a school year, at an afternoon tea—they were big on high tea at Finch—the dorm housemothers gathered us all in the main hall so we could begin building those cherished relationships that would constitute fodder for old-age reminiscence. That was where I met Cece. You know how some people look irreverent even though they seem to be conducting themselves in a normal manner? Cece had that look. She also looked like the tanned, healthy, blonde Southern California girl that was on the cover of my imaginary "How to Do It Right" handbook. Having already been married once to Gene Shacove, the hairdresser on whom the movie *Shampoo* was based, Cece was one step ahead of most of us in the sophistication department.

She and I hit it off because of our shared sardonic take on the upper-crusty, East Coast social scene that was heavily fortified at Finch. During a Scotch-and-tradition-soaked weekend at Princeton, Cece and I outraged the preppy boys by doing a spontaneous song-and-dance routine that we thought was a harmless bit of fun. They, on the other hand, thought it was completely "unbecoming" and asked us not to return to the campus in the future. The affronting performance consisted of Cece dancing by herself (fully clothed) in the middle of the room—are you shocked yet?—while I sat on the sidelines singing Chaucerian trash to my own guitar accompaniment.

The offending song went as follows:

I love my wife, yes I do, yes I do,
I love her truly,
I love the hole
That she pisses through.
I love her tits, tiddely-its, tiddely-its,
And her nut-brown asshole,
I'd eat her shit—chop, chop, gobble, gobble,
With a wooden spoon.

If one of their *male* college buddies had offered up that song, they would have just thought it was kind of stupid, but would they have asked him to leave and never come back?

Puh-leeze.

I also knew some other less offensive songs, having learned most of them from listening to records by black folk singers like Stan Wilson, Miriam Makeba, and Odetta. When Odetta was playing in Greenwich Village that year, I performed the sneak-into-her-dressing-room-after-the-show trick. Before she'd returned from the stage, I was already in there, playing one of her backup guitars. Unlike the rock stars of the following decade, she didn't have a gang of roadies dragging people away from her. Quite the opposite. She was alone and seemed genuinely flattered that someone was interested enough to weasel her way to the back of the club.

Since I have a low-end loud voice, I could relate to Odetta's style better than, say, a Joan Baez or a Joni

Mitchell reedy soprano. She encouraged my moderate ability and gently warned me that being a musician was sort of a hit-and-miss occupation. But she loved singing and told me that that was what kept her going when the jobs were few and far between. I wouldn't resume playing the guitar until many years later when the music business was no longer a life of hole-in-the-wall one-nighters.

Not that guitar was really my instrument, anyway. I mainly used the piano for songwriting. Occasionally I played it onstage with Airplane or Starship, but for the most part, people who had a better command of the instrument were the ones who played keyboard.

10

"Old" Men

During spring break, Cece went home to Los Angeles and I went tropical, spending a week and a half in the Bahamas with Rolli Miller, another roommate from Finch. She and I flew to Nassau to scan the beaches for boys, get blitzed on four-rum fruit drinks, shit-dance to the steel drum music, and tan our New York–white bodies. We flirted, albeit unsuccessfully, with two great-looking, bronzed, thirty-five-year-old bartenders who were both wearing gold studs in their ears. The ear jewelry, which was way ahead of the future eighties fashion requirement, made them seem romantic and exciting, like a couple of Caribbean pirates.

Neither of us got laid, but the experience was impressive enough for me to decide to spend my sophomore college year at the University of Miami in Florida—the closest I could get to the Bahamas. Obviously, none of my academic choices were designed to actually further my education. The most important attraction in selecting a school was how much *fun* might be involved. But sandwiched between Finch and the University of Miami was summertime in

HOLLYWOOD

When Cece asked me to spend a couple of months with her at her family's estate in Beverly Hills, I agreed. Since I'd spent most of my teenage years in the predictable monotony of Palo Alto, I'd never gone out with any "older" men on fast-lane dates, so Cece had to keep me on an invisible leash so I wouldn't wander off and land in somebody's bedroom. After all, this was the L.A. movie crowd; I was no longer dealing with inexperienced college boys.

The Luau, now a Mexican restaurant called The Acapulco, on La Cienega Boulevard, was one of Cece's favorite hangouts. She and I went there one night, and when I indicated an immediate interest in seeing the classic cars belonging to the older man (thirty years old to be exact) sitting next to me, Cece gave me a kind of wild-eyed warning smile. She was trying to indicate something she couldn't say out loud, and when I stood up and announced that he and I were going up to his house in the Hollywood hills, she gave me an even screwier grimace. I interpreted it as a congratulatory grin. Cece didn't stop me, but she wanted me to know that I might be out of my league with this guy. I dismissed all her facial expressions and went out into the night, actually thinking I was on my way to appreciate some antique cars.

College boys didn't try to jump your bones in five minutes, but this was a grown-up predator looking at the new young meat in town. And I was naive enough to be sucked in by the "Wanna see my Bugatti?" routine. Not three minutes after we got to his house, though, Cece showed up, all smiles and apologies. "I'm so sorry," she said to Mr. Older

Man Car Collector, "but Grace forgot that we have a private party to go to in Bel Air and we're two hours late already." Another wild-eyed smile in my direction and this time I understood it was the "Hello, Red Riding Hood, that's not your grandmother" look. As Cece and I drove off, she explained that, yes, my new friend probably would have shown me his private car collection—as well as his privates.

Cece's parents, Mr. and Mrs. Shane, had been married a long time and kept a well-mannered relationship. Like my own parents. But unlike my household, in the middle of theirs on any given day, you might find a pet monkey in diapers swinging from the chandeliers over some drunken actress sprawled on one of the beds, crying about a fight with her ex-husband. Cece's mother, calmly wearing nothing but black eye patches, might be found lying face-down, getting the house-call treatment in the massage room. Cece always seemed to take a rakish delight in whatever was happening. I never saw her get angry, but at eighteen years old, with a pleasant and well-heeled family to rely on, what's to get mad at? Like a teenager winning an MTV trip to a backstage band party, I felt like the lucky kid who'd won a trip to Hollywood.

Jill St. John, one of Cece's friends, often joined us to make a threesome. She was extremely intelligent and remarkably beautiful, and when we went shopping at Bullock's, she demonstrated the rich-and-famous ability to seek, find, spend, and acquire. When she spotted a throw pillow she liked, she bought twelve of them, one in every color. That kind of full-sweep spending was not a Palo Alto pastime. Her house included an indoor/outdoor swimming pool, a vast array of tropical fish, and a basement filled with miniature trains. Although she was the same age as Cece and I, she was already living on her own, and unlike most young people, she managed to refrain from any debilitating excesses. She had a mind like a steel trap and could give you details on subjects most people couldn't even pronounce. Lately she's become a gourmet cook. Mr. Robert Wagner is a lucky man.

Richard Anderson, another actor friend of Cece's, was a bit older (twenty-nine?) than we were, so I considered him ancient. Cece liked them well seasoned—she later married director John Huston, who was at least thirty years her senior—but as *I've* sprinted through the decades, I notice that I don't even feel comfortable with people my *own* age, let alone those who're older. The post-fifty-five set seems deadened by something or soured by the constant intrusion of reality. I probably project that same ennui to my daughter's friends; they must be thinking, *Poor Grace, the old party animal—she's sitting home again.*

Another missed opportunity occurred when Cece introduced me to a very funny and not yet famous Richard Donner, future director of the *Lethal Weapon* movies, *Ladyhawke*, *The Omen*, *Maverick*, *Radio Flyer*, and *Conspiracy Theory*, and the producer of *Free Willy*. He lived in a small, comfortable house in one of the canyons, and I spent an afternoon with him at home, chatting. If I hadn't had that stupid he's-five-minutes-older-than-I-am-so-he-must-be-dead attitude, I probably would have jumped his bones. Happily married now, he's a great director as well as a humane human being, and in his movies he's able to both entertain and inform without compromising either goal.

Hi, Dick! You reading this shit? You wanna make a movie based on the life of an animal-loving, shotgun-toting, eccentric, upper-middle-class rock goddess? No? Okay. Just a thought.

I accompanied Cece to lots of fancy gatherings, where I loved being the only "outsider" in a room full of Robin Leach subjects. We went to a party once where I saw Julie

Newmar, an outstanding example of the kind of beauty that drops your jaw. She stood talking to some people in the middle of the living room, and her bright red dress and shoes added to the Nordic Amazon shock value. Standing over six feet, she was taller than most of the men and towered over all of the women. I couldn't imagine what it must be like to be inside such a spectacular body and have a completely stunning effect on everybody within fifty feet of you at all times. There was no costume I could put together to imitate that.

But I *did* get to put on a showy outfit of sorts. Cece got a call for us to be "Kennedy Girls" at a Democratic party fund-raiser for JFK. We wore red-white-and-blue dresses with white straw hats and spike heels, and our function was to mingle, smile, and make the men with the bucks feel like they not only had it, but that if they gave enough of it away ... maybe—?

We weren't expected to screw any of them, but we weren't told not to, either. Cece certainly didn't have to do anything she didn't want to do to get wealthy boyfriends, and with my aversion to "old" men, we both managed to go home without putting out anything more than conversation. But for Yours Truly, meeting John Kennedy, even if it was only in a long, fast-moving line of starlet types, was the high point of the evening. This was my favorite summer vacation, and to top it all off, Darlene's ex-boyfriend, Johnny Schwartz, asked me out on a date when I stopped by Palo Alto to prepare for my trip to the University of Miami.

Insignificant events can take on monumental proportions when your head is full of practically nothing.

11

Convulsive Decision

The University of Miami. The humidity dropped me in my tracks (too much cold Norwegian blood?), the palmetto bugs swarmed in red, flying clouds fifty feet wide, splattering on my windshield like blood clots, and everybody on campus was an athlete. But, if you can't beat 'em . . .

I cut my hair short, bleached it blonde, got a Coppertone tan, wore white shorts and tennis shoes, and learned how to throw a mean shot put. Variety and eccentricity. I also acquired a king snake who stayed in my dorm room and ensured my privacy by being one of the world's least popular animals. In fact, the best athletic move I've ever witnessed was executed by a pudgy girl who, upon sighting the snake, jumped five feet in the air onto the top of my dresser in about one tenth of a second. She was not ordinarily agile, but the snake's presence called forth instant Olympic ability. Encouraged by that performance, I kept the snake, more for entertainment value than an actual affinity for reptiles.

Less intimidating attractions at the U of Miami were plaid madras sport shirts, Cuban music (Castro's fatigue-clad soldiers made up fifty percent of the nightclub clientele), lots of beer and umbrella-topped rum drinks, any sporting event (not my first choice for fun), and a huge linebacker from the college football team. We did a lot of quadruple dating—my dormmates and his teammates—usually centered around movies. Typically, the guys sat in every other seat because their bodies were so big, the normal setup would bring on claustrophobia. Swimming, boating, and attending the obligatory formal prom at the Fontainebleau Hotel completed the list of "must-do" activities. It was a tame and sunny year, during which I remember only two inclinations to deviate from the norm.

The first came when I was in a record store looking for "La Bamba" by Ritchie Valens, and happened to see an album cover with a picture of a guy having a picnic by himself in a graveyard. It was Lenny Bruce. I'd never heard of him, but as soon as I listened to the record, I knew I'd found a soul mate. He used and abused the English language, and he cracked jokes about the Catholic church, Adolf Hitler, the judicial system, and anything else that needed catharsis. In short, he *said* the things that most people only *thought*. When I first heard the album, my face hurt from laughing, and I dragged my friends into my dorm room to listen to this prophet of attitude. Their response was not as enthusiastic as mine, but I wanted to find more people like him to hang out with—fringe-thinking as a way of life.

Look out what you wish for—you might get it.

My second "deviation" was toward a lifestyle change that proved permanent. I received a letter from Darlene that included an article by the *San Francisco Chronicle* columnist Herb Caen. Herb's article was about the new scene—a Bay Area phenomenon that included "hippies," marijuana, rock music, and strange but pleasantly artistic postbeatnik behavior. Darlene suggested I come home to check it out. Since her instincts regarding promising scenes were always reliable, I decided to return to the West Coast, probably the most pivotal decision I ever made, considering where destiny ultimately took me.

It would be a while before people realized what had hit them, but within a decade, every section of the country would be tossed into the eruption and spit back out with a whole new paradigm to paddle around in.

12

Stupid Jobs

When I arrived back in northern California in the fall of 1958, I moved in with my parents on Hamilton Avenue in Palo Alto. The first order of business was to find a job so that I could support myself and move into my own place, but what could I do? Neither the knowledge I'd gained at Finch (don't drink your finger bowl) nor the partying skills I'd developed at the University of Miami were much in demand. I scanned the want ads daily, looking for a suitable job and asking myself the same question that had plagued me during puberty:

Where do I fit in?

I decided to apply for a job as a receptionist in a lawyer's office, where multifunctional phones were just starting to rear their ugly little heads. My job was about being polite while trying to remember how many people I had languishing on the hold buttons. I failed—I'm *still* terrible at doing two things at once. After watching me struggle with the advanced technology for a few days, my boss informed me that my "phone manner" was unacceptable.

I remember taking another short-lived job as a market-research guinea pig. After seating me in a dark room in front of a glass case containing three different cartons of aluminum foil, they switched on the light for a fraction of a second. When they turned it back off again, they asked me which box I'd noticed first. The point was to determine which color scheme would best grab the average housewife by the eyeballs and lure her into a spontaneous purchase. Ever find yourself unpacking the grocery bag and wondering why you bought the instant dustball warmer? They've got it all figured out at both the advertising *and* the shelf level.

As I continued to search the want ads, one caught my eye. It read like this:

> *Singer wanted for new record label. No experience necessary. Call 555-1225.*

My mother was a singer and I thought maybe I could squeeze myself into that job, whatever it was. I picked out a song that I loved and dressed to the nines for the tryout. Two men in a small recording studio with a closet-sized control room waved me over to a microphone to do the song I'd rehearsed. Unfortunately it was "Summertime." For an all-black record label? Bad choice, but I figured it would be worse to attempt a song I hadn't rehearsed. Through the double-glass window of the control booth, I saw gentle smiles—not condescending—just two black men watching a little white dufus squirming under the weight of her own self-inflicted hubris.

I didn't get a callback.

I'd always been a lover of art and I considered myself a fair illustrator, so when an advertising agency placed an ad in the newspaper for a graphic artist, I showed up for the interview, not knowing exactly what a graphic artist was supposed to do. But I explained that I had an idea for updating their Bank of America TV commercials. "How about a cartoon character to liven it up a bit?" I suggested.

"No," they said. "That would never work. The public doesn't want anything that frivolous when it comes to institutions entrusted with handling their investments. We have to convey the appearance of respectability and reliability."

I didn't get the job, but on the tube, two months later, I saw a cartoon symphony conductor pointing out the benefits of a Bank of America checking account with his baton. Did they steal my idea? *They* would have said no. After all, I hadn't said anything about a symphony conductor.

How dumb could I get?

13

Grace Cathedral

When I was five years old, I told my parents, "I'm going to be married in *that* church." I was pointing to Grace Cathedral, a neoclassical Episcopalian monolith that sits on top of Nob Hill along with the Pacific Union Club (rich guys only) and the Fairmont Hotel. At five years of age, of course, I didn't know what denomination it was, who went there, or anything else about it, but it was big and beautiful, and it had my name.

In 1961, it seemed fitting that Grace Cathedral would be my matrimonial church of choice. My decision to marry was not sudden. Rather, it was a natural progression of events, seemingly the right thing to do at the time. But nothing predictable had real longevity during that turbulent era. My generation, educated by the best public school systems before or since, was busy gathering the ingredients for a cultural stew that would feed reactionary efforts right up through the millennium. So when you consider the diverse mass of information we were receiving during the

Jerry Slick and I slice through six tiers of tradition
on our wedding day. (Ivan Wing)

time period between 1959 and 1962, and the evolutionary shifts that were occurring, it was probably inevitable that my first marriage would be temporary.

My parents, as yet unobstructed by their hedonistic daughter, had moved to a stately, fake Tudor structure covered with ivy and surrounded by ivy-covered neighborhood homes. My mother was doing volunteer work at Stanford Children's Hospital, playing bridge with the ladies, and taking care of my brother, who was a quiet but naturally busy nine-year-old boy. My father was chairman of the board at Weeden and Company, living a polite, unassuming existence. Jerry Slick's parents had become good friends with my parents, and the two families were in the habit of enjoying weekends together at the Slicks' beach house in Santa Cruz. My future husband, Jerry, had two brothers, Darby (author of the song "Somebody to Love") and Danny (who avoided rock-and-roll silliness altogether). The rest of the Slick family comprised Jerry's mother, Betty, a housewife who drank her way through the family gatherings, Jerry's lawyer father, Bob, and a basset hound.

Our decision to marry was inevitable. Neat and tidy? Not yet aware of what "complete personal freedom" meant, I was evaluating the long-run specifics. Jerry was bright and, like me, twenty years old. We had the same friends, our parents already knew and liked each other, we'd gone to the same schools, had come from the same social strata, had the same ethics and family background, and lived in the same small town. Does that sound like the ingredients for the perfect tight-ass, fifties, arranged marriage? I bought it and so did Jerry.

Was there passion? Nope. Just cultural imposition.

"Will you marry me?" Nobody ever said that lovely,

naive line. We just moved into the married state as if it was expected and irrevocable.

Even though Cece and Jill St. John didn't know Jerry, my getting married was a good enough reason to get together and knock back a few cocktails. The night before the wedding, the three of us had a low-key, three-woman bachelorette party in one of the bars at the Fairmont. No drunken debauchery, just a mild high to fuel the girl talk. The next day, I had the kind of wedding that women love and men hate—big, dressy, and full of relatives and friends acting out lots of rituals. The reception was held in the Gold Room at the Fairmont Hotel with cake and champagne, and, to me, it all felt natural, no second thoughts, no regrets. Just another workout on the treadmill of tradition coming to a satisfying end at sunset.

Throw the bouquet and say "Good night, Gracie."

After the standard honeymoon in Hawaii, we went back to the Bay Area. Then, at some point, Jerry decided, for reasons I can't remember, to go to San Diego State University. A beautiful area, San Diego was nevertheless populated by large groups of military-minded right-wing organizations. Jerry studied while I worked at a department store running a comptometer, a monstrous machine that calculates billing statements. For relaxation (?) we visited Jerry's cousin and her husband who weren't much older than we but were members of the John Birch Society. They were so right-wing, they made Charlton Heston look like a draft dodger. Although I wasn't particularly political at the time, it was hard to keep from laughing or just nodding off when they started with the here's-how-the-country-should-defend-itself harangue.

Our stay in San Diego was brief, thank God, because

Jerry switched to San Francisco State at the end of the first semester. But I was still faced with a need to make money, and had no well-defined skills. The last stupid job I tried before my twenty-five-year rock-and-roll stretch, was modeling for the I. Magnin couturier department. Living with Jerry in a ninety-dollar-a-month shit-hole apartment in San Francisco with rats in the basement and unpredictable plumbing, I was expected to show up at the store each morning, change into a different four-thousand-dollar outfit every ten minutes, and float around, showing rich old women the latest in overpriced European designer wear. If they liked something I was wearing, the head of the department, Madam Moon, a bullet-faced frogue with pretensions of social superiority, would measure their lumpy old bodies. Then, magically, with the help of her overworked seamstresses, she'd crank out a perfect copy of the original, transforming the outfit from a size six to a size sixteen. Mirrors don't lie, but denial systems rule—the old broads thought they looked fabulous and the I. Magnin coffers filled up.

One afternoon, an old dowager, cocooned in fur and rattling diamonds, came waddling over to me with her best four-martini tack and said, "My dear, you really *do* need to cream your elbows." What the fuck was she talking about? How dare she discuss dry skin? Her entire body had freeze-dried so long ago, the addition of moisture would have been a life-saving event. And *she* thought *I* needed a lube job? I was twenty-two years old. The only time a twenty-two-year-old is going to look too crispy is if she's been in a four-alarm fire. I'm now fifty-eight and still refuse to put cream on my elbows. Stubborn perversity.

Ironically, while I was busy looking for a "real" job, I

wrote my first song, without a clue that it was a precursor to my future. Jerry and I both got involved in a project with a mutual friend, Bill Piersol, an aspiring writer who'd written an interesting script treatment for an amateur sixteen-millimeter movie he named *Everybody Hits Their Brother Once*. A satirical comment on violence, Jerry filmed it while he was studying cinematography at San Francisco State, and it subsequently won first prize at the Ann Arbor film festival. I wrote a song for part of the succession of skits that made up that forty-five-minute reel, which was my initial experience at recording my own music—two layers of Spanish-style guitar picking that almost sounded like a cut from a professional sound-track.

One of the best parts of returning to San Francisco was getting back in circulation with our original group of friends—with a few new additions. Darlene Ermacoff had married a man named Ira Lee, who was literally possessed by a monster IQ. A handsome and eccentric part-time model/full-time student, he'd been a Quiz Kid, a contestant on the forties radio show of the same name. It was Ira who once told me (accurately) that I was an empty-headed WASP, and he proceeded to suggest reading material that might remedy the problem. I learned a great deal from him, not so much because of my thirst for knowledge, but because I was absolutely fascinated by his wild-eyed delivery of arcane details on every subject imaginable. His outbursts of enthusiasm became one-man performances lasting well into the night, and although Darlene was used to them and went to bed more often than not, I needed a tutor and he needed an audience.

Darlene and Ira and Jerry and I used to take road trips to

Mexico in an old station wagon, visiting the pristine beaches of Baja and, like all budding hippies, purchasing drugs. In those days, "south of the border" wasn't just a folksy phrase, it was the access route to a state of mind.

14

Use It

It was 1965, a couple of apartments later and a lot of stupid jobs under the bridge, when Darby, Jerry, and I went to a small nightclub called The Matrix to hear a headlining group called Jefferson Airplane. Marty Balin, one of the two lead singers, had started the club with the help of other band members and some marginal outside backing from a couple of doctors.

As I watched Airplane perform that night (they were an eclectic group that did electric folk-rock, blues, and pop), playing in a band like that seemed like the perfect thing to do. Get paid to make music, write your own songs if you feel like it, work for a couple hours a night, hang out with friends, and take lots of drugs whenever you want. When we got home that night and added up the numbers, we realized that the members of Airplane were making more money in one night than I was making all week at I. Magnin. It didn't take us more than about five minutes to start making plans to form our own band.

Jerry had an old set of drums collecting dust in his parents' garage. Darby already knew how to play the guitar. My untrained voice was at least loud enough to compete with the amplifiers, and a friend, David Minor, could sing and play a few chords. And he was a good-looking front man. Peter van Gelder played sax and Bard Dupont could at best find the notes on a bass guitar.

A name for the group? What about The Acid Fraction? No.

What about The Great Society? (Making fun of Lyndon Johnson's grandiose moniker for the U.S. population.)

It stuck.

At that time, fortunately for us (and unfortunately for the listening audiences), you didn't have to be very good to get jobs in the local clubs. So once we formed the band, we managed to work on a semiregular basis. Some nights, we'd be playing to three drunks who were too old and wise or too loaded to even bother looking at the stage. Other nights, the clubs would be populated with members of the various local bands, just hanging out. Once in a while, a marketing representative from a record company came in and blew smoke up my ass, saying things like, "You guys are great. I'm going to make you rich." One guy said he was going to make another Edith Piaf out of me.

How? By breaking my back?

The press vacillated between thinking we sucked and complimenting us on our originality. Good or bad, who's to say, but *original* is definitely what we were. Music lyrics were changing then, from the classic boy/girl romance stories to a wider variety of subjects, and we all took a shot at writing material. Pretty soon, the only "outside" song we did was "Sally Go 'Round the Roses." The Motown-style arrangement lent itself nicely to the East Indian rhythms Darby and Peter loved; it had a sort of repeated mantra in the title chorus.

Since all changes, no matter how small, are absorbed into and add impetus to the ongoing paradigm shift, nothing ever really slips away. The old themes and styles persisted as stitches in the unfurling tapestry, but they were hard to see. What caught the eye was all the newness.

At a certain point, the "Why don't you love me?" concept was pretty much put on the back burner, replaced by what we considered *relevant* topics: political, social, and psychological ones. In a short space of time, we learned more than our parents wanted us to know about things they'd been too timid to investigate. Or, to put it more kindly and accurately, our new forms of communication hadn't been available to them at a time when their minds were open enough to *"hear it."*

In any event, our parents' world was crumbling (a perfectly natural evolutionary process that they refused to acknowledge), so they kept saying,

"DON'T!"

and we kept asking,

"WHY NOT?"

The same question that was being voiced in England, Africa, South America, Russia, and China, according to each country's own parameters, became an almost tangible force in our lyrics. Both the joyful songs that celebrated new life and the wrenching shouts of labor pains were heard in the music, the press, the movies, the prisons, the churches, and the state rooms.

What concerns you? Put it in a lyric.

What country's style of music best suits the idea you're trying to convey? English? Spanish? Jamaican? Whatever it is, use it.

Global nation? Use it.

Does colored oil and water produce interesting images when you backlight it and project it on a screen? Great. Use it.

Are nude young girls shit-dancing a good example of freedom of expression? Sure, let 'em dance.

Does living with a bunch of friends who aren't related by blood feel more comfortable than living with your family? Yes? Then move in.

Does shooting a bunch of people in a foreign country for no good reason sound like a drag? Yes? Then *don't* do it, but *do* put it in a song.

Darby Slick's "Somebody to Love," which Darby originally wrote for The Great Society, is a good example of the shift that lyrics were taking. In the past, when people wrote love songs, they were talking about someone who would or wouldn't fill their personal desires. "Somebody to Love," which became a huge hit later when Jefferson Airplane recorded it, turned the old concept around. The lyrics implied that rather than the loving you're whining about *getting* or *not getting*, a more satisfying state of heart might be the loving you're *giving*.

> *Don't you want somebody to love?*
> *Don't you need somebody to love?*
> *Wouldn't you love somebody to love?*
> *You better find somebody to love.*

Cluster: Jefferson Airplane in 1968.
(Jim Wells/Archive Photos)

Darby wrote the words simply, without pedantry, suggesting that adhering to the old Puritan cliché "It's better to give than to receive" might actually make you a happier person. The idea of service and selflessness may sound like a tedious task reserved for bald monks, but the way Darby wrote the lyrics, altruism didn't seem like such a lofty and unattainable state. He gave people the impression that giving could even be an enjoyable adventure.

As had happened with the seemingly overnight changes in lyrics, the sudden, yet natural shift from the rigid dress codes of the fifties to the if-it-feels-right-wear-it free forms of the sixties didn't give me a moment's pause. Does anybody question going from the fourth to the fifth grade? Remember reading about that kid who dressed up all the time?

SHE'S BACK, SHE'S TWENTY-FOUR YEARS OLD, AND SHE'S GOT COSTUMES!

They ranged from a miniskirted, knee-booted pirate getup to a floor-length Indian caftan. I never wore tie-dyed T-shirts—too modern. I always went for the costume racks at the San Francisco Opera House or Western Costume Movie Rentals in L.A. If they didn't have what I wanted, I'd sew it myself.

Shades of Lady Sue.

I had the big buckled leather boots and belts made, and I got the jewelry from a secondhand store or a head shop. When all else failed, I got two extra-large paisley-printed towels, sewed them together at the top corners, stuck my head through the opening, and belted the front and back at the waist with an enormous five-inch-wide black rubber tire tread. No more couturier department for Grace. To this day, you can still see me in that towel outfit on some VH1 "Flashback" programs.

Lucky you.

My first experience with community living, a definite sign of the times, happened as a matter of convenience. I was with the other Great Society band members most of the time anyway, and to make the situation easier on us, we all decided to get a house together in Mill Valley. While this enabled us to play or practice day and night, the difficulties of communal living emerged quickly. What if one person wanted to sleep and the others were playing music?

What if you'd just had an argument with someone and couldn't get away from that person? What if someone wanted to use the bathroom and *she* was in there? It was the usual interpersonal problems multiplied by six or seven. The difficulties eventually outweighed the advantages and probably hastened the departure of David Minor and Bard Dupont from the group. It's natural that differences escalate in tight quarters. You don't have to watch five rats in a small cage to understand claustrophobia.

15

Peyote, Sweet Potatoes, and LSD

My group of friends spent a lot of time at Fay Roy Baxter's house. (No, he wasn't the one Airplane referred to in the album title *After Bathing at Baxter's*.) Fay Roy was a man who knew how to throw a party. He loved artists and musicians, so around twenty of us would gather at his house on the weekends for dinner and conversation while he ran in and out of the kitchen joining in the chat and preparing some of the best meals I've ever tasted. Great wine, candlelight, incense, marijuana, and interesting tablemates were a given at Fay Roy's.

A gathering at his house was simply *the best*.

When I was there, I felt as if I'd been transported back to the salons held by Gertrude Stein. Artists told each other elegant lies and engaged in spirited arguments over the integrity of some author or other. Listening to music through the pleasant alteration of hashish, we were young enough to think that we were the first group of people to really have a handle on IT—the next level of perception in human consciousness. And we thought that all those other "poor suckers" were just plodding along in the old survival grind. Arrogance, indeed—but it was fun buying into our self-created storylines.

Along with the regular jazz musicians, macramé artists, writers, and students gathered at Baxter's, there was also a chemical engineer named Nick who worked for a big oil company. A twenty-two-year-old Brit with pink cheeks, a placid grin, an easy manner, and a Rolls Royce (an appreciation gift from his deep-pocketed employer), he'd invented the glue that adheres those plastic disks (road bumps) to street dividing lines. But industrial-strength glue was not the only powerful stuff Nick knew how to make. After loading us up with all the existing information on the subject, he gave us "homemade" LSD.

Up to that point our group's experience with psychedelics had been pretty much confined to taking peyote, which was a "natural" plant—and that had only occurred a few times. It was at Baxter's house that we'd had our first taste. Peyote (a cactus that was already well known by the desert tribes of Native America), when boiled down to a concentrate, became a vehicle for going out of our minds. Or, in a more gentle interpretation, going from one plane of reality to another (and another and another). Our first peyote experience varied from person to person, but as well as I can use words to describe my earliest psychedelic shift in consciousness, this is how I remember it.

After swallowing the bitter-tasting cactus concentrate with a chaser of water, I sat still and enjoyed the initial sensation, a very subtle tingling or vibrating. Then I became aware of a large, inner area of air that was automatically collecting in my lungs and releasing over and over, without any help or thought behind the process. It reminded me of smoking cigarettes, so I pulled a pack of Marlboros out of my purse. After marveling at the ugliness of the art design, a pathetic blatant red-and-white attempt at flashy modern packaging, I took out a cigarette and lit it, just as I'd done hundreds of times before. But this time, it seemed like a very strange thing to do. As the smoke funneled down my throat, I felt a dry heat and then an interference with the air that was already in my lungs. I put the cigarette out and didn't light up another until I'd come down, about sixteen hours later. Feeling sort of nauseous (people usually throw up at the beginning of a peyote high), I went to the toilet bowl and arranged myself in the kneeling position, but nothing happened and the nausea slowly disappeared.

Since flying off the edge of a cliff or trying to embrace a moving vehicle is not an uncommon desire for psychedelic drug participants (it's not that people become suicidal, it's just that in such a state anything seems possible), just before the six of us had ingested the drug, we'd designated one of the girls, Dana, to be our "straight" person. That was fortunate indeed, since in the middle of our high, we decided to climb a mountain that was close to Baxter's house. Before giving us the okay, Dana discreetly scanned everyone's faces, trying to determine if we were capable of comprehending the functions of simple things like door-knobs, curbs, traffic lights, and so forth.

She finally voiced her approval, and after stepping out of the house (a monumental move into another world), it took us fifteen minutes to arrive at the sidewalk. There were just so many familiar objects that had suddenly taken on new importance, new vibrancy—and each flower, each square of cement, had to be appreciated at length. Children do this. Animals do this. Most adults forget how incredibly complex and beautiful the ordinary world is, but peyote was reminding us.

As we lay on our backs in the tall grass on the mountain, each person made a brief awestruck remark about the diversity and synchronicity of the clouds, the air, the trees, and the animals. Unlike the Marlboro package, it all looked as if it had been perfectly designed.

It and I became *this*.

This and them became *us*.

It was on that mountaintop where I first understood that you and I are only separated by one channel of a limited thought process. If I looked long enough, colors on the same object would slowly change in accordance with my ability to take in the transformation. My usual focused perspective was expanded. Instead of viewing certain things or people as passing scenery, as something inconsequential, the peyote made everything and everyone seem equally important. Suddenly I could see no isolation, no overabundance. It was all just energy, exhibiting itself in infinite dimensions.

We returned to relax at Baxter's house for a while, and waited until we got to a point where we could shift in and out of the various levels of phenomena. Then we decided to head back out to attend some other parties. On the way to the car, as I passed through the kitchen to go to the front door, I noticed a fat sweet potato on the ledge by the sink. I picked it up and watched it radiate. Yup, I could *see* a kind of living force in the usually dull-brownish appearance of that ordinary vegetable. It felt warm, as if the detachment from its ground home had done nothing to drain its own energy. I liked the feel of it in the palm of my hand, and even though I knew it was a thing separate from my body, it became an extension of me, like my arm or foot.

I took it with me to the various parties; I damn near introduced it a couple of times. But because many of our friends were moving in the same direction as far as the acceptance of unusual conduct, no one was particularly surprised about the inclusion of a sweet potato in the evening's guest lists. As a matter of fact, a few people asked if they could look at it for a while, and I'd watch as they sat in a chair and studied it. Perhaps they'd ingested some kind of chemical themselves that made them potato-friendly.

When I started to return to a narrower consciousness, my body felt puffy, as if my insides were too big for my skin. My nervous system was alert but worn out at the same time—a polarized condition that I balanced by eating some freshly baked bread and drinking two glasses of wine. All in all, it was a highly pleasant experience. Throughout the day, no one had experienced a freak-out or hyperventilation or any other symptom of chemical imbalance, so that ingestion at Baxter's turned out to be a perfect excursion into alternative planes of observation.

I've since learned that, like mutating viruses, psychedelic drugs such as peyote or LSD seem to match their performance to an individual's makeup. The risk varies depending on a person's emotional, physical, and spiritual state. For that reason or perhaps for some other, what a person experienced last week might not necessarily be what he or she will experience next month. Unfortunately, some people have taken acid either alone or in a situation where their vulnerable aspects were triggered, and the resulting hellish hallucinations took them off a rooftop—or to the nuthouse. In short, psychedelics can offer a spiritual gift or issue a death sentence.

Aren't you glad there are extremist human guinea pigs like me who've already performed the nuts-and-bolts experimentation?

16

The Scene

Most big cities are gray—out of necessity. Who can imagine an all-red city? The gray stuff is cheap and unjarring; cement is light gray, asphalt is dark gray, buildings are constructed in shades of gray in between, and most of the inhabitants are wearing muted colors so as not to offend at the workplace—browns, navy blues, dark greens, grays and beiges. City people don't talk to each other because everybody is a stranger; their faces look preoccupied with some kind of struggle, and their speedy pace suggests, usually rightly, that they're five minutes late to wherever they're going.

Big cities look like that now. They looked like that in the sixties, too.

In 1965, though, on the corner of one of those gray streets, Geary and Fillmore in San Francisco, the color scheme seemed to be changing . . .

Imagine it's Saturday night, and there's a line of what looks like a bunch of young multicolored circus freaks waiting to go into one of those gray buildings, the Fillmore Auditorium. It's hard to tell the girls from the boys. No one is wearing a suit, the crowd is animated, and everybody is talking to each other, even though they may have just met for the first time. The only visible sign of color on the outside of the building, besides the clothing, is a poster drawn in Day-Glo swirls. It reads, *Jefferson Airplane, The Charlatans, Moby Grape, and The Great Society.*

Jerry, Darby, the rest of the guys from The Great Society, and I play the Fillmore quite a lot, opening for some of the more popular groups like Jefferson Airplane. Before a performance, we stuff our gear into a station wagon, haul it up to the backstage area, and some of the kids come around from the line in front of the building to chat with us as we go in through the side entrance. There are no metal detectors, no security guards, no backstage passes, no VIPs at all. Everybody is "us."

When the door to the building opens, the last of the gray vanishes. At the top of the steps that lead to Fillmore's main hall is a wall of bright, intensely colored posters. They're so numerous, the wall itself is invisible. Art Nouveau has influenced these elaborate, colorful portraits of ladies with winding garlands of flowers in their hands, pointing to the elongated letters that spell out the names of the bands. The now familiar rose-crowned Grateful Dead skull can be seen on one poster, on another is the sepia-toned, oval-framed, Old West photo of The Charlatans. And in front of the wall stands a young man with long hair, blowing bubbles toward no one in particular.

As you walk onto the dance floor, you have the feeling you've just entered seven different centuries all thrown together in one room. The interior of the building is turn-of-the-century rococo, and a man in red briefs and silver body paint is handing out East Indian incense. A girl in full Renaissance drag is spinning around by herself listening to some Baroque music in her head, while several people in jeans and American Indian headbands are sitting in a circle on the floor smoking weed. Close by, a good-looking man in a three-musketeer costume is placing ashtrays on the cheap fifties Formica tables that circle the edge of the room. Over in the corner, people are stripping off their clothes, and while the acid is taking effect, they're getting body-painted so they'll glow in the dark as the night progresses. As for the ones who remain fully dressed, the predominant look for the boys is Clint Eastwood spaghetti Western or just T-shirts and jeans—but the flashing black lights make all the clothes, even the more normal outfits, look irradiated.

Rather than work for a big concessions company, the hawkers are self-employed, peddling their own handmade beads, vests, hats, drawings, and a variety of leather items. They don't yell at anyone; easy bartering is expected. There's no curtain on the stage, so people are moving equipment and wires around in full view of the audience. Sometimes they just stop what they're doing and jump off the riser to hang out for a minute with someone on the dance floor. Sometimes there are chairs, and sometimes there aren't, so people sit, dance, or lie down on the floor. Electronics and Indians, disco balls and medieval flutes. Day-Glo space colors and Botticelli sprites. The howl of an amplifier and the tinkling of ankle bracelets.

This is *not* Kansas, Dorothy.

But this *is Peter Pan, Alice in Wonderland,* Oz, Long John Silver, *Stranger in a Strange Land, Naked Lunch,* and *Be Here Now.* This is the American dream (for a few hours), with

Paul Kantner, me, Jerry Garcia, and Bill Graham organizing the flying objects. (John Olson, *Life* magazine © Time Inc.)

no color barriers, no ethnic rivalry, no dress code, no moral imperatives, no political hustling, and only one keeper— the show's intense but smiling dark-haired promoter, Bill Graham.

For everyone to be able to step out of the gray and into the circus, there has to be a human switchboard. That's Bill, the one who calls the shots so the carnival can explode into life. He's running around talking to fifteen people at once, pointing and yelling, laughing and frowning, one hand on his hip, the other on his forehead, eyebrows furled, when he suddenly spins around and yells up to the balcony,

"Tell Garcia he can't do another goddamned three-hour set next week or the cops are going to shut some barred doors on my ass!"

Bill's shouting at Jerry Garcia, or his angry hurling of chairs, or his being upset with Paul Kantner for being the unruly lion in the center ring is all taken in stride. *Someone* has to make sure the Fillmore stays friendly with city regulations or they'll close it down. *Someone* has to make phone calls and weasel the suits into thinking it's a "clean" venue for young people. *Someone* has to organize the flying objects into a business that eliminates the GRAY—that's Bill.

We do the experimenting, and he gives everyone the space to enjoy it.

By the time the Fillmore was in full swing, most of the musicians had moved out of San Francisco to live in Marin County. In juxtaposition to the crowded gray city, just twenty minutes north across the Golden Gate Bridge, Marin was a flourishing community full of fish restaurants, town halls, yacht clubs, cowboys, big sprawling farms, rich-guy enclaves, and small bookstores/bars for the resident artists. The Grateful Dead had a ranch in Marin where the various members of the music scene liked to gather, and I remember seeing Pigpen leaning on the ranch gate when we drove up the dusty road and parked up near the barn for one of their famous parties.

Pigpen, aka Ron McKernan, The Dead's first keyboard player, had a brief affair with Janis Joplin and was, in fact, the one who introduced her to Southern Comfort. Not as easy to get to know as other members of the band, he'd nod without saying anything, but he wasn't stupid or shy. Pigpen was just a quiet man who felt and looked more comfortable in this country setting than he ever did in the city.

The Dead ranch had a big swimming pool, and on this particular day, Jerry Garcia was unintentionally holding court near the trunk of one of the old trees down by the diving board. Wherever he was, a small group of people would gather to talk about anything and everything. Even in his twenties, he projected the wise old rascal image of an Eastern guru. As we moved closer, a sixteen-year-old girl ran by, laughing and waving hello.

No clothes, no makeup, no problem.

That was Girl, so nicknamed by her family because she was the only girl in a family of eight kids. Children and adults leaped in and out of the pool while watermelon, chips, and dips were spread out on the long worn-out picnic tables and thin streams of smoke rose up from the barbecue pits. Dogs, horses, guitar music, wheat-gold hills, and blue sky—the Novato farmland. It looked like the northern branch of the Hotel California, the mythical subject of the not-yet-written hit song by the Eagles.

I was curious about a cluster of people over by the barn. They were standing in a loose circle watching some guy bend and turn, snarl and laugh, his whole body in constant motion. As I got closer, I could hear what he was saying— but could I understand it? Phil Lesh, the bass player for The Dead, was standing in the circle with his arms crossed and a grin on his face, just watching this ball of energy go through his routine. I looked at Phil and there must have been a question mark stamped on my forehead, because he leaned over and said, "That's Neal Cassady, and if you stand here long enough, you'll catch up with all seven of the conversations he's having with himself."

Neal, the lead character in poet Jack Kerouac's *On the Road*, was one of the Merry Pranksters, a group of people based in Santa Cruz who'd traveled the country in search of everything in a graffiti-covered bus called Furthur. He and Ken Kesey (author of *One Flew over the Cuckoo's Nest*, inspired by his twenty-dollar-a-day job as LSD guinea pig for the CIA), Jerry Garcia and his wife, Mountain Girl, and several other happy, eccentric freaks put on some of the best musical gatherings.

Everyone comes, anything goes, and the music drives the action.

When the bus, Furthur, was inducted into the Rock and Roll Hall of Fame in 1997, a bystander was reported to have said, "Larry, Kesey and Garcia aren't heroes, they're criminals. And that's not a bus, it's a hearse!" Echoing what is probably "popular" opinion, there'll always be people who are afraid of living and afraid of dying. And there are always more of them than there are risk-takers, the people who bring innovation into every area, with or without drugs. Hunter S. Thompson, gonzo journalist, once said, "Living in San Francisco in the sixties was like being in Paris in the twenties." Kesey added, "The sixties aren't over until the fat lady gets high."

The musical events inspired by the Pranksters were called Trips Festivals, and they couldn't be managed by "regular" promoters; they were too purposefully fragmented and spontaneously erratic to fall into a classic "party" or "concert" category. We knew when and where they were going to happen, but after that, it was shifting chaos and Wavy Gravy party games. Wavy Gravy, aka the clown saint, who was also one of the Merry Pranksters, literally dressed in a clown outfit, complete with the big red nose, the wig, the painted lips, and the huge ears. Wavy was integral to all our concerts and events, the only clown I ever saw who was conscious, at each moment, of everything that was going on. He had a unique ability to show people the humor in all things and, most of all, in themselves. A gentle, funny, and helpful man, he was always around in a tent or a trailer, providing people with a place to come and relieve themselves of their seriousness. Wavy Gravy reminded you that you didn't have to be an adult; five minutes with Wavy and he could loosen up the strings and have you laughing at life in the most beautiful and disarming way.

Most of the early gatherings (often called happenings) were spontaneous and chaotic. There was an anything-goes kind of atmosphere—that is, until various business-oriented types saw there was money to be made by opening more halls and exposing the paying public to more controlled versions of the first rock parties. That was when the Avalon, the Carousel Ballroom, and even some of the "straight" concert halls started bringing in four- or five-group lineups featuring the Bay Area's young electric bands. As a member of The Great Society and later Jefferson Airplane I played them all, but Society, Airplane, and others like The Dead were still just local bands until the record companies read about "the new Flower Power explosion" in San Francisco. Free publicity, although somewhat too cutesy, was popping up in the national magazines like *Time* and *Life*. We'd dose the young reporters with acid until they thought a whole new world was emerging on the West Coast.

Maybe it was.

17

Initiation Rites

Not long after we'd formed The Great Society, we were approached by a couple of L.A. business/music men scouting for hippie talent. Jack Nitzsche, a Dutch Boy Paints look-alike, mumbled several things we didn't quite understand, but Howard Wolfe said, "Fifty-thousand-dollar contract with Columbia." We all understood that, signed an exclusive deal with him, and the result was that Howard got fifty percent of publishing for "White Rabbit," which he later sold to Irving Music. I still don't know exactly how it all worked, but one day, after The Great Society broke up, Howard Wolfe also "sold" *me* to Bill Graham for $750. Bill was now my new manager for a sum that was not bad for *him*, considering that Airplane's album *Surrealistic Pillow* cost eight thousand dollars to make and pulled in eight million in sales.

Concerning the split-up of Great Society, as far as I can remember, it happened after we'd played together for about a year. Darby Slick and Peter van Gelder had become so enthralled with the sounds of tablas and sitars, they were considering going to India so they could be near the source and study with the masters. At the same time, Jefferson Airplane singer Signe Anderson decided to move to Oregon to raise her child—away from the craziness of the rock community.

It was sometime in 1966, and I was up in the balcony at the Avalon Ballroom watching the crowd down below as they were slowly moving out after an Airplane concert, when Jack Casady, their bass player, came up to talk for a while. The rock-and-roll community was small, we all knew each other, we all went to clubs together, and we all watched each other play. So I was accustomed to hanging out and chatting with the guys from Airplane. But that night, seemingly out of nowhere, Jack said, "What do you think about singing with Airplane?"

My reaction to Jack was a calm (trying to be cool), "Yeah, that might work."

What was I really thinking? *ARE YOU KIDDING? FINALLY, I'M GOING TO BE ON THE FUCKING VARSITY SQUAD!*

I didn't say that out loud, but for me, this was an initiation, an invitation to hold what I'd always thought was a lofty position reserved only for supermodels, movie stars, and great physical beauties ad nauseam. It felt like the flat-chested, kinky-brown-haired sarcastic bitch was breaking down another barrier in Barbie Land.

Grace, take a bow.

My mother was the first in a succession of blondes who solidified my early belief that blondes were always the first choice and everybody else, except Elizabeth Taylor (who *was* a blonde for her part in the first movie of Taylor's I saw,

Little Women), had to stand in line for the scraps. Since I was blonde as a child, I'd figured things would be just fine when I was an adult, and until I was thirteen, my confidence in the successful transition was unquestioned. After all, I'd been born with the preferable hair color. If the prevailing color for female icons had been red, I would have been bedeviled by the likes of Botticelli's Venus on a half shell.

But that unlucky number, thirteen, was the year puberty kicked in, and instead of getting pimples, my father's genes came roaring into place. The fat, short, round-faced blonde that I was shot up from five feet, two inches to five feet, seven inches, my weight plunged downward, and my hair changed from a soft, textured curly blonde to fourteen inches of dark brown S.O.S. pad, all uncontrollable fuzz. All in the space of about two years.

Getting the weight off wasn't bad, but the rest of the genetic makeover had me inwardly screaming.

By the way, I've tested out my people-prefer-blondes theory. In the late seventies, I went to a bar in Mill Valley, California, once, with my own brown hair, my own unpainted face, regular clothes, and flat heels. I sat down for a half hour, and the only man in the room who spoke to me was the bartender. I went back home, put on a long black dress, makeup, high heels, and a long blonde wig. And then back to the same bar.

Instant popularity.

Come to think of it, maybe I was predestined to sport the darker look. During an acid trip, as odd as it was, I realized I had an almost eerie affinity for anything Spanish. In fact, I discovered that I could jam in the Eastern flamenco tradition easier than I could sing in the Western twelve-tone scale. I don't know where it came from, but the music, dance, architecture, and culture of Renaissance Spain is still burned into my psyche as if I had actually lived there. With no Spanish blood that I know of, and no Spanish influence (with the possible exceptions of California city and street names), I still gravitate to all aspects of that country as if it were my own.

Out of this same influence came the song "White Rabbit." The music is a *bolero* (Spanish) rip-off, while the lyrics were inspired by Lewis Carroll's *Alice in Wonderland*. In part the lyrics allude to the hypocrisy of the older generation swilling one of the hardest drugs (alcohol) known to man, but telling us not to use psychedelics.

Well, how about *their* medicine chests?

Patriarch has to get it all done *now*? Take some speed.

Is Mom nervous about the kids? The PTA? The burnt dinner? Take some phenobarbital.

Need some sleep? Take some barbiturates.

The athletes want to jump higher? Take steroids.

How about the addict who wants to forget his painful day-to-day existence? Take heroin.

Take booze to get into the party mood. Take Valium for the nerves; Tagamet for the ulcers.

Contrary to popular belief, the "adults" were the original experimenters with the ups, downs, and sideways manufactured by the "legal" drug dealers—Roche, Johnson & Johnson, Merck, Rorer, Eli Lilly, Yuban, Smirnoff, American Tobacco Company, and the list goes on. Fun with alcohol and cigarettes. Fun *and* deadly. Just like the rest of life.

Let's face it, we all want it—the smoke, the fat, the sugar, the booze, *and* the magic-bullet drugs to fix us up when all of the above have taken their toll. *Prevention* means you have to be responsible for your own health.

Fuck it, we want a Big Mac.
But—

One pill makes you larger
And one pill makes you small,
And the ones that Mother gives you
Don't do anything at all.

These were cautious mixed messages that seemed to be the way our parents dealt with the world. After listening to Miles Davis's and Gil Evans's *Sketches of Spain* about fifty times without stopping—a manic marathon of obsessive behavior—I went to my old red upright piano (with about ten keys missing), and crammed *Alice in Wonderland*–inspired lyrics into a *bolero*-style march that I called "White Rabbit." Being totally honest with myself, I think I missed the mark with the lyrics, because what I'd intended was to remind our parents (who were sipping on highballs while they badgered us about the new drugs) that *they* were the ones who read all these "fun with chemical" children's books to us when we were small.

And if you go chasing rabbits
And you know you're going to fall,
Tell 'em a hookah smoking caterpillar
Has given you the call.

Peter Pan sprinkles white dust on everybody and suddenly they can fly—cocaine.

Dorothy and her band of sweet misfits (a rock-and-roll band?) are off to see the wizard and they get off on poppies—opium.

Suddenly they encounter the fantastic Emerald City—a psychedelic wonderland.

Which brings us, last but not least, to the biggest druggie of them all, Alice, who uses chemicals that literally get her high, tall, and short—DRINK ME, EAT ME. She takes a bite out of the Caterpillar's "magic" mushroom (psilocybin) and pulls a toke from his hookah (hashish). The girl is thoroughly ripped all the way through the book. And our parents wondered why we were "curiouser and curiouser" about drugs.

> When logic and proportion
> Have fallen sloppy dead
> And the White Knight is talking backwards
> And the Red Queen's "Off with her head!"
> Remember what the dormouse said,
> "Feed your head. Feed your head."

Whether or not the lyrics imparted what I wanted them to, the song still represents some of the attitudes of an era, so I suppose it was successful in a symbolic framework. With the spiritual/sexual warmth of "Somebody to Love" and the strange hybrid of "White Rabbit," I brought two hits to the already popular set list of Jefferson Airplane.

18

Knobs and Dials and Wires

Signe Anderson was finishing up her last performances with Airplane when I started rehearsing at Jack Casady's and Marty Balin's apartment in Haight Ashbury. Since the group already knew their material, they didn't need the practice.

But I did.

Mostly when we got together, though, it was about conversation and listening to other people's records, so I had to find other ways to get familiar with the music. Airplane was the first San Francisco band to sign with a major label, RCA, and since they'd already recorded *Jefferson Airplane Takes Off*, I could practice along with the album. But only some of the numbers they performed live were on that album, so to get a feel for their stage routine, I'd go and watch them whenever they were playing.

Signe was still one of the lead singers, but one night at the Fillmore, Bill Graham came backstage all worked up.

"Where's Signe?" he yelled. "You guys were supposed to go on five minutes ago!" I knew what was coming next. "Say, Grace, think you can do the show?"

"Uh, can we wait for another five? She might be stuck in traffic," I said.

Signe never came.

When I stepped out onto the stage at the Fillmore to sing with Jefferson Airplane for the first time, I was scared shitless. Airplane was extremely popular at the time. The group had become an integral part of the current scene while The Great Society was still working its way up the ladder. What terrified me was not the fear that I lacked the talent, or even that I lacked knowledge of the material. I knew the songs because I'd been listening to them for a long time. The audience at the Fillmore knew me, they'd seen me many times with The Great Society, so I wasn't afraid of their acceptance or of fucking up the lyrics.

My problem was that I detested performing without lots of rehearsals, without meticulous preparation. I'm still that way. I like to practice whatever it is I'm about to do until I have the technical side down perfectly. Only then do I feel free to express myself. I'd imagined my first performance with Airplane would be well rehearsed, that when I replaced Signe, it would be a pat changeover. But there I was, ready to start singing, with very little preparation and, hence, no self-assurance.

Even so, I stepped out onstage with plenty of attitude, calculated, looking casual, walking slowly, careful to keep my hands relaxed and by my sides, no fingers twitching. I gave the audience a smile and a silent look that said, "I know I'm new, I know you're used to Signe, but I'm here now." In a certain way, it felt natural to be there and I tried to look like I belonged, like I had the situation handled. Of course inside I was a nervous wreck.

I didn't realize how much louder Airplane played than Great Society. With the low-tech monitor speakers, I couldn't hear a thing except the amplified guitars—I didn't have any idea what notes I was singing. That's rough for a singer, not to be able to hear yourself. When you play a guitar, you have frets that are always in the same place, so even if you can't hear yourself play, when you hit those frets, you can be sure, by finger placement, that you're playing a specific note. With piano keys, it's the same. But a singer has an invisible instrument, and if you can't hear yourself, you can't be sure what the hell you're singing.

That night, I just hoped that whatever I was doing was somewhere near the music that the band was playing. When the set was over, I knew it had been awful, but Airplane's road manager, Bill Thompson, in particular, and all the guys in the band, in general, were very encouraging. Someone said, "We have a tape of it—you want to listen?"

"No," I said quickly, not interested in hearing back a performance that I knew had sucked, "but I *do* want to step up the practices. And let's do them plugged in, instead of those deceptively audible acoustic rehearsals."

When a band *is* in sync, and everybody is playing well and feeling good, there's nothing like it. You, both the audience *and* the performers, *become* the power of the music. It's a biological as well as a spiritual phenomenon and it still happens to me when I'm riding around in a car or sitting at home listening to 130 decibels of speaker-cracking music. An almost tangible shift in feeling happens as I go from thick to weightless. It's like swimming in scuba gear with a twenty-five percent nitrous feed.

The first time I recorded in the big Studio A at RCA on Sunset Boulevard, I felt like a kid who loves horses getting paid to ride a stallion for a couple of months. Four gigantic Altec speakers were set up so we could literally feel the playback, the technology could squeeze or explode a sound, and the engineers could get whatever sound you wanted if you could just explain it to them. There were countless knobs and dials and wires to mold a song into an aural vision, and I was fascinated by all of it. Along with the stationary equipment, the guys in the band were starting to experiment with all the new gadgets that were coming out on a daily basis for the electric guitar. Rick Jarrard, our producer, was a company man, and between his ear for how the completed song should sound and our desire to make it unique, the finished "product" worked for everybody—the suits *and* the kids. During the making of *Surrealistic Pillow*, even when I wasn't recording, I was in the studio, just watching and listening to all the machinery transform the simplest noise into an all-enveloping sound. It was Jefferson Airplane's second album (following *Jefferson Airplane Takes Off*), but it was *my* first, and I didn't want to miss a second of the process.

If you're wondering what the title *Surrealistic Pillow* means, it's one of those names that leaves the interpretation up to the beholder. When Marty Balin asked Jerry Garcia what he thought of the studio tapes, Jerry said, "Sounds like a surrealistic pillow." Asleep or awake on the pillow? Dreaming? Making love? The adjective "surrealistic" leaves the picture wide open.

What went on outside the studio during that time certainly dipped into the surreal world. We all stayed at the Tropicana, a cheap motel on Santa Monica Boulevard, where we had semi-kitchenette setups and complimentary smog. On one of our first nights in L.A., we were coming back to our rooms, when we heard what we thought was a dog howling. On the balcony, crawling on all fours, was a totally nude Jim Morrison, barking at the moon. Oblivious to the contrast between his "natural" state and the urban slum look of midtown L.A., he kept up the dog act even after Paul Kantner stepped over him to get to his room.

When I asked Paul what he said to Morrison, Paul answered, "What do you say to a guy who's becoming a dog? Nothing." Jim was so willing to take himself completely to the *edge* of human experience, I found his "performance" both fascinating and frightening. I tried to imagine what kind of curiosity could take someone to those extremes without the overwhelming fear of "Maybe I'll never get back." But get back to what? Who's to say which is the preferable reality?

I sometimes see guys dancing down the street, singing and talking to themselves or some imaginary person, and my first thought is, "Too bad, they're nuts." But what do I know? Maybe they're happier people than I'll ever be. My judgment is based on a set of cultural ideas that clearly reflect a cautious norm. I have to regularly remind myself that without the freaks—without the Wright Brothers, or Mozart, or Jim Carrey, or Gandhi, or Le Petomaine, the famous "fartmeister"—existence might be very gray indeed.

During our stay at the Tropicana, I was not only getting to know the music business, I was also getting to "know" my fellow band members. Although, as far as the state of California was concerned, Jerry Slick and I were still married, I hardly ever saw him anymore. Between his work (film) and mine (music), the chances of our even colliding at an airport were slim.

For better or worse, I've always been driven primarily by my passions—for art, architecture, music, learning. I suppose it's selfish, but it's the way I operate, and the sixties rock-and-roll scene in San Francisco, which was all about passion and freedom of expression, was irresistible to me. My marriage with Jerry, on the other hand, was a throwback to the fifties way of life, which heavily impacted Jerry's and my relationship. There was no passion there at all, there never had been, and when I started performing and making music, I found a lifestyle I was far more attuned to. It was the way I'd pictured my life when I was a child. Though Jerry and I wouldn't divorce until 1971, in 1967 I already felt like a single woman.

The sixties idea of sexual freedom was something I actually related to quite easily, despite my earlier programming. To me, switching to the new lifestyle was like changing costumes—was that so difficult? Who wants to wear the same thing every day? Similarly, even if you *love* bananas, you probably wouldn't want bananas at every meal. A little diversification is what we look for in every other area, so why not in bed? At least, that was the thinking at the time, and it made sense to me. So it wasn't surprising that musicians, because of their talent, humor, and proximity, made up the majority of my lovers. When you're in a band, you see more of your fellow band members than you do your blood family, so it stands to reason that I'd end up honing in on the guys I sang next to night after night. During my Great Society and Airplane/Starship years, it seemed like I was married to seven people at once.

I always ignored the old dictum "Never ask a boy out,

always let them ask you." Ask them *out?* How about asking them if they want to FUCK? The Tropicana didn't lend itself to romantic encounters, but if you just ignored the surroundings, things could get downright enjoyable. For example, I knew that Jack Casady was in his room one morning; it was too early to have gone anywhere and too late to be asleep. Using the excuse of having no corkscrew, I called his room for assistance. But wine at 9:00 A.M.? Now Jack is a friendly and helpful sort, so he personally brought the corkscrew over to my room.

Even though Jack and I both considered ourselves sophisticated, the conversation that took place when we knew we were about to make love in five minutes consisted of smiles, jokes, and innuendoes. Basically, we were two embarrassed and horny people, and exactly what we said I don't remember, but the general drift was one of circling anticipation—touch, move back, close in, silence, laugh, get face to face, and come in on the kiss that moves everything to horizontal.

He was an extremely well hung man, and I'm sure Jack's wife, Diana (whom I know and like very much), will forgive that blunt description of the man she didn't even know at the time. But I also was friends with a girl Jack *did* know at the time, a woman named Miranda. A companionable sort, Miranda had also "known" some of our road crew, Paul Kantner and others. Our group obviously had a lot in common, so we had made a point of getting to "know" each other. After I got back to San Francisco and mentioned to Miranda the incident with Jack and me, she said, "Well, *you* get him in L.A., and *I'll* take him in San Francisco."

Okay.

Did Jack feel like a piece of meat being handed around by two sexist sluts? I don't think so. We weren't saddled with the politically correct social/moral restrictions that would later predominate in the Age of AIDS. We were all friends, and one of the possible activities you could do with a friend was have sex. We also had cures for all the sexually transmitted diseases of the time.

As Paul Kantner said many years later, "Forget about 'The Summer of Love'; it should have been called 'The Golden Age of Fucking.'"

19

Lather

Spencer Dryden was my next lover, although I never planned these things. It just wasn't my usual procedure to see someone and take him straight to bed; I needed to let things develop. I once had a girlfriend who was more than happy to get nude and get down right away if she saw somebody she liked, and I was always sort of envious of that spontaneity because it has always taken more than visual input to make me want to join a man. I *do* recognize beauty, but I think a Redwood tree is beautiful and it doesn't make me want to straddle a branch. If the looks-mind-humor package is all there, *then* something kicks in and the hormones start moving. Slowly. This has never been a moral decision; it's just that I'm an eighteen-wheeler and it takes more mechanisms to put me in gear.

Spencer did interesting fills and had a good sense of timing, but he wasn't a power drummer. He played the way his mind worked, always aware of what was going on but more comfortable in the spaces where imagination could flourish. About five feet, nine inches tall with a slight frame and finely chiseled features, he was not only the smallest of the guys, but also the most delicate. Easily hurt and fast to retreat into his own world, he would spend hours writing and drawing ideas for quirky songs that the band would never play. At age twenty-nine, he was older than the rest of us, but at the same time, he seemed like a child. With his big brown eyes always expecting an invisible reprimand, Spencer was perpetually the outsider. He'd played in L.A. strip clubs, doing hours of pounding monotony for the skin trade, and the rest of the band seemed to just tolerate him, out of some vague automatic distaste for the L.A. sensibility, or what they perceived to be L.A.'s *lack* of sensibility.

I, on the other hand, thought he was a beautiful and solitary spirit, inhabited by his own mischievous characters. Even with that sadness in his eyes, he laughed easily. He seemed to be waiting for humor to save him, and he had no trouble with women who wanted to make love to him and mother him at the same time. If I'd had more of the latter instinct, we probably would have stayed together longer.

Spencer's and my common ability to dismiss reality and jump capriciously into the moment was our immediate and sustaining attraction. Our first night "together" began on a bus in the rain, heading to a hotel in Manhattan. The band and crew were laughing and fooling around in back of us, while Spencer and I were sitting side by side and face to face at the same time, hunched down in the seats, giggling in the conspiratorial way little kids have of letting you know its none of your business. It seemed like the bus seats got bigger and bigger and we got smaller and smaller, allowing us to hide from grown-ups' eyes and speak our own language.

I went to his room right after we checked into the hotel.

The rest of the night was darkness, illuminated only by the soft glow of the city lights coming in through the curtain. He wanted it that way—wanted to create a place where nothing could intrude. Gentle and imaginative, he made love the way he thought, the way he played. I wrote the song "Lather" about Spencer, and about all of us looking at the impending age of thirty through the eyes of a bunch of perpetual children.

Lather was thirty years old today,
And Lather came foam from his tongue.
He looked at me eyes wide and plainly said,
"Is it true that I'm no longer young?"
And the children call him famous
What the old men call insane,
And sometimes he's so nameless
That he hardly knows what game to play

Spencer and I moved into an apartment below Jorma Kaukonen, Airplane's lead guitar player, and his wife, Margaretta. I have an interesting eight-by-ten publicity shot of the band standing in front of that building on Washington Street in San Francisco. At first glance, it appears to be a standard group photo. But although I'd prepared to pose for the shot standing beside Spencer, at the last moment Paul was seized by what turned out to be a prophetic impulse and hoisted me up on his shoulder.

That photograph was taken by Jim Marshall, one of the San Francisco photographers who shot virtually all of the Bay Area bands. Granted, he was good at his job, but he got some of the best animated "posed" shots because we all tried to make the boring business of standing around for photo sessions less tedious by fucking with him. He usually didn't think we were funny, and that made it even better, because when we messed with Jim's head for two hours, we'd be cracking up, and he'd get *real* smiles and laughter out of us.

During the time I was seeing Spencer, Jim set up a photo session with Janis Joplin and me. When Janis arrived at my apartment in advance of Jim, we concocted a plan to be serious—no matter what Jim said or did. What ensued was hours of Jim saying, "Come on, you guys, smile." He tried to tell jokes and just be his kind-of-silly self, but Janis and I continued to do the serious routine, thinking Jim would eventually lose it and quit. He didn't, we didn't, and the Grace and Janis side-by-side, grim-looking photograph has shown up on calendars, books, and posters all over the world. No matter what Jim Marshall said or did or what we said or did in return, he always managed to get shots that worked.

Despite the calculation that led up to that picture of Janis and me, if you look closely at it, you can see the dissimilarity between our two personalities. Younger than I was, Janis appeared far more world-weary—as if her dreams had already been altered by disillusionment. Even though it was hot that day, she was wearing a dress, a beaded cape, four pounds of jewelry, and a fur hat—the full hot-mama mask. I, as yet untouched by the same sadness (I'd experience *that* much later in life), was in a Girl Scout uniform, making fun of the suburban club I'd never joined. My face looked like a soft version of "Try me, sucker." I was self-contained, and I thought I knew how to manipulate the props into the scene I wanted to play.

Janis knew more than I did about "how it was," but she lacked enough armor for the inevitable hassles. She was open and spontaneous enough to get her heart trampled with a regularity that took me thirty years to experience or understand. On the various occasions when we were together, she seemed to be holding in something she thought I might not want to hear, like older people do when they hear the kids they love saying with absolute youthful confidence, "Oh, that'll never happen to me." Sometimes you know you can't *tell* them how it is, they have to find out for themselves. Janis felt like an old soul, a wisecracking grandmother whom everybody loved to visit. When I was with her I often felt like a part of her distant family, a young upstart relative who was still too full of her own sophistry to hear wisdom. Did we compliment each other? Yes. But not often enough.

Contrasting with Spencer, the thin man in black, was David Crosby, with his Southern California Sun Boy ebullience. Everything about and around him had the natural exuberance of juicy ripe fruit. David's home in Laurel Canyon, with its rubbed wood, hand-carved figures of boats and whales, and beautiful acoustic guitars lying around everywhere, was the quintessential retreat for a man who liked to hide out in the open.

Open doors, open windows, and open refrigerator. Open mind, manners, and morals.

When Paul and I went to visit him during a week off from recording *Pillow*, David had two or three golden nymphs with trays of food and Michuocan moving quietly around the house, while he played his latest songs on a guitar that was almost as beautiful as the women who lived there. He loved them. They loved him. For David, at that time, two women together were what love was all about. I was later to sing a song by David called "Triad," which his own band rejected because of its reference to living as a threesome.

"What can we do now that we both love you,"
I love you too—I don't really see
Why can't we go on as three
You are afraid—embarrassed too
No one has ever said such a thing to you.

I didn't understand his band's objection. If everyone's happy about it, who cares? It was just a song, anyway, and what's the value of songwriting if not to bring up fringe topics, ideas that everybody thinks about but lacks the guts to express openly?

Some of the fringe topics that we all wrote about then and over the following years, included the following:

Possible space travel: *Blows against the Empire*
 —PAUL KANTNER
A sexual threesome: "Triad" —DAVID CROSBY
Television addiction: "Plastic Fantastic Lover"
 —MARTY BALIN
Stand-up comedian as clergy: "Father Bruce"
 —GRACE SLICK
Clashes with the police: "For What It's Worth"
 —STEPHEN STILLS
Drugs: "Heroin" —THE VELVET UNDERGROUND
Change: "Break on Through" —THE DOORS
Gay issues: "Lola" —THE KINKS
Poverty: "We Gotta Get out of This Place"
 —ERIC BURDON

20

Jailbirds

We were now full throttle into the twenty-four-hour lifestyle that built or destroyed rock musicians. For a while Bill Graham was our manager, but after he'd booked us into three different cities in one day, we decided that his powerhouse management and our interest in having some time to rest or goof off were at terminal odds. Bill Thompson, who'd been our road manager, moved into the position of full-time manager, nurse, confidant, psychotherapist, and fellow freak.

Graham accepted our shift, and this preservation move probably saved our lives, because *all* the members of Jefferson Airplane are still alive, a rarity among the rock-and-roll groups of the sixties. Whether or not we could have made mounds of money with one of the L.A. or New York pros is now a moot point. Bill Thompson was, and is, a friend, who stayed with us through every strange development that occurred in the band over a period of thirty years. In fact, he still negotiates contracts and conducts legal business for the Airplane/Starship entities, with varying degrees of appreciation from the band members.

There were no big audiences or predictable venues then, as is the current situation with rock tours, so some of our early jobs were truly strange. We played in places where the people didn't even know who or *what* we were. On any given evening in the Midwest, you could find us warming up in a country club where we were viewed as base entertainment right up there next to a bearded lady. The audience of rich hog farmers would just stand there with their mouths open, wondering if we might explode or turn inside out—or engage in some other hideous act that would *really* get them off. You've got to remember, the gap between "straight" and "freak" was so wide then, we weren't even considered human in some southern states.

One bust occurred in New Orleans, which, compared to the rest of the South, was actually quite loose. There was flagrant drunkenness, entertaining misuse of political power (is that redundant?), and the ever-expanding population of musicians and freaks in the Crescent City. We checked into our hotel, and within a few minutes everybody, except me, gathered in Chick Casady's room. (Chick, Jack's brother, worked with the band taking care of the equipment.) I wanted to wash off the traveling first, before the fun started.

But the so-called fun took an unexpected turn. Refreshed from my shower, I strolled down the hallway and knocked on Chick's door, expecting to find my comrades hanging out, getting high, making snide remarks at the TV, talking about amplifiers, and getting ready to check out the local clubs—as usual. But no one answered. Someone in the crew came by and told me the guys were all in jail. Apparently, they'd wedged towels beneath the door—their usual modus operandi—but the scent of pot had somehow penetrated and wafted into a security guard's nostrils. Everybody in the room had been arrested for drug possession and taken to the local precinct.

My concern for hygiene had saved me; I was the only one who missed the Jazz City slammer. The next night, after Thompson managed to get everybody out, fifteen hundred high school students dressed in classic prom gear came to hear the "jailbirds" from San Francisco do "acid rock."

Did they know what it was?

No.

Did they know it was okay to stand up and dance?

No.

They sat there instead, in polite clumps of corsages and stiff tuxedos, clapping for songs that encouraged the complete annihilation of every aspect of their constricted little lives up to and including that peculiar point in time. They could hardly help it; what did they know?

But dumb adults were another matter. Wealthy contributors to the established art museums would receive invitations to concerts that were put on by the "Friends of Culture," or some other cloying title, where they could see radical new *mishigas* without having to leave their upper-class neighborhoods. The Whitney Museum, my case in point, was filled with lots of furs and diamonds one afternoon, while the patrons patiently waited to see the drug-addled psychedelic trend from the West Coast: Jefferson Airplane. Having been to Finch College, I knew this well-heeled crowd before I even saw them.

One of the newest electronic innovations was a cordless microphone, and the night of our Whitney Museum appearance was the first time I got to use and abuse this liberating device. Someone put it in my hand and informed me that it would likely carry from the top floor all the way down to the room where we'd be playing. I was fascinated and inspired, so in the elevator, on the way to the ground floor, I let the straights have a warm-up talk. Before the music began, before they could even see who was ragging on their ass, I spoke into the mike, "Hello, you fools. You got Rembrandts on the mantel and a Rolls in the garage, but your old man still wouldn't know a clitoris from a junk bond if you had the guts to show him your twat in the first place."

I added other congenial remarks that made people just want to love me no matter what I did, following such a friendly introduction. I might add that none of the other band members were as prone to warming up audiences the way I was. They were *musicians*, while I was a perverse clown.

Was any of my outrageous behavior fueled by drugs? You betcha. Chemicals destroy inhibitions *and* basic body functions, if administered in the right proportions. Since I'm damned near sixty years old, I can now say with relative impunity the same kind of flippant shit I dished at the Whitney, but would I encourage that sort of "self-destructive" behavior in the nation's youth? Of course! We're overpopulated.

Back when LSD was circulating, I had to constantly look out for the invisible dosers. Since acid was tasteless, colorless, and effective in very small quantities, it was easy to slip someone a hit without their knowledge. Surreptitious dosing was not an activity in which I engaged, but if one of the guys set down his 7-Up bottle in the dressing room, the doser, usually a member of another band, might put a little acid on the bottle's lip. The next thing the thirst quencher knew, the walls were dripping green slime, he thought he was Napoleon, and it was time to go onstage. Since I've never liked soft drinks (easily accessible open containers), the dosers never got me, but an honest dose was had by all of us in Fargo, North Dakota.

We were backstage, in semidarkness, waiting to go on, and our road manager, Bill Laudner, brought out the usual clear plastic drug tray with dividers in it to separate one powder from another. One section held vitamins, while the others held, respectively, a nasal decongestant, crystal Methedrine, cocaine, LSD, and some popular headache remedy. We thought we were each taking a couple of snorts of cocaine, but due to the lack of lighting, the entire band made the mistake of honking up enough acid to make the whole night a complete joke.

About fifteen minutes into the set, I looked over at Marty and noticed that his face was decomposing. The drug was beginning to kick in, and we started giving each other goofy smiles that said, "That wasn't cocaine, was it?" The Fargodome added to the weirdness of the situation with its inverted saucer shape that positioned the audience up in the air and the performers down at the bottom. To the band, it was like being on an operating table in a surgical observation room.

I always loved Jack's bass sound, so during the beginning of his solo, when I was supposed to be playing the piano, I just stopped and turned around to face the speakers, not thinking about whether that abrupt move would mess up the continuity of the song. I'm sure each member of every sixties band has stories about drug silliness onstage, but fortunately, our audiences were usually as fucked up as we were, so they pleasantly went along with whatever was happening.

Those were the good old days.

Ah yes, children. Those were the times before everybody "became powerless and our lives became manageable."

Before consistent togetherness became "codependent."

Before black people started killing each other over "Who's got the music?"

Before white people discovered "politically correct."

Before a pat on the butt became "sexual harassment."

Before you couldn't fix your computerized life if your ass depended on it—*Newsweek,* June 2, 1997.

Of course, the "fabulous free psychedelic sixties and early seventies" were not all fun and games. Consider the following:

Young men were killing each other in a dipshit war in Vietnam.

Students were being shot to death at Kent State.

Cops were using clubs and tear gas on peace demonstrators.

Birmingham was trying to shut up black people by sending in dogs and fire hoses.

And our president, attorney general, and leading civil rights leader were all being struck by assassins' bullets.

The sixties were a time when people with electric guitars naively but nobly thought they could change the whole genetic code of aggression by writing a few good songs, and using volume to drown out the ever-present whistling arsenal.

So much for acid. It may have been illegal, but it never made me any enemies. Alcohol was the "fun" chemical that fueled most of my outbursts of congenial conversation, like the cordless mike incident at the Whitney Museum. That's the *legal* beverage that causes husbands and wives to kill each other, prisons to fill up to capacity, highway death rates to soar, six-figure missed work days, and self-inflicted hospital admissions. Without my use of alcohol, Marty Balin might not have said in an interview: "Grace? Did I sleep with her? I wouldn't even let her give me head." God only knows what offensive behavior of mine he was reacting to. I can't remember, probably because of the alcohol. Without alcohol, I'd be richer by two million dollars that went to pay lawyer's fees. What an interesting ride it's been, folks.

I stayed away from heroin, not out of any moral or righteous decision; it just didn't look like much fun. The first person I saw nodding on the stuff was an excellent guitar player who'd come to the studio where we were recording, to visit and listen to us play. When I got there, anticipating meeting him, I found him sitting in a chair, head drooping to one side and drool trickling from his mouth. (I know you're wondering about who he was, but trust me, you wouldn't know his name even if I mentioned it.)

"What's wrong with him?" I asked one of the guys.

"He's a junkie. But he just had a fix and he'll be okay in a minute."

"If he wants to sleep, why doesn't he go to bed?" I asked.

A grin was the answer.

I was interested in drugs as a means to enjoy or alter the

waking state. I simply couldn't figure out why anyone would take the trouble to get the money, get the dealer, get all the paraphernalia, get sick, go into a coma—and then consider it an experience they'd want to repeat.

21

Monterey Pop

It wasn't until I heard The Beatles' album *Revolver* that I started liking their music. A friend phoned when the Mop Tops were appearing on the *Ed Sullivan Show*, and said, "Wait till you see these guys. They're wonderful!" What *I* saw was four guys in their twenties wearing matching cute outfits with matching cute hairdos, singing a too-cute song, "I Wanna Hold Your Hand." If I had been twelve years old, they might have been impressive.

At the time, my idea of rock and roll was The Rolling Stones—craggy wiseguys playing flat-out rock with seriously offensive lyrics, each of them making their own decisions about what to wear and how to look. I loved how Jagger *defied* his audience to join in the fun. The women who were my contemporaries were either folk sopranos or blues singers, categories that didn't fit Yours Truly. Jagger's bad-boy-with-attitude persona was something I understood. I didn't copy his singing style or mannerisms, but, from watching him perform and listening to his music, I learned how to let it out and damn the censorship. Jagger and The Stones were the only element I missed at the Monterey Pop Festival.

The rest of it was perfect.

Outdoor concerts are common now, but when Monterey Pop happened, I'd never seen anything like it. Produced by Lou Adler and The Mamas and the Papas, it's the only festival I can think of that was excellent in every way.

It was June 1967. In the beautiful setting of the Carmel coast, the audience area was on a large, grassy lawn surrounded by cypress and pine trees. Unlike most summer concerts where the sun shone down mercilessly, here the big tree branches broke up the light into soft beams, making everything look like a Disney version of Sherwood Forest. In back of the trees, around the perimeter of the seating space, were about thirty small booths, individually decorated with colored silks and cottons and hand-painted banners, showing off every kind of original creation—from one-of-a-kind boots and belts to framed paintings by amateur artists. Even the stalls selling food and concert items were quaint and uninfected by corporate logos and pitchmen.

I had previously heard most of the musicians at Monterey Pop on record, but I had never actually seen them live, from Otis Redding to Ravi Shankar. The lineup boasted an all-inclusive representation of "new" music. Black, white, East, West, rock, blues, instrumental, pop, and folk—the three-day list of performers was made up of nothing but headliners. You may have seen some of the performances in the film *Monterey Pop* on VH1 or MTV. One clip of Jefferson Airplane has the camera on Yours Truly, mouthing the lyrics of the song "Today," but it was Marty's song and *his* voice on

"Jimi Hendrix" (Grace Slick)

the soundtrack. Since I knew his phrasing, I used to just sing along while I was playing the piano, and the engineer, who knew my habits, would turn my mike off. But in the film, my lips match Marty's vocals perfectly, and it appears *I'm* the one singing. Twenty-five years ago, Marty probably wasn't too happy that no one caught the editing mistake and that my lip synching appeared in the final film version, but I'm sure he finds it mildly amusing now.

"Nobody had ever heard anything like it." That was John Phillips talking about Jimi Hendrix's performance at Monterey. I watched him play the guitar with his teeth, use the mike stand for slide guitar, bang into the speakers for feedback, and finally set his guitar on fire with lighter fluid. None of the theatrics could overshadow his incredible musicianship. And the fabulous outfit! He wore a perfect sixties costume: Spanish hat, Mongol vest, ostrich boa, English velvet pants, silk ruffled paisley shirt, pounds of handmade jewelry, and Western boots. If any musician represented that era, it was Jimi Hendrix.

At Monterey Pop, within seventy-two hours, you could see The Who, Buffalo Springfield, The Dead, The Mamas and the Papas, Country Joe and the Fish, Big Brother with Janis Joplin, Jimi Hendrix, Laura Nyro, Ravi Shankar, Quicksilver Messenger Service, Simon and Garfunkel, Paul Butterfield, Otis Redding, Jefferson Airplane, and the band that wrote the song about it ("Monterey"), The Animals.

We all combined to create a peaceful and extraordinary offering (even the police cruisers had orchids on their antennas). And I felt lucky to be there, observing one of the great examples of human celebration.

22

Woodstock

On August 15, 1969, two years after Monterey Pop, Woodstock took center stage, both in my personal history and in collective history. It's an event that has been reported on, analyzed, sung about—even re-created twenty-five years later. Everyone has a take on that magical moment in time.

"The sun rises on a new hour of creation—we are the Woodstock nation." Nobody and everybody said that in one way or another, from the stage, from the audience, from the heart.

> "We are the Woodstock nation."
> —ABBIE HOFFMAN

> "Warts and all."
> —GRACE SLICK

And there *were* warts. When we arrived at the concert site in upstate New York near the towns of Liberty and

Woodstock, despite the initial feeling of having arrived "home," it was clear that the as-yet-unfinished site needed a lot of work and faith to support the half million young people who'd soon be camping out there for four days.

It was construction mania. Thirty tents, fifty-foot towers for spotlights, overflowing hotels, rain-drenched muddy roads. The structure that would be a stage for forty acts was still lying around in pieces waiting be assembled. The scaffolding, sheets of plywood, and pile of two-by-fours would, in a matter of hours, become the big Erector Set platform that would support ten different bands at a time—nine waiting and one playing. It was to be a constant show from beginning to end. No intermissions. No breaks for sleeping, for peeing, for anything.

Guys in hard hats with walkie-talkies were pointing and shouting, while Chip Monck, the young lighting director, was answering five questions at once. "Please don't climb on the metal towers," he bellowed over the PA system. "If they fall, it's fifty feet of metal crashing into five hundred people." Big rolls of plastic sheeting were brought out to protect the electronic equipment as drenching rain suddenly and chaotically shifted everyone's plans. The skies would empty off and on throughout all the days of the concert.

Was it really going to work, this gigantic dream?

I'd been blissfully unaware of the extent of the financial fuck-ups going on around the Monterey Pop Festival, but it seemed that Airplane, Big Brother, and a couple of other bands had had to hire attorneys to find out what happened to the profits. The lawyers for the promoters said the revenue had been directed toward "charitable purposes," but what about television syndication? No money was ever distributed to any of the bands and donations to charities were unrecorded, if they had occurred at all.

We didn't want a repeat performance of that one, so our manager, who'd learned the hard way, was determined to do it differently this time. When the negotiations for Woodstock started, Bill Thompson went to the wire in demanding that his bands be paid *before* they performed. The promoters resisted, spouting stuff about "peace and love." But Thompson came back with how he'd be feeling a lot more peace and brotherly love *after* he'd been handed a check. It was a good move, collecting early, because we heard later that six hundred thousand dollars in bad checks eventually bounced on the bands who hadn't been paid prior to performing.

Woodstock clearly wasn't about money, since most of the bands didn't take a lot of money away from it, so what was it really about?

On the outer levels, it could be experienced as either nerve-racking chaos or joyous confusion, depending on your level of tolerance and drug ingestion. There was plenty of the latter—Owsley, the master acid chemist, was giving the stuff away, and the pot smoke could be detected for miles. In between the music, over the loudspeakers came the soothing voice of the event's bad-trip caretaker, Wavy Gravy, advising, "Don't take the brown pills," or, "If you get confused, come to our tent and we'll help you see humor in the chaos."

You could wear nothing or everything. Either choice of "outfit" would honor the nameless spirit. Or you could try a little of both. Adorn yourself in the full regalia of a sorcerer, roll in the mud, let the rain splash it all away, and then take all your clothes off and dance.

I wanted to be clear—light—no color. I chose white. White pants and a white leather dress with fringe that swayed when I moved, just right for the first gathering of the tribes, our first verbal declaration to the world that we were more than isolated misfits.

In the past, in all the other cities on two continents, whenever we entered a hotel, we were the minority freaks—proud of it, but still the outcasts. But when we walked into the Holiday Inn in the town of Liberty, New York, not far from the Yasgur farm, where Woodstock was held, the world of rock and roll literally filled the hotel. Wall-to-wall long-haired, loud-mouthed, laughing, screaming freaks—no longer the minority. We were, in fact, a growing representation of an inevitable shift in consciousness and ideology.

I spent the day of our performance at the hotel in a quiet, kind of thoughtful state. Everybody else was playing pool and getting fucked up, but adopting my usual habit before a performance, I'd chosen to go inside myself, making a mental list. Where were we about to perform? How long would the set last? What did I need to do about the accessories on my dress? If I sat, would the shells break or the feathers get crushed? How did I want to present myself, and how did I fit into the ceremony? Should I try to be one thing or another? Or should I just leave it all alone? I knew one thing for sure: I wanted to look like a strong but fluid representation from the Coast, so I wasn't about to get so fucked up that I looked like a freaked-out slob.

There was no more road access to the concert site because of the relentless rain, so a helicopter flew us from the hotel to the platform. We soared down over a field of muddy but smiling faces a little before 9:00 P.M. That was

Woodstock: haggard but happy, Janis and me. (Time, Inc., collection)

when we were supposed to perform, and I felt magic in the blue-black night as we got out of the helicopter and placed our feet on the stage. But due to transportation and scheduling fuck-ups, we didn't go on until sunrise.

Seated for nine hours in a darkness broken only by the towering white beams of spotlights that flowed downward from the sky, I was a part of a congregation of musicians from the tribes of a temporarily undivided state. No bathrooms—my body, seemingly obeying a higher order, shut down and I had no need. No chairs—we gathered on the floor of the gigantic stage to watch and be watched without the heavy cover of imperatives. After arranging ourselves in

an arc around the center stage, engaged in a nondenomi-
national rite, food seemed to come from nowhere. We par-
took from each other's stash of fruit, cheese, wine,
marijuana, coke, acid, water, and conversation.

Were we, the bands, there to invoke the spirits? The
gods? Were we pagan? No labeling was necessary. We were
all shamans of equal power, channeling an unknown
energy, seeking fluidity. I felt like a princess in a benign
court—one without thrones or crowns. I could see "royalty"
in every direction. The audience was just more of "us." The
performers were just more of "us."

We seemed to take turns representing each other—
sometimes someone else slept for my tired body. A friend
danced when I could only stand, and I spoke when
someone else felt like it was time to listen. My focus shifted
all night long; sometimes it was on the stage, at other times
it was on the audience. At still other times, it was somewhere else altogether that was impossible to describe. So
much of Woodstock's appeal was the chance to simply
come together and touch what we knew had already taken
birth. It was something that had formed from the energy of
the invisible collective consciousness. It was shades of
Huxley, Leary, the surrealists, Gertrude Stein, Kafka—the
inexhaustible list of artists who'd encouraged multiple
levels of observation. It was *our* turn. We were ready to
breathe, ready to celebrate change.

Woodstock was especially intense for Crosby, Stills and
Nash, who up until that time had only played together
twice. This was their first large-scale performance as a
group, and they were determined to get it right. As it
turned out, they were *so* good, it was amazing, and I was
jealous of their preparation. They'd obviously rehearsed

their harmonies to perfection. They demonstrated a kind of professional blend I'd hoped Airplane would develop.

And then there was Jimi Hendrix's rendition of "The Star-Spangled Banner." He played it as a cry, solely with his guitar, using no words. With no anger on his face, no sign of annoyance or of sympathy, he played the national anthem as it had never been played before, expressing *all* of the aspects. He offered not just the traditional "my country, right or wrong" rendition, but something else that showed us—via screaming, sliding notes—the truth about our beautiful but fucked-up nation. It was an interpretation none of us would ever forget.

Strangely odd and at the same time ordinary images of those days remain in my head: Jackie Kaukonen, Jorma's sister-in-law, playing poker with Janis Joplin and Keith Moon; The Band all dressed in black, walking single file to their rooms, looking like Amish grandfathers; The Grateful Dead, Joan Baez, and Ravi Shankar at the front desk waiting for their room keys; Dale Franklin, Bill Graham's secretary from the Fillmore East, standing in the lobby with a clipboard directing "traffic."

I really believed the whole world would look like that in about sixteen years—the different skin colors weaving in and out of the tapestry, the unrestricted language and lack of cultural animosity, and the beautiful power of our main language: rock and roll. The blend of African American, Native American, Scottish folk, East Indian, Irish, Spanish, and even classical music all folded into German-Japanese electronic technology to produce art for everybody, our endless anthems celebrating the differences and similarities of the new global family.

At 6:00 A.M., I stepped up to the mike. "All right, friends.

You have heard the heavy groups. Now you will see morning maniac music. Believe me, yeah. It's a new dawn. Good morning, People."

We started our set with "Volunteers." For the moment, the rain had stopped, and it was the dawn of one more new day and the dawn of a fascinating point in history. I looked out at a mass of half a million children covered in wet mud, some celebrating, some sleeping, some making love with each other, oblivious to the people around them. Plastic sheeting protected clothing and bodies, paper bags sheltered heads. A few guys danced, tossing around their muddy, long hair, but no matter what anyone was doing, we were all focused on the same thing.

I hardly remember singing, and I'm sure it wasn't my best performance. I'd been up all night, my eyelids were at half-mast, but it hardly mattered because good and bad had disappeared for four days and nights. The audience was completely appreciative, no demanding attitudes with their applause, total acceptance when one group stopped and another began. There was no competition. We were all just there, grateful to be a part of all of it: the beauty, the misery, the exhaustion, the exhilaration, the mud, and the glory of dawn.

Did the gigantic dream work? It not only worked, it remains a magnificent symbol of an era. The musical execution of most of the bands was far from perfect, but the spirit was so powerful, it overrode all technical considerations.

We are all accustomed to big outdoor concerts these days; they've become a part of our culture. But not so in 1969. Woodstock, the first of its kind, represented the split between what we had come from in the fifties and what we were becoming in the sixties. Today, the mere name "Woodstock" immediately conjures an image of a specific point in time where social theory became practice, where for four days and nights in the spirit of acceptance, celebration, and profound ritual, wherever we were, we were all different—and we were all the same.

23

Altamont

Monterey, then Woodstock. And now, ladies and gentlemen, the hot flash of festivals—Altamont.

Pageants, especially those that rouse the passions, often take the form of ritual: they're repeated again and again. That was part of the problem with Altamont—trying to repeat Woodstock. Too many aspects of the Woodstock "ceremony" were circumstantial and therefore impossible to reenact.

During our performance at Altamont I forgot to wear my contact lenses—maybe I just didn't want to see it. The concept was a gigantic Grateful Dead/Airplane/Rolling Stones San Francisco–style concert in the park. But from the earliest planning stages—and leading up to the death of a man in the audience—this event was doomed. In transitioning from idea to practice, it became a series of last-minute downgrades, all pointing to disaster.

When the concept was first emerging, Paul Kantner and

I went to Mick Jagger's house in London to discuss when, where, and how. I'd never met Mick, but the reputation of his group's excesses preceded him. I knew that he and his band were really out of control, much more wild than our group was, and in the taxi with Paul on my way over there I was pretty uncomfortable.

"What's the matter, Grace?" Paul asked.

"It's Mick. What if everybody's shooting heroin and screwing knotholes in the wall or something and I have to sit there and act cool?"

I was afraid we'd be walking into a roomful of foppish junkies engaged in unnatural acts with elegantly dressed ninety-pound groupies, loaded on drugs I'd never heard of. Paul didn't pay me much attention, and by the time we rang the doorbell, I was practically hyperventilating. But good old Mick revealed a different side to his persona; he opened the door in an expensive business suit. I exhaled as soon as I stepped inside. The place was immaculate; Mick had magnificent Oriental rugs covering hardwood floors with Louis XIV furniture and expensive artwork hanging on the walls. He was like a kid dressing up in his rich daddy's accessories. He offered us no dope, just tea. There were no groupies, either. Or unnatural acts. Or fooling around. It was all business.

We sipped tea and discussed the concert idea for about an hour and the whole meeting was so crisp and professional, it totally blew me away. It turned out Mick had gone to business college, and apparently, when he told you he'd be talking business, that's *all* he did. He was one of a small group of rock stars—Frank Zappa and Kiss's Gene Simmons were also members of the club—who never got irreparably jerked around financially, because he paid close attention to what the managers and record companies were doing when it was time to shuffle the deck.

A smart businessman.

The entertainers who *didn't* bother to figure out the sleight-of-hand tricks played by the suits are now hiring pro bono lawyers to try to get back the royalties and perks that slipped away while they were "sniffing up" their assets. Incidentally, if it weren't for Skip Johnson—Starship's lighting director, my future husband of eighteen years, and still my good friend—I'd probably be joining the rest of them in a breadline somewhere, wondering what happened to all the money that flew out the window. Skip closely watched the managers, lawyers, accountants, and record companies, and he spoke up when I missed the errors because I was too busy having "fun." He had the uncanny ability to get ripped at night and show up at the office the next day. Like Mick, he could say thank you to the compliments and still read the fine print.

After hearing Mick's thoughts on how a concert of this kind might be set up, Paul and I reassured Mick that "our people" would stay in touch with "his people." And we left feeling like we'd just had a meeting with a very young art patron, rather than the crown prince of British hedonism. We thought, Hey, *if Mick is this together, maybe this thing can work.*

Wrong.

We'd wanted to hold the concert in Golden Gate Park, but two days before it was supposed to happen, the city of San Francisco said no to the park permit. Sears Point raceway was the next option, but the owners wanted one hundred thousand dollars in escrow from The Stones. Understandably, Jagger said no. Finally, we found Altamont. Located about forty minutes outside San Francisco, Altamont was an ugly, brown, flat, open expanse of land with no tree cover and no personality. Definitely not a pastoral setting. And obtaining a permit for even that was a hassle. We finally got it, but as Paul later reminded me, "We took Altamont out of desperation."

The concert was scheduled on what turned out to be a weird, gray-red dusty day in the muggy dead-grass flatland in the middle of nowhere. The sun never came out. Granted, it rained through most of Woodstock, but this dullness was worse than rain. I wore a pair of blue pants and a blue jacket—nothing striking, no princess posing. This time, I settled for looking like just another guy in the band because the anticipation of another glorious event had been flattened by the constant hassles.

Flying in from Florida after doing a gig the night before, we'd had no sleep, so we were far more concerned with keeping our energy up long enough to make it through our set than with how we looked. There were a couple of trailers near the stage serving as overloaded holding pens for any and all bands, crew, managers, and Hell's Angels, who were acting as security. With a mass of people shuffling around, trying to organize either themselves or some aspect of the production, the atmosphere was closer to traffic at rush hour than an outdoor celebration.

I later told an interviewer, "Woodstock was unruly, but Altamont was reigning chaos." The Hell's Angels were roaring drunk and ready to ignite even before the concert started. Jefferson Airplane went on second, after The Flying Burrito Brothers, and in the middle of the set, my contact-lens-less eyes could see a blurry scramble over on stage left where Marty usually stood. I walked to the drum riser to ask Spencer what was going on, but he just kept playing with a terrified look on his face. Then I walked toward Marty, but he wasn't there. After jumping off the stage to help some poor guy who was being pummeled by the Hell's Angels, he'd apparently made a big mistake by yelling "Fuck you!" at one of the bikers.

"Nobody says 'Fuck you!' to a Hell's Angel," the drunken biker shot back.

"Fuck you!" Marty repeated, without losing a beat.

Our crew gathered around Marty and for some reason, the "Angel" backed off and later apologized. But the problems didn't end there. Mick Jagger, dressed in a black satin cape, was singing "Sympathy for the Devil" when life imitated art and another fight broke out. Toward the end of The Stones' set we left by helicopter, and my enduring memory of Altamont is Paul's line when we looked down at the audience near the stage. "It looks like someone is being beaten to death," he said. He was right—in the hospital the man died of inflicted wounds.

Ralph Gleason, *San Francisco Chronicle* columnist, reported, "In twenty-four hours, we created all the problems of our society in one place: congestion, violence, and dehumanization. The name of the game is money, power, and ego."

"Janice Joplin" (GRACE SLICK)

"Jimi" (GRACE SLICK)

"Jerry Garcia" (GRACE SLICK)

"Alice & the White Rabbit" (GRACE SLICK)

24

Ladies (and Gentlemen) of the Canyon

By 1967, Che Guevara had been assassinated, *Sergeant Pepper's Lonely Hearts Club Band* was the overwhelming hit of the summer, and our album, *Surrealistic Pillow*, had made it to No. 3 on the *Billboard* charts. We started doing promotional TV shows, but the speakers on home TV sets weren't built to carry the new high-volume sounds we were making. Consequently, the music sounded trapped and "tinny." We wanted people to hear the *real* sound of full-spectrum electric rock, not a watered-down jumble of small-speaker crackle.

But radio and TV talk shows help sell records—"so get out there and market that stuff!"

In the dressing room at *The Smothers Brothers Comedy Hour,* I'd never seen so much makeup—everything from black to white and all the shades in between. I was already white, so piling on more white grease paint would have been redundant. But black—that's the right color for singing "White Rabbit," I thought. I wasn't interested in some funny Al Jolson look, though. I wanted to get it as real as possible. The trouble was that my features were angular and not right for the part, so apparently none of the viewers even noticed that I was in special makeup. Since nobody wrote in to the show and said, "What the hell was that?" they must have thought I had on some jet black tanning lotion or that the color on their TV sets had gone haywire. Maybe it was just getting harder to shock the couch potatoes.

When we were living in L.A., doing various TV shows, playing live, and recording our new music, we spent about half our time up in Laurel Canyon. Musicians such as Graham Nash, Joni Mitchell, Frank Zappa, Stephen Stills, and David Crosby, as well as hundreds of others, had flocked to the canyon as a pastoral relief from the flatlands of Hollywood. The guys in the different bands would hop into an array of fast cars, and at night, usually fueled by cocaine, they'd race across Mulholland Drive on the way to friends' parties.

Frank Zappa's house in the canyon, which I visited several times, looked exactly like a troll's kingdom. Fuzzy-haired women lounged in long antique dresses, and naked children ran to and fro while Frank sat behind piles of electronic equipment, discussing his latest ideas for orchestrating satirical hippie rock music. Never a druggie, Frank openly made fun of the very counterculture he was helping to sustain. While the San Francisco artists were creating posters with pictures of flowers, fair maidens, and placid Indian gurus, he was into something quite different. His first poster showed him with his pants down around his ankles, squatting on a toilet. Now that's *my* kind of tasteful commentary.

If only I'd thought of it first.

In those days I made a habit of putting on makeup, shaving my armpits and legs, and wearing dresses or skirts, but the language that came out of my low-end voice was a counterpoint to the refined image I might otherwise be projecting. As my mother so quaintly put it, I tended to talk "like a truck driver!"

My parents' Edwardian background and their experience living through the Depression had produced certain criteria for social accceptance. My father had achieved financial success through hard work; my mother had dedicated her life to her family; and they exhibited neither Jewish nor Italian cultural stamping. Which means they lived by an ethic where you simply don't fly off the handle—ever! Hence, when I began "making it" as a rock star and engaging in outrageous behavior, they were seriously conflicted. My father's response to my newfound celebrity was almost nonexistent, while my mother let me know she liked some of the softer songs the group did, because that was how *she* liked to sing. Of course, none of the softer songs were mine, so basically my parents' reaction to my so-called success was divided between admiration for my financial accumulation and disgust for a lifestyle that was completely contrary to their sense of what was appropriate "for a lady."

A woman who *did* bow her head and blush, although she was very talented and self-reliant at the same time, was Joni Mitchell. She somehow managed to put it all together. When David Crosby took me to the studio where she was recording, Joni was sitting quietly in a chair between takes, singing a soft song for anybody who wanted to listen. When she was finished and David introduced us, she seemed so fragile, I thought she'd break into bunches of rose petals on

153

the floor. That first impression was ultimately wrong—she is a strong woman. But, that first time we met, she seemed like the most sensitive person on the planet, and I couldn't bring myself to fuck up her serenity by being my usual sarcastic "truck driver" self. I saw her recently at a restaurant in L.A. and I was still too chickenshit to deal with someone who was musician enough to record with Charlie Mingus.

Joni lived with Graham Nash in the canyon for a while. In fact, "Our House," Graham's classic hit song, was written as an ode to the relationship he was having with Joni. But as we've all experienced, something changed and "the two cats in the yard" became one cat in town and the other cat in Wyoming. Spencer Dryden later told an interviewer that when I was in L.A., I was having an affair with Graham. I wish. I don't know what made Spencer say that; maybe he was reading my mind. Graham prefers them blonder and quieter.

Too bad for me.

I don't remember whose house it was, probably because I never saw the inside of it, but one night in Laurel Canyon, I drove up to some kind of party that was going on. Before I got out of the car, I saw Stephen Stills, standing out in front of the house by himself, and when I waved, he came over and got into my car to talk. Three hours later, this funny, talented man had poured out the sad story of his breakup with Judy Collins. It sounded like "Suite Judy Blue Eyes" had been the love of his life, and since it was rare to hear a man being that honest about how he *felt*, I was almost honored that he'd confided his feelings to me. I say "almost" because I was beginning to feel like I was the skinny substitute for "the sweet fat girl" who gets the sob stories instead of the heroes. But in my experience, men generally feel more comfortable telling *any* woman how much they hurt, rather than running the risk of seeming weak by showing sorrow in front of another man.

Perhaps PBS (public television) was correct when they once called the sixties "the Age of Anxiety." We all had a lot to be anxious about. Along with a deeper sensitivity emerging in both men and women, our parents just didn't get the ironic connection whenever three-hundred-pound Kate Smith did a loud, maudlin version of "God Bless America." That was the perfect end of *their* era, a demonstration of "Yup, it's over. The fat lady *has* sung. " This was during a time when the garish tailfins and bloat of the fifties were prevalent in a country made rich from a world war.

It was about a nation that needed to go on a diet, a nation that needed to get back in touch with its core.

When the joke of it all was being exposed in art that reflected the depth of a soup can (tell it like it is, Andy Warhol), Laurel Canyon had its own particular form of budding artists: a group of girls who worked in plaster. These artists, known as the Plaster Casters, got their hands on more rocker dicks than the well-known groupie Pamela des Barres, or me or anybody else in the world for that matter. Touting their castes of rock star penises as a sincere artistic endeavor, the girls managed to lure more than a few willing subjects. No surprise there, of course—what big-egoed rock star *wouldn't* want his cock immortalized in soapstone?

Although I wasn't there during any of the actual artistic endeavor, I imagine the procedure must have gone something like this:

The girls (I have no idea exactly who they were), would get the rock star's dick in a comfortable position. That varied for each gentleman, who was offered his handjob of choice—serve yourself, or may we serve you? Next, they'd slap some clay on the erect body part, and after it had hardened into the desired shape (the clay, not the dick), they'd crack it open and take it off. While the rock star relaxed after his ordeal, they'd glue the mold back together, pour the plaster into the clay mold—and wait. Once the plaster had hardened into the container shape, veins and all, they'd break off the clay and there it was—a perfectly immortal plaster specimen.

But I've never see one—have you? No knockoffs, no limited editions, and certainly no originals. The story about these dedicated female artists is so legendary, everybody has heard it or told it, but

WHERE ARE THE DICKS?

If you know of their whereabouts, please send them or any pertinent information to my editor, Rick Horgan, c/o Warner Books in New York.

I wonder, will plaster rock star dicks eventually become valuable artifacts from an anxious age? Or will they just fetch a wry smile, be viewed as yet another item—like pet rocks and 3-D glasses—that earned its five minutes of fame?

Hey, have you heard the one about the disappearing dicks?

25

Reruns

We'd arrived in L.A. armed with the success of *Surrealistic Pillow*, while the increasing publicity touted Jefferson Airplane as being in the forefront of the new music scene. When it was time to record our next album, *After Bathing at Baxter's*, we rented the same mansion The Beatles had used during one of their stays in the Hollywood hills—a big, typical Southern California home with a pool and an underground bowling alley extravagance. The mansion housed our band members and their entourage for the entire six months it took to record the album. Unlike when we'd recorded previously, we were now awash in money, cars, parties with L.A. bands, and new fans hanging out at the studio and in the bedrooms.

The sales of our records broadcast a message that was impossible not to hear: a whole lot of people understood what we were saying and what we meant. And a whole lot equaled success. Artistic success? Who was talking about *art*

anymore? The discussion had moved to the bottom line—
it was about continuity, the charts, the numbers.

In 1968, RCA was paying for all our studio time (that
was the policy then), so we could relax and get weird. Each
member of our group developed his own piece of the puzzle
in the ongoing quest *not* to become a rerun. Unavoidably,
there was a tendency toward deliberate eccentricity. By the
way, the title *After Bathing at Baxter's* was not a specific reference. It came to us quite spontaneously, out of the mouth
of Gary Blackman, a poet friend of Marty's. Gary used to
hang around a lot, and one day, he said, "Hey, why don't
you name this album *After Bathing at Baxter's?*"

Okay.

During this time of excess, the various band members let
most of the business details ride, complaining only occasionally to our mates, instead of taking the problem to the
right source. Except Paul. He was the one who talked to the
managers, producers, CEOs, agents, and record company
toadies. He always showed up at the studio as early as I did,
and his presence in his favorite flowing medieval cape
would immediately change the atmosphere. Conversations
would go from casual to "Look out, the principal's here,"
though not in such a way that the familiar school routine
was interrupted. With his military straight back and a pot-
head's colorful take on the world, Paul presented an
intriguing paradox.

At this point, he was becoming a power figure to me.
He'd question every move the producers or the suits made,
and even if his judgment wasn't always on the mark, at least
someone was guarding whatever integrity we thought we
had and wanted to preserve. Don't mistake me, he could be
a major pain in the ass, but if he was on your side, the oppo-

sition was in deep shit. Romantically, he and I hadn't yet connected, but the union was closing in—the band probably saw it before we did.

There wasn't much time to contemplate much of anything. As soon as we finished *After Bathing at Baxter's,* we immediately went on tour. We'd had offers to go to Europe based on the popularity of *Surrealistic Pillow,* but concert dates in America and the excessive time we'd spent recording *Baxter's* had held us up. As soon as we were free, we took about a week to buy some new underwear and then zipped over to "do" the continent, co-headlining with The Doors.

In one of the Scandinavian countries, Airplane was offered the use of a big boat to cruise around a lake—a good opportunity to appreciate the scenery from the vantage point of about three hundred mics of acid per person. During the course of the day, we stopped the boat to explore a small island and swim around in the water. I was the only one left on the boat with Paul, who was sitting by himself, looking off into the distance. It was not one of those peaceful, contemplative moments. I could tell by the way I felt—jittery and distorted—that *he* might be experiencing the same point in the LSD high where things can get really peculiar. As much as for my own benefit as his, I went over and put my arms around him—but the extra feeling of sexual attraction was a surprise to me. The acid was clarifying some aspect of our friendship that I'd been previously unaware of. After we traded comments on the strangeness of the drug, the beauty of the water, and so forth, the strangeness diminished and we resumed our separate paths for the rest of the day.

• • •

Another country. Another night.

"We're going to the red-light district, you wanna come?" the group asked me. Frankfurt had an area of prostitution that was more like a Gene Kelly set for *An American in Paris* than the usual sleazy appearance of hooker hangouts. There was a huge cobblestone courtyard surrounded by quaint two- or three-story apartment buildings. Men and women lounged around on the windowsills or walked around the ground floor area, showing themselves and waiting for a trick. As we were crossing between the front entrance and the large yard area, a girl came toward us screaming and yelling, threatening me with a knife. As if he was Errol Flynn, Paul whipped off his blue leather cape and swirled it in front of her like a bullfighter. I guess she thought I was infringing on her territory. We concluded that my presence was upsetting the status quo, and we went off to more hospitable nightlife.

Now Paul had become both the strong and sensitive "leader" of the group and the mythic hero figure for Yours Truly. But still the relationship took only platonic forms.

26

Strawberry Fuck

During that tour in Europe where we were co-headlining with The Doors (one night they'd open the sets, the next night it was Airplane), my most vivid memories are of Paul, but I also remember Jim Morrison.

In London, the Doors/Airplane concerts took place in an old structure called the Round House. Located at the end of a railway line, the interior of the house had a floor with radiating tracks, and there was a huge turntable-type machine, originally used to turn the big locomotives around. It looked like some kind of gigantic record player made out of iron, and although the sound was cavernous, the atmosphere more than made up for it.

Images of The Doors performing there are still vivid in my mind. No colors, all black, except one spotlight on Jim's face. Both of his hands holding the mike right up on his mouth, eyes closed and silent. You could see him just waiting for ignition to come flying up through his body. The long silence was full of music he could hear, but

"Jim Morrison" (Grace Slick)

everyone else only *felt*. Then, in a sudden step backward, arms lifting out to the sides, he yelled, "FIYAAHH!" The audience let out a collective scream, relieved by the explosion they'd been anticipating. Most of them had never seen him before, but he had the ability to draw people into his mood without opening his eyes or his mouth.

I was always fascinated by the way he seemed to go from one side of his brain to the other, ignoring all the synapses in between. It was just like his lyric, "Break on through to the other side." And beautiful? He looked like a rabid Johnny Depp, perfectly formed and possessed by abstraction. I'd been backstage before and after all the shows, talking easily with members of both of the bands, but when I directed a remark to Jim, I usually got back a colorful non sequitur.

"Jim," I'd say, "did you see that broken chair by the speaker system?"

With a pleasant smile and pupils dilated to the very edges of the iris, he'd respond with something like, "Lady in smoke shop, nobody for broken, chair broken, chair broken."

He inhabited two places at once, and although I knew there was some pattern of events going on in his head that connected what I'd just said to what he was thinking, it never made sense. I'm sure that the people who knew him well must have heard normal dialogue out of him like, "What time does the plane arrive?" But I never heard anything intelligible I could respond to until I was able to see what he was like alone, away from the frantic energy of the music halls.

We co-headlined in Frankfurt, Copenhagen, London, and Amsterdam, and I can't remember which country we were in when it happened. But I *do* remember strangely isolated things like the color of the rug in the hotel hallway (rose pink and maroon) and the nervousness I felt standing in front of the door to Jim's room.

It's daytime, he's probably asleep. If he's asleep, then he won't answer my knock, and I can go back to my room and stop shaking. What if it's the wrong room? Oh, fuck it.

I did the "secret knock," which he wouldn't have known anyway because it was Airplane's private signal, the opening beat to one of our songs, to let each other know that it was one of us standing outside the door. I was surprised when Jim didn't even ask, "Who is it?" Instead, he turned the handle and pulled the door all the way back so I could see him and the whole room. He smiled. "What's up?"

I wish I could remember my answer, but some specifics about the past are clear while others are vague. Since I had no idea that anyone would *care* about this thirty years later, I never kept a diary. In fact, if I'd known the enormous impact Morrison would have on future generations, I might have been tempted to wear a tape recorder. I also wish I could tell you that *he* came to *my* room to hustle *me*. But it didn't happen that way. I was, once again, the perpetrator.

Either the hotel had sent them up as a complimentary food tray, or he'd ordered them from room service, but either way, there were strawberries sitting on a plate on top of the coffee table. I went over to look at them, just for something to do, while I tried to figure out what to say next. Jim flopped on the bed and watched me. I brought the strawberries over to the end of the bed, and then, for some stupid reason, I put my finger into the middle of them. There was an extraordinarily cold and hard center. Frozen strawberries. *Thank you, Baby Jesus, for a topic to guide my conversation with Mr. Non Sequitur.*

"Okay if I put this plate on the radiator?" I asked. This was Europe, 1968. No central heating.

"Sure, but it's not on," he said, one of the most coherent

remarks I ever heard from him. After I set the plate of strawberries on the cold radiator, he crawled over the top of the bed, reached down, picked one up, and squeezed it till it turned into juice in his hand. He laughed and did it again to another one and kept on laughing. Words are hard to respond to, but laughter makes its own sense. I can play this, I thought, and I relaxed.

It wasn't 9½ Weeks with Kim Basinger and Mickey Rourke using food as erotic lubricant; it was more like kindergarten play—mud puddles and Silly Putty. Smash it, shove it around, not on each other, but we just individually tried to make a bigger mess than the other could. He outdid me by smearing the strawberries all over the cream-colored bedspread, but then suddenly, the private stories in his head made him stop and go over to the top dresser drawer. He opened and closed it without putting anything in or taking anything out, and he came back to where I was kneeling at the end of the bed, still playing in the fruit tray. I didn't ask him what the dresser move was all about; I was afraid I'd be stepping on that *Fantasia* tape that seemed to be running in his cranium.

This was new. Like making love to a floating art form with eyes. I'd never had anyone "study" me like that. It wasn't the standard evaluation of body parts. He seemed to be appraising the distance between us as if it was an invisible garment that needed to be continually breached with each motion. With our hips joined together and his body moving up and down, it felt like he was taking a moment each time to circle the area between our bodies with his eyes and consider the space that separated us. He was a well-built boy, his cock was slightly larger than average, and he was young enough to maintain the engorged silent connection right through the residue of chemicals that can threaten erection.

At the same time, he was surprisingly gentle. Somehow, I'd expected a sort of frantic horizontal ritual. It's interesting: the most maniacal guys onstage can be such sublime lovers. But everybody has to stop being a jerk sometimes. Jim mystified me with that otherworldly expression, and at the same time, his hips never lost the insistent rolling motion that was driving the dance.

When he did look *directly* at my face, he seemed to be constantly searching for the expression that might break the lock, as if I might be wearing a disguise. I'm not sure what I mean by that, but I can say that it was both intriguing and disconcerting, waiting for him to ask me if I was someone else—an impostor or a product of his imagination.

I have no idea how long I was there, but there was no lying around afterward having a cigarette, dreamily looking at each other. I knew I should leave before I got caught—we both had other relationships—and I felt like an intruder. I dressed as fast as I could, without looking like it was a race. Jim didn't seem to notice; he appeared to be totally unconscious, just lying there motionless on the bed. But naked, with eyes closed and without moving a muscle from his completely immobile posture, he said, "Why wouldn't you come back?" Since I hadn't said anything about coming *or* going, I didn't know what he expected to hear, so I went into proper Finch College mode and said, "Only if I'm asked." He smiled, but he never asked.

Because I have the Robin Williams disease—If-You-Can-Remember-the-Sixties-You-Weren't-Really-There-itis—I've blanked on what *country* the Strawberry Fuck was actually in, so I called author Danny Sugerman, who probably knows more about The Doors than they know about themselves.

"What countries did we play with The Doors?" I asked him.

He gave me the Frankfurt, Copenhagen, London, Amsterdam list.

"And where, if you could possibly figure this out, would we have been when I fucked Jim?"

Danny took a long pause, and then he said, "You know, Grace, I'm glad you're telling everybody you screwed Jim. You can't believe the amount of ugly women who've claimed to have fucked him."

Backhanded compliment.

Since Danny was only thirteen when all of this was going on, he could only come up with answers by process of elimination. "It couldn't have been Amsterdam," he said. I agreed, because on the first day in Holland, the two groups had gone on a loose trip to a downtown area. We'd been told there were a lot of head shops and interesting things we couldn't get in the States, and we all wanted to check it out. The kids on the streets of Amsterdam recognized us, so while were walking around, going in and out of the stores, they'd come up and talk, handing us various drugs as gifts of thanks for our music. Most of us just said "Thank you" and put whatever it was in our pockets for later. Jim, on the other hand, stopped, sat down on the curb, and did it right up. Pot, hash, coke, whatever. I thought he was ingesting an overly interesting combination of chemicals for that night's concert.

I don't know about The Doors, but it was the first time most of Airplane had tried "poppers" (amyl nitrate), and because of the legality of so many drugs in Amsterdam, it was a temptation for everybody to overdo it. We all ingested heavily, but Jim was the champ. An all-day, all-night consumption of everything available had turned him into a running pinwheel. Airplane opened that night and he came flying onto the stage during our set and collapsed. Dancing toward death, he was rushed to the hospital, and Ray Manzarek, The Doors' keyboard player, had to do the singing that night. Jim recuperated through the next day and was back onstage for the following evening's performance; that he lived as long as he did was amazing to me. But when we were in our twenties, we all thought we were invincible, and those short overdose situations came and went as part of the territory. It wasn't until death started picking us off on a regular basis that we started reflecting on our mortality. I don't think Jim ever thought of himself as a possible future drug casualty. It was always the other guy. "Not me. I won't die. I'm different, not like they are. I know what I'm doing." We *all* thought that way.

It was the reverse of Chicken Little—the sky would *never* fall. Some people *did* get the message, but most of us kept right on behaving as if we were made of steel.

27

The Big House

When Airplane returned from Europe to San Francisco, we spent a lot of time in the big Victorian mansion we'd acquired. We called this place the Big House, because for us, it was. The whole Victorian package, it featured four floors of activity, including an office, a kitchen, six bedrooms, a parlor, a dining room, a living room, a foyer, plus a carpenter/martial arts expert/coke dealer. He made his "office" in the basement, which also housed tools, a small bed and desk, and a couple of jumbo-sized nitrous oxide tanks. The members of the band would go down there from time to time and sit in a circle on the floor around the big blue metal totems, while our road manager, John Scheer, adjusted the six-spigot contraption on the top that allowed a group of people to get high, all at the same time. The "laughing gas" made us dizzy enough to pass out, so staying on the floor was a less painful way of enjoying the experience.

Jorma, for some reason, preferred to stand. Having hit his head twice (to the point of bleeding) on the sharp metal conduits at the top of the tank, we could never figure why he kept resuming his upright standing position. It's one of the few stupid things I've seen him do. Extremely bright and pragmatic, Jorma normally conducted himself with more restraint than the rest of us. Not to say that he wasn't into the extremes of the time as much as anybody else, but he was generally the most quiet and self-contained member of the group.

The main floor of the Big House had the typical baroque excesses of cut-velvet wall covering and pink carpets, carved wood paneling, and painted cherubs on the ceiling. The dining room accommodated our pool table, and the furniture ranged from cheap Louis XIV couches to a hand-made wooden torture rack/dining table and an unplugged electric chair. I had the macabre items specially made, because the juxtaposition of happy dining and instruments of death tickled my dark fancy. We actually put David Crosby on the rack one time, strapped him in by his hands and feet, then turned the wheel that pulls on all four limbs at the same time. We realized how well designed it was when David's laughter turned to anguished screams.

Peace and love.

We used the second floor for offices, and I lived in the master bedroom (also on the second floor) for about four months. I was still seeing Spencer, although our love affair was cooling off, but on the road as well as at home, I've always maintained separate rooms from my partner. That way, each individual can sleep, play music, eat, be quiet, watch television, or party without disturbing the other.

I've always gotten up at about 4:30 every morning; it's

my own peculiar ritual. Lying there in the dark for hours until the guy woke up would drive me nuts. Besides, it's sexier to make love in someone else's room; things get much more interesting when I can visit the man's territory for a while. Private quarters also help to avoid the old "Did you leave the cap off the toothpaste?" routine or "When are you gonna turn off the damn TV?" They lighten up the situation, leaving me free to argue over more important issues than who left the wet towels on the floor. Without that setup, each of my relationships would have ended in about a week.

The top floor of the Big House looked like a salon from a fancy turn-of-the-century house of ill repute. Lots of small rooms (for getting a quickie?) around a central area (which one of these girls would you like?) and one large bedroom (for the Madam?), where Paul took up residence. From Home of Tramps to Enrico Caruso's residing there on the night of the big earthquake of 1906, the Big House had seen it all.

Originally white, we painted it black—not as a tribute to The Stones song "Paint It Black," but just to bring dark flavor to the neighborhood. With four big stained-dark columns in front, it looked like the Addams Family mansion.

I spent some strange days at the Big House; I actually met my friend Sally there one night when she was waiting for Spencer in one of the small upstairs bedrooms. Sally, a groupie (the groupies weren't necessarily mindless idiots), is now a lawyer, living in Texas with—surprise!—another musician husband. She and I talked for a couple of hours when we first met, and I liked her sense of humor and her sharp mind.

I felt that Spencer and I, as an item, were pretty much over, but it was another night at the Big House when my suspicions were confirmed. I walked in the front door to find Spencer and Sally in the living room, watching a video (which Spencer had taken earlier that evening) of Sally dancing around naked. I had a twinge of one-more-blonde-with-big-tits-grabs-the-spotlight envy. But considering my new interest in Paul, and my ongoing friendship with both Sally and Spencer, plus the fact that I was still married to Jerry, the viewing of the homemade peep show was more humorous than devastating.

Sally and Spencer tied the knot at the Big House. Our manager, Bill Thompson, got a mail-order preacher's license and married my ex-boyfriend and my new girlfriend there, followed by a lavish party attended by rock-and-roll types and San Francisco freaks of all descriptions. I was living off premises at that point, so I decided to leave on the early side. When I got home to Sausalito, though, I received a concerned phone call. "You've got to come back to the wedding party," a friend said. "Paul's losing it on LSD."

Paul losing it? Oh, Jesus, I didn't know what to think, or what I could do, but I went back to see if I could help. When I got to Paul's top-floor bedroom, he was sitting on his bed, legs crossed, in his usual ramrod-straight position, rolling a joint. This was freaking out?

"How's it going?" I asked. "Someone said you weren't doing so well."

"Everything is so confusing," he replied.

That was the extent of any "bad acid trip" I ever saw. Just momentary confusion. Of course, I'd *read* about people *really* losing it, like Art Linkletter's daughter, who

172

committed suicide by jumping out a window while she was high on LSD. When Mr. Linkletter was interviewed on a TV program some years later, he accused Timothy Leary and me of killing her. Tim and I had never even met her, but our reputation as unpaid cheerleaders for LSD led Mr. Linkletter to arrive at his conclusion. When I heard Linkletter accuse me, I tried to call the TV station. I wondered how many celebrities who'd been *paid* to pitch alcohol had been accused of the millions of traffic deaths attributable to alcohol over the years. Probably none. I wanted to talk to the man, to remind him of the more serious alcohol situation and the hypocrisy associated with it, but the lines were jammed with other people who had their own opinions. I suppose Linkletter's grief would have prevented him from really *listening* to me anyway.

Later, Leary released this statement:

> *I've talked in the past about the weirdo oxygen-snorting fish who advanced evolution. But let's be honest. Some fish aren't ready to sniff oxygen. Most of them know who they are. It's been said, for instance, that LSD causes panic among people who have never tried it. Still, if I have prematurely coaxed some fish ashore who were really not prepared for the experience, I now express regret for not refining our invitations with more care.*
>
> —TIMOTHY LEARY (and GRACE SLICK
> by association)

On another occasion, at the Big House, I almost *did* kill somebody. I came in late one night, opened the front door,

and the furniture had been tossed around the room like discarded toys. It looked like some kid had thrown a tantrum,
but it was very quiet. No crazy party had gone on here—I
would have known about it—so I figured it must have been
a crazy person.

Fear.

I remembered that Paul kept a gun in his nightstand, but
that was three floors up. Where was the person who'd
caused the chaos? Was he or she still here and armed? As
quietly as possible, I made it all the way up to Paul's room.
Then I heard footsteps behind me. I grabbed the gun with
mindless resolution and aimed at the door, fully intending
to fire on sight.

"Good girl," a familiar voice said, complimenting me on
my ability to protect myself. David Crosby strolled into the
room.

"Good girl, my ass," I retorted. "I almost blew your head
off."

David had obviously come into the house *before* me, and
after the screwball had trashed the place. Since neither of
us knew at the time whether or not the nut was still in the
house, we couldn't do anything but sneak out, wondering
who'd done all the redecorating and why. We later found
out that the mess had been created by a crazy "fan" who had
some gripe about us not responding to his desire to join the
band.

Since I didn't fire the gun, Crosby is still around. And
happily for me, my ears didn't suffer the same kind of
trauma that took place after an afternoon of shooting in the
woods with The Dead, Airplane, and assorted Bay Area
musicians and artists. We weren't aiming at animals; we
were just bouncing bullets off planks of wood that we'd

nailed to the trees. I should have worn target practice head-gear, because my ears were ringing for days.

Of course, it never occurred to us semiconscious musicians that self-inflicted ear assaults could wreak havoc with a key requirement for our "profession": hearing.

28

And the Winner Is . . .

In 1968, when we were recording *Crown of Creation*, we were still new enough at the business of delegating authority that each member of the band wanted to control his own knob or fader on the board.

For those of you who don't know the ins and outs of a recording studio, "the board" is a slanted desk with an enormous number of knobs, faders, dials, wires, VU meters, and electric gizmos that both record and mix the music. "Mixing" happens after the song is completed, when the volume of each instrument gets placed at precisely the desired level in relation to the overall sound of the piece.

Usually, the producer is the master of the board, but of course, each of us wanted to be louder than everybody else. That meant six egos were busy sending the meters into the red, indicating OVERLOAD. Add to that consistent snorts of cocaine, and you have a formula for major cost overruns if not chaos. Apart from its expense and its tendency to cause people to babble, cocaine also has a tendency to make musicians want to try at least seventy-five different ways of mixing a song before they'll surrender to a popular opinion that the fifth take was just fine. That can be great fun if you have $250 an hour to throw away on studio time, or if you have a couple thousand dollars to get everyone else in the room as fucked up as you are.

I know I've fried my share of engineers by replaying a particular song in every possible permutation of sound until the janitors imposed their vacuum cleaners on me at dawn. God love the patience of all recording engineers. Producers and stars will argue or walk when they get miffed, but the engineer stays right there until the end. It was during one of these six-man mixing sessions that Paul's and my hands were constantly touching due to his fader being located right next to mine on the board. After about forty-five minutes, I still had my hand on the fader, making adjustments that had nothing to do with the song. I just wanted to see how long it would take before the skin-touching registered as a proposition. It *did* make Paul friendly, not to the point of making lewd remarks, but I noticed that he'd begun moving to the left a bit more, talking in my direction, keeping his hand on the knob even when the tape was rewinding—that sort of thing. Slow buildup. But not yet.

What *was* building was the popularity of the group, and we were suddenly being approached by various film people who were interested to see if we could join forces and make some money together. The director Otto Preminger was one of those people. He apparently thought he was a certi-fied hippie because he'd been doing some psychedelics at radical chic parties with Leonard Bernstein. Burning to direct a comedy about the counterculture, he talked up my being in a movie called *Skidoo*, about an old guy (ultimately played by Jackie Gleason) who takes acid. Unfortunately— or perhaps *fortunately* for those moviegoers who would have had to sit through my performance—there was something so absurd about Preminger's cocky presentation, I said no thanks to his offer of a role.

I also turned down what was eventually Lauren Hutton's role in *Little Fauss and Big Halsy*. Hollywood was still making mass-appeal color trivia infused with Doris Day cleanliness—not exactly my area. But in 1969, Airplane said yes to a collaboration between the group and Jean Luc Godard, thereby bringing together two bizarre artistic elements.

Here's something to do if you have a band and you want free publicity: play 150-decibel rock music from a rooftop in midtown Manhattan. We did it, deciding that the cost of getting out of jail would be less than hiring a publicist for the same "volume" of public exposure. Speaking of exposure, do it nude. That last part we didn't think of, so Jean Luc Godard, shooting from across the street through the window of the office of Leacock-Pennebaker studios, filmed us, fully clothed, as we perched on the roof of the Schuyler Hotel.

When we were ready to begin, Marty took his microphone and shouted, "Wake up, New York. Wake up!" The actor Rip Torn, in a bright red scarf, and Paula Matter, dressed in a bedsheet, arrived to join us. Unfortunately, they weren't the only ones who showed up. After two songs, "Somebody to Love" and "We Can Be Together," a cop appeared and told us to stop the music because we were disturbing the peace. We figured it would make a better film if we kept on playing, so we did, while cars screeched to a halt, pedestrians froze in their tracks, and office workers leaned out the windows waving. Five more cops showed up and started shoving Rip and Paula around. When they resisted, they were arrested and taken to the Eighteenth Precinct.

And the band played on.

The film, called *One American Movie*, opened at an art house in Berkeley on December 17, 1969, to this review by film critic Ralph Gleason:

> *It is a fascinating sequence—the film, itself, actually only a work print of a series of interviews plus some footage of Rip Torn which hints at what the flick might have ultimately been, does something which I find quite important—in a way, it is an exact mirror of the political scene today. . . .*
>
> *It is a collection of open-end raps which eventually becomes boring. If it were not for the presence of the rock band and the fact that its footage is not only interesting visually, but also listenable, the whole thing would have been hard to take.*

But, Ralph, you've heard the old line "You had to have been there." Some jokes exist for their own sake, and most of us thought that the film was meant to be a comedy of errors. Maybe tighter editing would have helped, or the addition of at least one cop with a lamp shade on his head. But the incongruity of it combined with the illegality were enough to make the entire production a worthwhile farce—as far as I was concerned. And there was another plus: Siskel and Ebert would have hated it.

By the way, decades later the rock group U2 did the same thing in L.A. in the process of shooting a video. There were no arrests.

One more Hollywood turndown for me: Milos Forman's *Ragtime*. This time I was offered the part of a radical Communist rabble-rouser, which wouldn't have been a big stretch for me. Unfortunately, it cut into our touring time and I declined. My movie career was short, uneventful, and over in one poorly reviewed underground flop.

No Oscars for Grace.

No Grammys either. We were playing in Florida once, and the word was out that I was GOING TO GET A GRAMMY. In fact, it was supposed to be a sure thing. *So sure that cameras were set up onstage the night of the awards. There was a monitor showing the ceremony in L.A., and the idea was that we'd stop the concert when the winner—me—was revealed, so I could blush, look humble, and say thanks to my Aunt Frieda, Uncle Trot, etc. But when the announcement finally came, the presenter said, "And the Grammy goes to . . . Linda Ronstadt!"

The camera guys onstage looked confused, the audience booed, and I was pretty embarrassed. I remember thinking, *What kind of "inside" information made someone sure enough of my win to go to the trouble of interrupting our set, shutting up the audience, and dragging cameras onstage? Hot tip, indeed.*

The screwup left me standing there with vinyl on my face. I knew people were looking at me to see how I'd respond, so I immediately flashed that no-problem-isn't-this-an-amusing-fuck-up look so we could finish the rest of the set without everybody feeling sorry for Grace. The truth was that although not getting "the coveted prize" was awkward, I didn't feel sorry for myself. I was saved by the part of me that was disdainful of the straight world's award show circus. Besides, when you compare notes, Ronstadt *does* have better pipes.

My second Grammy nomination was for "Female Solo Album" or "Female Rock Star with the Best Teeth" or "Female Rock Something or Other." These were the days before there was a major category called "Best Performance by a Female Rock Singer." In the early eighties, rock was a subcategory, so this particular category, as well as having a name not worth remembering, wasn't even televised. As I remember, the event took place in Radio City Music Hall in New York, and I went to the actual ceremony. But I was beaten once again—this time by Pat Benatar. I never *was* able to pile up those statues, but I'm grateful the Grammy guys considered my efforts, when they easily could have avoided me altogether, what with my lazy and somewhat sloppy attention to cranking out the hits.

As well as never winning a Grammy, I also have never been able to get a grip on the Top 40. When it *did* happen with a song that I recorded, it was either written by someone else (Darby Slick, Diane Warren, Bernie Taupin) or a one-hit fluke like "White Rabbit." My inability to successfully mainstream *anything* hasn't bothered me much, but *had* I achieved mega–mainstream success it would have been an interesting test of the distorted pride I seem to take in my idiosyncratic behavior.

My "Mainstream Star of the Year Award" acceptance speech would have gone something like this: "Thank you for your amusing lack of taste in popular icons."

I *did* get four Bammies (Bay Area Music Awards), but

that's a ballot-stuffing process. All you need to do is get enough of the same people to write in to the award office seventeen times. I wasn't aware of "the award-winning procedure" until about the third nomination, when Jackie Kaukonen, the group's executive secretary, who was then married to Jorma's brother Peter, was giggling in the office one day about how many nice people were going to great lengths to get grocery clerks, distant cousins, and parolees to send in votes for Yours Truly.

Scour the country for ballot-marking. No sealed Price Waterhouse envelopes. Just good old Bay Area clout.

I *did* legitimately win three wooden bears in a toy store raffle in Tiburon a couple of years ago, however. Not for any particular talent—just luck of the draw.

With so many performances and my style of shouting out the lyrics as loudly as I could, my voice was suffering, a condition for which I place a great deal of the blame on deficient monitor speakers. Or the lack of them altogether. All of it was rough on the pipes. Before monitor speakers became available at all, I had to scream every night to hear what notes I was singing over the amplified guitars. When they were cheap or broken, which was the case far too often, I wanted to destroy them. Which is exactly what Roger Daltrey did when The Who, Airplane, and B.B. King played at the Tanglewood Festival. When I watched Daltrey kick the monitor speakers and toss them in pieces off the stage, I cheered. It may sound like I'm overreacting, but since the speakers are the only means by which singers have to hear themselves, they're extremely important—*if* the singer cares how the performance sounds.

All that screaming created nodes on my throat, and between concerts, rehearsals, touring, and recording, if I had a minute, I would have Dr. Ripstein (perfect name for a surgeon) rip another one out. I had three operations in about three years, and after each surgery, I couldn't talk or smoke for about six weeks. In order to avoid a fourth trip to the hospital, I asked a singing coach if there was anything I could do, short of quitting singing altogether, to keep from destroying my throat. She asked if I smoked *menthol* cigarettes.

"Yes."

"Well, smoke if you have to, but lose the menthol."

"Okay."

I don't know if it was the switch to regular cigarettes or the increasing technology of the monitor speakers, but after 1970, I had no more problems with nodes.

It was sometime after I'd recovered from the second node removal that we played the International Center in Honolulu, Hawaii. We rented a grand Spanish mansion right on the beach and enjoyed tropical flowers, piña coladas, and hot sun cooled by misty showers—the whole brochure.

One afternoon, Jorma and Margaretta and Paul and I went for a long ride around the island in a jeep. This was the first time I'd had a chance to be with Paul outside a work situation or a fully packed party. Instead of being his preoccupied self, on this day he was animated, relaxed, and apparently unconcerned about the girl he had waiting back at the beach house. I was still hanging onto a dead relationship with Spencer (also back at the house, shades down, nursing a hangover), and the last vestiges of loyalty kept me, once again, from going with the moment.

It didn't take me long after that, however, to get uncharacteristically domestic by offering to make Paul some dinner up in his room. He brought the champagne, I brought the meat and potatoes, so to speak, and as Bill Thompson remembers, "When they came down the next morning, she had a sheepish grin on her face, he looked pretty satisfied, and I thought, 'Oh no, here we go again.'"

PART

Two

29

Dosing Tricky Dick

While Paul and I swiftly became a unit, the right-wing Republican situation was offering us great pickings for sub-cultural entertainment. When Airplane performed at the Fillmore East in New York, I wore a Hitler outfit and Rip Torn joined us up onstage dressed as my buddy, Richard Nixon. We enjoyed the brief satire so much that Paul and I went to see Rip Torn and his wife, Geraldine Page, to discuss doing *Richard III* (the idea was that Rip would play Richard Nixon playing the Shakespearean king) in the round with rock band accompaniment. We dropped the idea when we learned more about the logistics involved. It would have taken the support of the Sultan of Brunei to get the production on the road. But dreaming up the idea was almost as much fun as the actual performance would have been.

Another grandiose "Get Nixon" idea we came up with was the "Let's Dose Dickie" trick. That one wasn't carried through to conclusion either, which was probably fortunate since the repercussions might have been more than we bargained for. But the planning stages were pretty exciting.

Tricky Dick Nixon, as he was fondly referred to by people not part of his inane circle, had a daughter, Tricia, who had attended Finch College about ten years after my stay at the "bow and curtsey" academy. Which led to Yours Truly, of all people, getting an invitation to tea at the White House.

One of the other Finchettes, Mrs. David Busby, who'd been a suite mate of mine, was in charge of passing judgment on each alumna's character—or lack thereof. It seems that she was warned by all the proper ladies who'd heard of the notorious Grace Slick *not* to send me an invitation because I'd become a "lefty," one of the drug-crazed antigovernment hippies from the San Francisco rock tribes. But poor sweet Mrs. Busby stood up for the Grace she remembered. Going against the counsel of the other Finchettes, she sent me the invitation. When she asked me who my "escort" would be, I quickly said, "Mr. Leonard Haufman."

Mrs. Busby recalls, "The man's name made an impression on me, but it never occurred to me that she was talking about Abbie Hoffman. I just wrote down his name and listed it with the others I was sending to the State Department for clearance."

The next morning, Mrs. B. got an urgent call from the White House. "What's the problem?" she asked.

"The problem, Mrs. Busby," the security guard told her, "is Grace Slick."

I was pretty good friends with Abbie at the time. In fact, he, his wife, Anita, and Paul and I occasionally used to get together to discuss politics and pranks. One time, we all took a trip to Gettysburg, where we listened to tape-recorded information that came crackling out of boxes that looked like parking meters. Push a button and hear some glorious interpretation of the Civil War slaughter that made that particular cemetery such a popular tourist attraction.

Abbie, a political activist, was later wanted by the FBI, CIA, AT&T, BLT, and several other important government agencies, so he had to go "underground" for quite a while. At one point, he hid in Paul's and my house in San Francisco, where he engaged in subversive terrorist activities like entertaining the kids at China's birthday party. He loved the *idea* of this country (theory and practice often being diametrically opposed), but the manner in which the original documents of freedom had been mangled to steer corporate/military interests drove him close to clinically insane. I believe it was grief for a nation that finally killed him. If all of us had been *that* concerned, "political sins of omission" would no longer be a problem.

So when I was deciding on an escort for the White House, I invited Abbie because I couldn't think of anyone who'd be more delighted to visit the seat of Western power. The day of the tea, I tried to flatten Abbie's hair—he had a big afro and we didn't want to look like a couple of screaming hippies. But when I got through with him and he put on a suit and tie, he looked like a hit man for the Mafia. Really, he looked awful, more intimidating straight than when he wore his American flag shirt.

The Finch alumni lined up in front of the White House in their camel-hair coats, the obligatory round gold pin on the lapel with matching gold earrings, medium-heeled beige shoes, panty hose, and long, camel-hair skirts with beige silk blouses. I stood in line beside Abbie in my black fishnet top with three-by-three-inch patch pockets just covering my nipples, a short black miniskirt that went all the way to the beaver, and long black boots that reached up to my thighs. Looking like a pimp and a go-go girl, the two of us couldn't have been more thrilled to have been invited to Nixon's White House, because unlike the beige crowd surrounding us, we had a personal agenda.

In our pockets was more than enough powdered acid to get a lot of people very high, but we weren't interested in a lot of people. Richard Milhous Nixon was our mark. Having been trained in formal tea etiquette at Finch, I knew this would not be a sit-down affair. There'd probably be two very long tables set up with a large tea urn at one end, maybe a coffee urn beside it, and people would stand around, sipping and conversing with each other. The plan was for me to reach my overly long pinky fingernail, grown especially for easy cocaine snorting, into my pocket, fill it with six hundred mics of pure powdered LSD, and with a large entertainer's gesture, drop the acid into Tricky Dick's teacup. If I missed, Abbie was my backup. We knew we wouldn't have the pleasure of seeing Nixon tripping (LSD takes a while to kick in), but the idea that he might be stumbling through the White House a little later, talking to paintings, watching walls melt, and thinking he was turning into a bulldog, was irresistible.

Although it was raining outside the White House, staining multiple pairs of Gucci shoes, the security boys detained everyone, thoroughly checking their identification and giving them an appraising eye.

"Excuse me, miss, but may I see your invitation?" one of the guards said to me. "And your ID."

He took my invitation with the name Grace Wing on it, and my driver's license, to the security booth and came back. "I'm sorry, Miss Wing," he said. "You can't go in."

"But I have an invitation," I argued.

"Look. We know you're Grace Slick and we consider you a security risk. You're on the FBI list." I hadn't done anything subversive that I knew of—it must have been some of my lyrics. And God only knows what they'd dug up on Abbie.

The guards finally agreed I could come in, but only by myself. Abbie would have to stay out. I told them I never went anywhere without my *own* security guard, and Abbie added, "I wouldn't let Miss Slick go in there alone, because I understand they lose a president every three years. It's a dangerous place."

Abbie and I left, and Mrs. Busby went to the tea sans revolutionaries. But to everyone's surprise, the social secretary said, "Go back and find them. Mrs. Nixon and Tricia really want to meet her." Unfortunately, we were long gone. I read that Tricia later commented, "If she had to come with a bodyguard, I feel sorry for her. She must be really paranoid."

Not as paranoid as your daddy was when McCord, Liddy, and Dean copped out on his unsuccessful wiretapping trick.

Nixon never got the ride of his life, but Abbie and I had vivid images of reading in the newspaper that he'd suddenly taken ill and was spending a few days at Walter Reed, the army hospital where the CIA would have hidden him away until they figured out what made him crack. Of course, from what we later learned about Nixon, he walked around the White House talking to pictures anyway, so maybe nobody would have noticed much of a change.

I'll concede it now, the LSD thing *was* an irresponsible and dangerous plot. At the time, though, we were so fired up about Vietnam, so incensed that some pitiful malformation of mental functions was making the old men in power assume we should kill our young, able-bodied boys for no reason, we didn't care *what* it took to get the president's attention. We'd hoped that after he got through acting crazy, Tricky might contemplate his navel for six hours and decide that government just wasn't the way to go. What if he really saw the truth, shifted gears, and left politics? It was a good thought, but ultimately, we didn't have to dose him. He overdosed *himself* on love of power, driving himself out of office without any outside help.

30

Small Busts

Nixon wasn't the only asshole to get busted. Yours Truly and friends have had ample opportunities to enjoy the accommodations offered by police departments from Florida to Hawaii. I don't know why, but any time I saw a badge, something in me would snap and all I could see was some goof who took smelly shits just like everyone else, having the unfair advantage of firepower. All the haphazard violence of nature, illnesses, fires, and accidents never bothered me as much as someone pointing a Magnum at me and telling me to STOP!

Streetlights going red—that kind of stopping was okay. But when cops pulled out guns on *my* property (Tiburon), on *our* stage (Ohio), and on *my* friends (Paul, in San Francisco), I immediately turned into some Wild West character.

The problem with "justice" is that if you have the money and the attorneys, you can very often skip the time behind bars that most people have to serve. Classic case in point: the O.J. double-murder scenario. The members of Airplane went to jail, and relatively often, but never for long. The lawyers would converge, the bail would be paid, and we would walk—usually within twenty-four hours. Sometimes we were at fault, sometimes not.

You decide.

Busted in Florida

All cities have different curfews, and on this night in Florida, we played too long. When the cops turned the power off in the middle of a set, Paul picked up a battery-powered bullhorn and exhorted the audience "not to let the heat take control of the show." He went to jail, and as usual Thompson arrived with the bail. But while Paul's freedom was being negotiated, he slipped a shitload of LSD into a bottle of bourbon that was sitting on an officer's desk. When the bail was paid and Paul was free, the cops were about to experience the total disintegration of life up to and including the unfortunate decision to bust someone who was holding a lot of acid.

Busted in Dallas

I said the word *fuck* onstage and the cops got it on tape. I'm sure you would agree that it was a good thing we had uniformed individuals protecting the nation from that sort of insurrection. Inundated by compliments on their live recording techniques, they decided to let it go if I cleaned up my language. Of course, I agreed.

Ya, that'll happen.

Busted in Ohio

They *knew* we remembered Kent State and they didn't trust us. All along the front of the stage stood a row of twenty-five officers, arms linked in riot style, creating a barrier. Their heads covered with bulletproof visors, their hips loaded with clubs and guns, they formed a line between the audience and us like a bizarre group of armored, hairy chorus girls. After the show, Chick Casady objected to the cops' overzealous handling of an unruly fan. I saw them mace Chick, so I went over and objected to their treatment of my friend. They maced me. Paul came over to object to their treatment of me. They maced Paul. The three of us were escorted to jail where the bail was set and the attorneys were called in to rectify the situation.

Busted in Ohio, again

They loved us in that state. Paul saw someone in the audience being roughed up by security, so he jumped off the stage to investigate the reason for the pounding. In the ensuing fracas, Paul, who was still carrying his "hard body" guitar, swung around and accidentally (?) jammed the security guy with the business end of the guitar. We went on playing, promising the powers that be that we'd deal with the matter after the show, but as soon as the set was finished, we hid Paul in the bottom of a van and drove him out of state—FAST.

Busted in L.A.

A patrolman saw a ladder on the side of a wall at the Tropicana, aka the Howling Morrison Hotel. What it was doing
there, no one ever found out, but it looked suspicious, so they
investigated the area closest to the top of the ladder by
peeking in the window of a room that happened to be registered to Airplane. The hookahs that had been purchased earlier that day were clearly visible through the thin hotel room
curtains, so when Jack Casady came back, he was greeted by
patrolmen. He was taken to jail for possession of both hashish
and the colorful paraphernalia that went with it.

Busted in L.A., again

Twenty-four years after the hookah incident, Jack ran afoul
of the law again. Sitting behind the wheel and acknowl-
edging that he'd had too much to drink, he pulled over for
a curbside power nap. When the flashlights lit up the red-
eyed bass player smelling of barleycorn, the cops turned on
their red lights and took him for a second visit to the West
L.A. police department.

Busted, almost, in San Francisco

Paul and I were on our way to play tennis (what?—yes, he
swears it's true, although I don't remember ever willfully
deciding to do something as physical as playing tennis) and
a plainclothes cop with his plain car decided he didn't like
the particular speed at which Paul had chosen to drive.
When the officer began pursuit, Paul didn't know it was a

cop, so he sped up and began to lose the guy. After some harrowing intersection moves, we came to an impasse. Boxed in at a dead end, Paul spotted a black-and-white and went over to tell the "real" cop that there was a screwball following us. While Paul was discussing the chase with the officer, the incognito fuzz jumped out of his car and stuck a gun through the window on my side. Aimed at Paul's head, the weapon got pushed aside by the black-and-white, who told Columbo, "Don't get fancy, it's only Paul Kantner and Grace Slick." They let us go.

That was before the mere mention of Paul's or my name caused the cops to start putting on the handcuffs as soon as they realized they'd stopped either one of us.

It was good while it lasted.

Busted in Monterey

Owsley, "the people's LSD chemist," gave Paul and Jack a horse dose of a drug called STP, supposedly a powerful psychedelic, which turned them inside out and backward. Paul got into a car and managed to get home to San Francisco, where a couple of hits of Thorazine brought him down to a semblance of normalcy. But Jack had the misfortune to be found by the local constabulary thrashing around in a mud puddle doing his version of the Jim Morrison wolf howl. He didn't remember anything after that until he came to in a Monterey jail cell, totally nude, clinging to the top of the bars like a monkey.

Better living through chemistry.

Busted in Hawaii

In order to publicize our concert in Honolulu, Paul did an interview with the local newspaper. The reporter came out to our big rented Spanish home and made notes of the location of the house, while Paul smoked weed during the conversation. When our address and Paul's drug use appeared in the newspaper article, the police sent out three large individuals to sneak up over the seawall and come in on the ocean side for a mass arrest. They simply couldn't pass up the opportunity to bust the entire group in one fell swoop. Paul, who was strolling on the sand, saw the cops lurking, they saw him strolling, and the hula began.

While they tried a choke hold on Paul (his formidable chin prevented them from getting a good lock on his neck), he managed to let out a 150-decibel yell to let us know all was not well and we should hide the dope. We got the message in time, they didn't get us, but they *did* claim that Paul was smoking the joint that they were holding in evidence. Paul was taken to the precinct where he was given a free night's lodging in a holding cell. Paul's cellmate was a black man who had no money for bail, so when the Airplane lawyers showed up the next day, Paul had them pay his new friend's bail and brought him back to the beach house for dinner that evening.

More (or less) busts

I got nailed three times for drunk driving without ever being in a car—I'll explain that later, along with a 1994 shotgun incident. Back in 1969, however, I *was* actually guilty for driving under the influence—of speed (the velocity, not the drug)—but I avoided getting arrested. I'd taken my Aston Martin up to about 150 mph on the straight road near Soledad Prison, when the black-and-whites started chasing me. Since their engines weren't quite as tweaked as the machine I was driving, they had to radio ahead for a roadblock. When I reached the point where two squad cars were stopped in the middle of the highway, it seemed like a reasonable idea to pull over. The blues got out and came over and, to my surprise, completely ignored me. Unable to take their eyes off the fabulous machine I was driving, one of them said, "We'll give you a ticket for eighty mph if you let us look at the engine."

No problem.

I popped the hood latch and the CHP stood around pointing and chatting about the James Bond car that had just outrun their Dodge Darts or whatever the copmobile was that year. Amazing what a good movie star car could do for your traffic tickets. Probably not anymore, though—the fuzz have gotten blasé.

So if you're wondering what the Airplane members did (besides getting arrested) with their new fast cars, fast women, fast drugs, gold albums, and gold credit cards, it went like this:

Jack and Jorma took plenty of pharmaceutical speed and went speed skating in Finland.

Marty went off to be an "honest" artist—creating art that suited his muse.

Spencer was fired for incessant complaining.

And Grace and Paul moved to the "one-horse" hippie community of Bolinas, California.

31

China

Paul and I were spending the night at the Sheraton in New York (although Paul swears up and down it was some other hotel) when I decided that having a baby would be a good thing. The sixties had come to a close, the seventies were dawning, and music had taken up residence in the smaller areas of my brain, far overshadowed by purchasing power. Paul and I were living together in our new beach house, acquiring lots of expensive accessories: a hand-tiled pool, a geodesic dome, a gold Mercedes, a black Porsche, and a small recording studio in the lower floor of the beach house. It was the right time for a baby.

I imagined that the combination of Paul and me would be pretty interesting, since both of us are fairly strong and obnoxious, and it turned out that, for better or worse, our daughter China *did* end up inheriting both of those characteristics. When we were getting ready to make love in New York that night, I told Paul, "I'd really like to have your child. You don't have to marry me or take care of it or any of that kind of stuff," I added, "because I can do that myself."

Paul gave me that smile, the one where only one corner of his mouth goes up. Clearly, he was game, and he loved children. I had no idea if I was ovulating that night, but we knew we were making love to get pregnant, which made it very sexy. Later, when I counted back the days, the timing would have been just about right for it to have happened that very night.

I was comfortable having sex during my pregnancy; I viewed it like feeding the baby. You know, sperm must be healthy. It's protein. So I just went ahead and did it, because what are you going to do, poke its eyes out? I don't think women are set up that way. I've seen pictures of the way a baby sits in your stomach, so I always figured, as long as you didn't bonk the fontanel in the wrong spot, it was okay with me.

So, pregnant and planning in our Bolinas house, I arranged the brass crib next to the antique wooden cradle (a gift from Bill Graham) in a pink room that was already filled with infant necessities and other presents from family and fans. It was a peaceful and expansive time during which we tried to build the "perfect" atmosphere. A child was coming.

As part of the preparations, I bought a small house down the street from our main residence to accommodate the baby's nanny, Pat Dugan. A wonderfully easygoing woman, she was recommended by Bill Graham, who had hired her to oversee the food concession at the Fillmore Auditorium. She was exactly what we needed; she was great with children (she had four of her own) and she had a talent for cooking that would make Wolfgang Puck's grub taste like a bad day at Burger King. Besides her unusual desire *not* to learn to drive, she was one of the most normal, wonderful people I've ever met, before or since. To this day, she still has never driven a car, preferring to find her way to places with the help of friends or public transportation, a rare behavioral pattern for any Californian.

I wrote some lyrics and a few pieces of songs during the time I was pregnant, but most of my energy was focused on what I was determined to be: the atypical mother. *This* child would see it all, I promised myself. She'd have the education and the freedom to investigate *all* cultural forms. No religious or social imperatives would be imposed on her Aquarian mind. No instructions on how to make the perfect Martha Stewart melon balls—unless she *asked* for that kind of silly domestication. And I'd ask her, "What fascinates *you?* What do you want to *do* when you grow up?" Not, "Whom do you want to marry and how many children will you have?" She'd travel and learn, love and laugh, and experience all of it with an extended family of artists who'd show her, by example, that anything was possible.

Before my daughter arrived, I went on two rock-and-roll road trips, fat with child, trying to sing some budding right-wingers out of their my-country-right-or-wrong mindset. At the time, I really thought (hoped?) that the Republican party would just break up and dissolve in its own denture cleanser.

Youthful optimism and determination.

Riding high, sometimes literally, I was living a sixties romance novel. Paul and Grace, the unmarried romantic harbingers of "the Dawning Age of Aquarius," were touring, saying it like it is, and waiting for a child to arrive. Some people probably thought that touring while I was pregnant was a foolish idea, but I thought it was fine. In fact, I couldn't imagine *not* doing it.

Since performing was such a huge part of who I was, I saw no reason to stop. I wore those big Middle Eastern caftans to free up the expanding gut, I ate for two, I flaunted my radical unmarried status, and accepted all the "May I carry that for you?" assistance I could get. People become very pleasant and helpful around pregnant women. Open the doors, fire up the torpedoes, let's cover the planet with the greediest species on earth.

At about 10:00 P.M. on January 24, 1971, while Paul and I were entertaining a coke dealer and his wife at our home (no, I didn't do cocaine while pregnant), I said, "Paul, saddle up the mare, we're going to Jerusalem." It was time. We drove forty-five minutes from Bolinas to French Hospital in San Francisco, where they took me to a cell with a gurney in it. When they offered me a three-milligram Valium, I almost laughed out loud. For a person like me who'd literally wallowed in a pharmacopoeia, three milligrams of *anything* was not about to do the job. And incidentally, that was the last drug of the evening, not by any choice of mine.

I'd previously told my doctor that when I was ready to give birth, I wanted an anesthetist to administer copious amounts of whatever they had in stock to kill the pain. But the anesthetist never showed up. In the spaces between the contractions that were turning me into a rictus-faced gargoyle, I inquired as to the whereabouts of the missing drug dispenser.

"Oh, he isn't here yet," the various nurses informed me, something they continued to say all night long. I hadn't taken any La Maze or La Modge or whatever-it-is classes, because no matter what kind of cute tiny breaths you practice, I figured that in the final analysis, you've got a mass the size of a cantaloupe coming out of a hole the size of a fifty-cent piece.

That simple bit of physics means PAIN.

I told myself that women had been doing this thing called childbirth forever. Don't worry about it, I kept thinking. Remember that it's only a few hours of hideous groaning and then you have a whole new person to love. So I had my daughter by natural childbirth, an accidental route I'd definitely not chosen.

I'd been warned that newborns do not look like the Gerber baby. They said "it" would probably be a blood-covered, squalling, blue-faced, wrinkled mess, so I was ready for a remnant of some atomic mishap. But she was a lovely, smooth-skinned, pink-and-white being, content to just lie there and be cuddled and admired by her mother.

On January 25, as I held my newborn baby in my arms, a Spanish nurse came into my hospital room to attend to antiseptics and linens. She was holding a framed certificate that looked like a high school diploma, and she said, "We give these to all the new mothers. You see, it says where she was born, what time, and the name of the baby goes here." She pointed to an empty line in the document. "What is your baby's name?" she asked.

I noticed a crucifix around her neck and spontaneously said, "god. We spell it with a small *g* because we want her to be humble."

It was only a few hours after my baby had arrived, I was holding the miracle of birth in my arms, and I was already messing with somebody's head. The nurse asked me to repeat what I'd said. I obliged her. After hearing it a second time, deciding that the blasphemy was real, she haltingly entered "god" on the parchment, probably expecting to go through her life repeating novenas for her participation in this profanity. When she was through filling in the irreverent name, she ran to the telephone to call Herb Caen, the same beloved *San Francisco Chronicle* newspaper columnist who'd inspired me to leave Florida many years prior. He published the information about the birth and the supposed appellation Paul and I had chosen, which would, by virtue of the deity's extensive popularity, make it impossible for my daughter to live up to her presumed given name.

Her real name is China. San Francisco has a large Asian community, and Paul and I had observed that the Chinese follow spiritual practices that seem to offer more equanimity than the fear- and guilt-ridden dogmas of the Judeo-Christian ethic. Thousands of years before the Western Bible was written and rewritten and burned, and rewritten again during the Inquisition, the Oriental people had realized that the yin/yang or 50/50 take on human existence produces more acceptance and self-control. To Paul and me, this seemed a better alternative to the "damned if you do, damned if you don't" ethic that permeates Western civilization. And aside from the fancy polemics, China is the name of a delicate and feminine form of artistic expression in clay, as well as useful eating utensils.

Seemed like a good combo.

Since I never paid much attention to the couplings of other celebrities, I didn't know that Michelle Phillips, another rock-and-roll mom, had named her child Chynna. In fact, I didn't know that Michelle even *had* a child. Several years after the birth of my daughter, when someone asked me if I'd made the spelling different from the name of

Michelle's daughter on purpose, the answer was no. In fact, I was so intent on being original with my daughter's name, if I'd known Michelle's kid was named Chynna, I probably would have called mine Xlopdy. Circumstances were such that two of the very limited number of couples in the sixties rock world who played together and loved together just happened to give approximately the same name to their firstborn girl.

A million to one.

32

The Chrome Nun

There was yet another reason Paul and I developed respect for the Eastern way of life. We'd seen the movie *Enter the Dragon*, and both of us were completely taken by the ease of movement and calm self-assurance that Bruce Lee displayed through the use of kung fu. A powerful but graceful form of martial arts, kung fu uses *all* of the body/mind systems, rather than just the upper-body jabbing of Western boxing. Again, because of adherence to the whole, a Chinese fighter must also learn to heal.

Balance.

The students of White Crane kung fu, the form that Paul and I studied briefly, were taught *both* the fighting *and* the healing arts. Yin and yang. Black and white in one circle. Unfortunately, being on the road most of the time made it extremely difficult to maintain the rigorous "workouts" that produce a martial arts adept. The practice has to become a way of life, and I'm afraid I didn't have the discipline to make it a top priority. I think I preferred *watching* the hard work of physical and mental training rather than actually doing it.

Ron Dong, who was both a friend and a teacher of ours, occasionally came on the road with us to perform an intricate grouping of moves using large swords slicing through the air at lightning speeds. He also attended to everybody's medical needs, taking out his acupuncture needles and "magically" erasing problems that could not be fixed by Western medicine. Acupuncture is now becoming recognized as a formidable medical practice, but when we were going to Master Long's studio in San Francisco in the seventies, Westerners still considered it some goofy offshoot of all the other alternative methods.

Byong Yu, another Eastern master, taught us a martial arts form called tae kwan do, a more direct and leg-focused form of karate. There's a line in one of Paul's songs, "Ride the Tiger," that synthesizes a conversation we had at dinner one evening, when Mr. Yu was discussing the differences between East and West:

It's like a tear in the hands of a Western man,
He'll tell you about salt, carbon, and water,
But a tear, to an Oriental man,
He'll tell you about sadness and sorrow or the love of
*   a man and a woman*

I don't think Byong Yu was accusing all Westerners of being coldhearted chemical engineers, but the heavy emphasis we place on technology in this country clearly bothered him. Of course, Korean and Chinese politics didn't seem to reflect the Asian spiritual ethic. Maybe that's why Master Long, Ron Dong, and Byong Yu were *here*—they were hoping the best of both cultures would somehow join, allowing each continent to benefit from the union.

Looking back on it, I find it interesting that while many of our contemporaries were studying at the feet of seated Eastern gurus, Paul and I gravitated to a more aggressive physical practice. All forms were headed in the same direction, though. For everyone, the goal was balance.

In my personal life, the balancing act of being a new mother and making records was made easier by the fact that for the first six months after China was born, we didn't tour. While Paul and I made a "duo" album titled *Sunfighter*,

Sunfighter: China and me in 1971. (AP/Wide World Photos)

which featured fat baby China's picture on the cover, I cared for my daughter during the day and Pat, her nanny, took the nights.

Rolling ocean, small town, new baby, visits with Grandmother, new record, no drugs, and no pressure.

This too shall pass. When I stopped breast-feeding, the liquor crawled slowly back into my bloodstream. Having help both with the baby and the paperwork at the office, I was able to juggle the remainder of my time in the best rock-and-roll tradition. ("Rock-and-roll tradition" could be an oxymoron, but, God knows, there are plenty of traditional morons in rock and roll.) By the time Paul's and my second duo effort, *Baron Von Tollbooth and the Chrome Nun*, was being recorded, I was back in full swing and displaying a certain sangfroid.

The title of the album was taken from David Crosby's nicknames for the two of us. "Baron Von Tollbooth" was a reference to Paul's facetious pride in his German ancestry, while "the Chrome Nun" evoked my tendency to engage in armored dogma. We constantly proved David's nicknames true, so we mounted no resistance to them.

David had a beautiful "wooden ship" called the *Mayan*, which he had anchored in a remote, pristine lagoonlike pool of tropical heaven about thirty miles off the Florida coast. After Airplane played Miami, Paul and I took a seaplane out to where David and several of his tanned, blonde, voluptuous nymphs were practicing the art of nautical Shangri-la. The guitars, the plates of fresh food, the marijuana, the nudity—I liked everything about it except that last part. Damned if I was going to be the only dark-haired, flat-chested, skinny white geek to throw myself up for the brutal physical comparison. For the remainder of the visit, the Chrome Nun was the only one wearing clothes—a conspicuous cover-up.

I'm still that way. Ninety-five degrees in L.A., and I'll be the only one not wearing shorts. If you want to let *your* fifty-year-old cellulite flap around, that's *your* problem. I find it offensive. I don't want to look at yours and I don't want you looking at mine.

Keep your city beautiful—wear slacks.

But I must say, I'm getting better at dealing with the blonde mythology that seemed to show up in my life at

Archetypal twentieth-century blonde and, coincidentally, my cowriter, Andrea Cagan. (Juliet Green)

every turn, and which still does. When I look at a photo-graph of Andrea Cagan, this book's coauthor, she seems like a composite of every blonde nymph who crossed my consciousness over a period of fifty-eight years. Ironically, these impossible role models with their unattainable beauty have consistently turned out to be among my best and brightest friends.

And sometimes much *more* than friends.

Leave it to the Cosmic Master Painter to give me a blonde child, who went through puberty without turning brunette like me.

What's a mother to do?

33

Fanatics and Fans

Even when China was a child, I didn't have bodyguards. What for? On tour, I was always surrounded by men, and when I was home, the people in San Francisco were friendly, but not invasive. The exceptions to the rule were strange indeed.

We were annoyed when a radio DJ who'd lost all sense of proportion jumped Paul's and my fence in Bolinas on a semiregular basis. Sometimes we'd find him standing in the backyard; sometimes he'd be in the house. Eventually, Paul got tired of it. On "DJ's" final visit, Paul asked him to leave by pointing a gun at him. Not to be deterred by a lethal weapon, the man just kept walking toward us. When Paul shot about five bullets around him in a circular pattern, his response was, "We must have a misunderstanding."

Uh huh. Fearless stupidity.

Two other fellows, unknown to each other or anyone else for that matter, decided (independently) they were China's father. The first climbed up the outside of a New

York hotel to the nineteenth floor, crawled in the window, then turned on the tube and spread himself out on *my* bed, waiting for me to return from a concert. Airplane had booked the whole floor for that particular date, but the hotel guard who was stationed near the entrance hadn't seen anyone. When Paul and Bill Laudner walked me to my room that night (I still maintained my own room), there was this guy just lying there.

"Hi, Grace, I want to see my daughter," he said, right in front of Paul. The guys were amused; it was so goofy, nobody was taking him seriously—except *me*. I wanted him the hell out of my room. He was "escorted" out of the building and spent an evening hanging out with NYPD Blue.

The second stalker, who'd maneuvered himself to a dangerous precipice overlooking the bay in San Francisco, also wanted me to admit he was China's father or he'd jump off the cliff next to our house by the Golden Gate Bridge. Some part of me wondered why we didn't just let him jump, but reason took over. We asked the fire department to bring the suicide nets, and it took them quite some time to get hold of the man without triggering a dive.

Rather than committed lifetime stalkers, these two were more into one-night stands. Lucky for me. Maybe I should have been nervous about that kind of insanity, but with so many people around at all times, I tended to find it entertaining—*pathetically* entertaining.

Of course, it did occur to me that perhaps I should be offended. Most celebrities have stalkers who're more interested in *them* than in their immediate family members. Did the obsession with China imply that I wasn't interesting enough on my own to stalk? Or might these guys have created the "father-of-China" thing as some kind of proof they'd boinked a rock star? I used to get lots of fan mail from prisoners and people in nuthouses. It was a bit easier to understand someone wanting to correspond with a person who *seemed* to have a larger area of freedom and mobility, than to make sense of guys who were willing to kill themselves over an impossible (they apparently weren't afraid of DNA testing) claim.

On the other end of my fanatical-fan spectrum were two benevolent fans who were almost twins but who had no knowledge of each other's existence. The first, Vincent Marchilello, gave me a reproduction antique doll during one of his visits backstage—with the result that I developed an interest in dolls that eventually became so extensive, my house looked like a toy store. Vince was a good-looking Italian man who was always polite, and although he was a persistent fan, he never showed any tendencies toward the stalker-type MO.

The second benevolent fan was named Vincent, too— Vincent Marino (or Vinnie, as I liked to call him). He was also sweet, good-looking, generous (he sent me every panda article, picture, magazine, and trinket available to Western man), Italian, and East Coast, and eventually he became one of my best friends.

The moral of the story: Some fans are frightening, some are family.

Back at the beginning of "Now I'm famous" in the sixties, I'd never heard of stalkers or tabloid journalism. If the lowbrow newspapers or gossip columns focused on anybody in particular, it was probably people in the movie business who were trying to maintain a certain amount of decorum. Rock-and-roll musicians could have cared less if they were caught with their pants down, so to speak—so we were less interesting to the press. But now it's a different story entirely. Constant invasion of privacy is driving people nuts, not only entertainers but notable people from all walks of life. I think paparazzi should have to get a signed release for any picture they take.

I understand about First Amendment rights, but the First Amendment was written by people who never had a clue that cameras, if used improperly, could *cripple* freedom. The new photo machinery and zoom lenses that are available to any goofball make it harder and harder to endorse limitless freedom of expression. From the somewhat harmless "organized" chaos I saw in the sixties and seventies, to the nineties death of Princess Diana, the stalking and rummaging around in people's garbage for cheesy information has escalated to insane proportions.

Supply and demand? That's a big part of it. As long as we read the rags, they'll continue to flourish.

My personal reaction to one of those in-your-face photographers was to be *more* disgusting than he was. At a concert back in the sixties, I was in a coed bathroom taking a pee, when I heard a guy ask, "Can I take some pictures out in the hall when you're through in there?" I *was* through, so I opened the stall door and pulled up my shirt, exposing one of my boobs, and said, "Here you go. The left one's a better shape than the right one, so take the shot now!" He did, and it appeared in the rock magazine *Creem.*

Sure, being famous can be fun, but when you have to resort to bodyguards, killer dogs, armored cars, and Fort Knox security systems, it makes you wonder. Today, my own home is situated so that there's no way to get to it except through an electric gate that closes behind anyone who enters. And if they look scary, I press a button and the gate becomes electrified, meaning that if you touch it, you're toast. Nice and friendly, but I was robbed three times in my relatively well protected Mill Valley house. This time around, I've made a vow: no robbers, intruders, paparazzi, or nuts (except me) get in or out without searing results.

Welcome to the modern world.

34

Silver Cup

Think of Jefferson Airplane as a silver cup. By the early seventies the marks of neglect were showing on the cup. But its owners were at once unwilling to give it up and no longer interested in polishing its exterior. Nor did they put it to much use. It waited on a shelf, quietly collecting a streaky tarnish, for someone to restore it to its position at the table of feasts, while each servant in the house thought it was the other's job to tend to the chalice.

Nineteen seventy-two was a good year for cracks in the wall and shredded documents. It was a year that sent Tricky Dick to a second term in office, and G. Gordon Liddy to prison for his stoic G-man tactics on behalf of Tricky Dick. Those of us in the rock-and-roll community had continued to write and sing our political views to a public that just didn't want to believe that a president could stoop to wiretapping. From our point of view, *anybody* the Democrats came up with to run against Darth Vader would be just fine. One of the hopefuls was George McGovern.

Old George, wanting to bridge the generation gap, con-tacted us, wondering if we'd meet with him in the lounge of the hotel where we were playing, somewhere in the middle of the country. Most us agreed to hear him out, but Jorma was lukewarm about this political get-together. On the pre-text of encouraging his participation in the barstool hustle the following night, I went to his room to practice my cajole. In reality, I wanted to go to bed with him, but killing two birds with one stone didn't seem like a bad idea. I began to talk about McGovern while we loosened up with one drug or the other, but I quickly proceeded to forget about *anyone's* candidacy . . . at least for that night. As I recall, though, everyone *did* eventually come down to the bar to listen to the man-who-would-not-be-king speaking in sincere tones about his hopes for our divided nation.

I slept with Jorma only that one time, but after a long recording session one night, he and I decided to interact in a different way, by racing cars on Doyle Drive. A number of people like me have thought that this straight wide road would be a good place not only to go faster than the speed limit, but to defy its history of brutal accidents. Unfortu-nately, I found out—the hard way—that it's called Deadly Doyle Drive for a reason.

Race until you land in a hospital, which is precisely what I did.

The combination of the rain and the oil on the street caused my car to slide sideways at 80 mph into a cement wall. The impact threw me over to the passenger's seat, so I was one of the rare exceptions to the seat belt rule: if I'd been wearing one, I'd be dead today, because the driver's side was crushed. It must have scared the shit out of Jorma, having to go up to the crushed car, wondering what kind of a mangled mess he'd find.

At the hospital emergency room with a head concussion

and a split lip, I remember asking the nurses for "cocaine, for the pain, of course." They just shook their heads (some addicts never give up), and knocked me out with something so strong I can't remember the entire next week that I was in their care. They wanted me to be *very* quiet so they could do tests and allow my head to heal.

Head injuries aside, I enjoyed spending time with Jorma because I loved him. In fact, I loved *all* the men in Airplane, and I *made* love to all of them. That is, the ones who were in the original lineup. Except Marty. Exactly why we didn't make that final connection, I don't know. There were times when I thought it would have brought a beautiful truth to the duets we performed onstage, but that sort of fantasy wasn't strong enough to cut through whatever aversion Marty might have had to consummating an artistic partnership. He might have just thought I was a jerk. At any rate, we both maintained enough of a distance that singing together sometimes felt like a competitive sport.

I still enjoyed Marty's presence, though, *and* his music. I think "Today" and "Comin' Back to Me" are two of the best love songs ever written.

> *I saw you—comin' back to me,*
> *Through an open window where no curtain hung,*
> *I saw you—comin' back to me*

In a way, Marty's capacity for love reached me through his songs. And *that* was the main attraction—the music. Each member of our band—and probably most bands for that matter—had the exquisite ability to appreciate and produce sound that *communicated*. Whether an individual likes the sitar or bagpipes, Old English lyrics or "punk shriek," everybody listens to someone calling on their

Marty, Yours Truly, and Paul at a free concert in Golden Gate Park.
(People Weekly © 1975 Michael Alexander)

humanity through music. For some, it's the purest form of expression, for others a brief passing delight, but it exists like no other art form in every culture, in all languages, giving voice to anyone who wants to sing. And when we sing together, everyone becomes perfect for a while.

But only for a while.

The unrest in the group was emerging in a visible way. We were starting to pair off—Jack and Jorma, Grace and Paul—or retreat as individuals: Marty into his own world, and Spencer into relationships with the women in his life.

We were in a new decade where the style of the old cup was being outmoded and replaced by a more physical and material disco sound. Airplane's promise was becoming exhausted. Or perhaps it was just like every other human contract—there's a time when the initial passion and novelty fades and attention turns to that which has not yet been experienced. We want a new game, a new job, a new government, a new husband, a new mistress, a new art form.

Although at this point we didn't discuss it out loud, we were all thinking similar thoughts. Without the constraints of Airplane, the possibilities seemed bright.

For Jack and Jorma, as Hot Tuna, they could . . .

For Grace and Paul, doing albums together, we could . . .

For Marty, working solo, he could . . .

And on and on.

The big chariot was getting cumbersome, and everyone saw some kind of freedom in the solo wild horse.

We made our next two albums, *Bark* and *Long John Silver*, in this irritated state. Back in 1967, when we were making *After Bathing at Baxter's*, Jorma had driven a motorcycle right into the studio (while Jack was recording), waving at several people sitting on the floor getting high with a nitrous oxide tank. But now, in the early seventies, even the fun of frivolous mutual excess was missing from the recording sessions. We just couldn't get a good bacchanal going for lack of interest in what we'd become. The desire to give the best performance had been reduced to barely compliant execution. The music was splintered. Each member worked on his or her own material, then put as little time as possible into everybody else's work.

Our new drummer, Joey Covington, was a fresh-faced Oshkosh B'Gosh blond farmboy whose enthusiasm at being in this famous group didn't rub off on the old regulars. We thought he was young, strong, and hopelessly naive. Jorma let not only the band, but the record-buying public as well, know of his dissatisfaction with Airplane, with his song, "Third Week in the Chelsea."

So we go on moving trying to make this image real
Straining every nerve not knowing what we really feel
Straining every nerve and making everybody see
That what they read in the Rolling Stone has really
    come to be
And trying to avoid a taste of that reality . . .

All my friends keep telling me that it would be a shame
To break up such a grand success and tear apart a name
But all I know is what I feel whenever I'm not playin'
Emptiness ain't where it's at and neither's feeling pain

It was difficult to avoid the truth. I remembered that in 1970, prior to the two final Airplane studio albums, Paul had made a "solo" record called *Blows against the Empire* that had been a refreshing experience. Jerry Garcia, Graham Nash, Mickey Hart, Jack Casady, David Crosby, and several other musicians from the local bands had joined in on that strange opus about living in a floating space city. Everyone had made suggestions and offered both talent and input to the effort, making it a pleasant process and, I think, a very unique record.

Spillin' out of the steel glass
Gravity gone from the cage
A million pounds gone from your heavy mass
All the years gone from your age . . .
The light in the night is the sun
And it can carry you around the planetary ground . . .
And the people you see will leave you be
more than the ones you've known before

Hey—rollin' on
We come and go like a comet
We are wanderers
Are you anymore?
        "Starship" from *Blows against the Empire*

The long faces and malaise of the subsequent Airplane albums suffered in comparison. Whether you were talking about Jack and Jorma, or Marty, or Paul and me, whatever we did away from the group was infused with more enthusiasm than anything Airplane was doing. But you don't just ignore a record contract; RCA could have sent pit bulls with law degrees to the West Coast for a dinner of rock stars. But actually, they were almost accommodating. When it was obvious that no one wanted to keep drinking out of the old cup, RCA spent the next few years putting out compilation albums and efforts from the Airplane off-shoot groups and pandering to our desire to have our own record label called Grunt.

It was a dark time for us; even the studio in San Francisco that we used for *Bark* and *Long John Silver* was depressing. Located in a San Francisco slum, there were bars on three corners and a methadone clinic on the fourth. Paul once stopped his VW bus to run into the studio and get something (it took him all of about five minutes), and when he got back, his bus was gone.

The fracturing of the group was something over which I had no control, so I jumped into the bottle to hide. I used cocaine to keep the booze going, and after long days and nights in the studio doing very little but drugs, I was getting fat and sloppy. After recording until the early hours, coming out into the sunrise with a hangover compounded the disintegration of both my own integrity and the cohesiveness of the band. I was figuratively what we had predicted—dead at the age of thirty.

One good thing about my body was its refusal to be shit-faced on a regular basis. After a night of drugs and booze, I'd have to (and want to) give it a rest. I've never liked being loaded on a daily basis, but being straight consistently wasn't particularly interesting, either. At that point, I was doing as much drinking as I could without becoming totally nonfunctional. Apparently, I did a fairly successful job of blotting everything out because I don't remember much about the albums or the road trips. My only hope seemed to lie in the possibility of a band being formed from the various musicians who'd performed on Paul's record or our duo albums.

In retrospect, Jefferson Airplane's breakup was not so much any*one's* fault, as it was simply the end of an era. I can see that we were unwilling to make a smooth transition into the next phase, but then I can think of other people who had an even tougher time with crossovers. (Marie Antoinette and Czar Nicholas come to mind.) As individuals, we weren't mortally wounded by the split; we were just a bit trashed around the edges. Each person had to deal with the next rung on the ladder in his or her own way and according to his or her own emotional abilities.

We were all afraid. After all, it was an ending. But my reaction to the dissolution took on more strident and obnoxious proportions than those of the rest of the band members. Some people recognize their own fear immediately and act accordingly. In my case, it happens a little differently. Because of the stoic household in which I was raised, my programmed reaction to fear, pain, or sadness is convoluted; I don't even apply it in the right direction. When I start to feel any of the above emotions, it's as if the moment it registers in my brain, I flip it around and become a half-assed warrior. Then a few days later, I take that repressed fear and get busy ripping up New Zealand, when I'm actually angry at Germany. Miss Directed Anger.

So, in the end, while some people sulk, others retreat, and still others party, I drink a whole lot and run my mouth.

PART
Three

35

Seacliff

The daily two-hour drive along the winding country roads that lie between San Francisco and Bolinas got to be tedious. The distance from the city combined with having a new baby in a one-doctor town made our idyllic ocean house less of a retreat and more of a dangerous and time-consuming extravagance. But Paul had had his eye on this place in the Seacliff area of San Francisco that looked out over the bay and the Golden Gate Bridge. So we took our nanny, Pat Dugan, her children, our child, a dog, and two cats and moved into the home that Paul loved.

An impressive structure, it would have made a better home for the Danish embassy than for our family, I thought. From the street, with its plain lines, clean, sparse land-scaping, and a spectacular view extending from the bridge all the way out across the Pacific Ocean, the house looked like a one-story wood and stone Scandinavian/Japanese mix. But it was actually a large five-floor house, resting on fifty-foot pylons that were designed to sway in the event of one of San Francisco's infamous earthquakes.

The house gained a measure of protection as well from the presence of three or four black men who sat all night, fully armed, in a car that was parked in front of the man- sion next door. The neighboring dwelling was owned by a Muslim leader, who, though he lived there, rarely showed his face. Sometimes when I came home in the middle of the night from recording or carousing, if I'd had enough liquid or chemical fortification, I'd get up the nerve to talk to the "security guards" for a while. They were nice guys, intelligent and patient with my questions about their artillery and their religion. When I finally went into my own house, they probably "dissed" the screwy drunk honky, but they never let on that my presence was unwanted or annoying.

The living room of our new home became a rehearsal hall for the band that would eventually be called Jefferson Star- ship. With its twenty-foot windows looking out onto the bay and the bridge, the house served as a perfect working/living space—perfect for everybody but me. It was too big and too busy—there were just too many people passing through. I went out as often as I could, to be alone and to avoid the duties that I imagined fell to me as "Mistress of the Man- sion." I assumed I was expected to play gracious, eccentric hostess to the multitudes. In fact, there were no expecta- tions. Everyone was too wrapped up in their own lives to consider what I should be doing, and the truth is that my presence wasn't a necessity for the carnival to maintain operation. Still, I felt the self-inflicted pressure.

Paul maintained an aerie on the top floor of the house, writing songs, watching TV, talking on the phone, playing

Paul Kantner, China Kantner, . . . and who's the outsider?
(Roger Ressmeyer/© Corbis)

with China, and presiding over everything from his favorite spot in the middle of the extra-large California King bed. Occasionally, he and I went out together to have dinner at Vanessi's or to do some aimless clubbing, but for the most part, I went out solo. I'd get in my Aston Martin (the James Bond machine that I'd purchased in 1967) and drive around until I could think of an interesting target for my particular mood. I could never stay still as long as Paul could; I had to be moving in a car, walking around the Japan Center, going to movies, hanging out in Marin County restaurants, or searching out people who'd satisfy my quest for external diversion.

One night, Paul and I took our friend Bad News Brown (an iron wedge of a man who, several months earlier, after being shot in the back, had taken *himself* on foot to a hospital) to North Beach. When Paul got bored with nightclubbing early and decided to go home, he asked Bad News to watch out for me. Anybody who can take that much lead pepper and keep moving was obviously a fine bodyguard, but when I told him "I vant to be alone," Bad News reluctantly gathered up his iron bulk and left.

We were in some boring bar, and after he exited, I noticed a table full of Oriental men speaking an Asian dialect I'd never heard. Extremely well dressed in the Las-Vegas-silk-suit-with-big-cufflink style, they seemed to be dead serious about whatever they were discussing—no laughing, lots of quiet pauses, and then frantic dialogue. I watched for about fifteen minutes and then decided to crash the party. "What language are you speaking?" I asked.

They smiled, invited me to sit down, asked my name and my age, and then continued to speak in their own dialect, never telling me exactly what it was. Intensely curious, but trying to play the quiet, demure female that I imagined was appealing to Oriental men, I sat for another fifteen minutes, saying nothing but looking pleased at just being allowed to be in the company of men.

Yeah, that's me.

Suddenly they all rose and gestured for me to follow. Since they knew I had no idea what they were talking about, they obviously felt safe having me tag along. A pretty Western trinket is I'm sure how they viewed me. We walked for several blocks until we arrived at a more secluded restaurant. Our group filed into a stark, lime-green back room with a round table piled high with guns, and we all sat with four other men, who looked a bit less charming than my companions.

Arms negotiations, weapons for sale.

I suddenly realized that I was watching a Chinatown gang argue over how much for how many. When they'd concluded the deal, one of the men took my arm, walked me out to his car, and escorted me to a hotel. We checked into a room together, but before anything could happen, I complained of an intestinal disorder. He surprised me by bowing graciously and walking backward out through the door. I stayed at the hotel that night, afraid to go home and tell Paul where I'd been. He wouldn't have believed the story, anyway, or that I hadn't banged one of the guys, so I told everybody that I'd been boozing all night with my friend Sally.

When I wasn't busy helping strange Asian men with their arms negotiations, hanging out at the Japan Center became something of a habit. I loved the food, the cleanliness, and the quiet respect that permeated the Oriental marketplace. I often went to the movies there; I followed a particular series of Japanese films called *The Blind Detective*, starring a stocky middle-aged man who, despite his lack of vision, managed to rout the bad guys with, among other things, a baby carriage equipped with Gatling guns. He'd pretend he was just a nice old man walking his grandchild, then open up on a group of killers, sending a massive spray of bullets from his harmless-looking perambulator. In the same way that Americans would shortly become addicted to *Rocky* sequels, the Japanese were crazy about this continuing saga. For me, part of the appeal was that the Japanese notion of censorship hadn't yet caught up with the Western Puritan ethic. For example, the detective's girlfriend enjoyed sex with him by seating herself naked in an open-weave rattan basket hanging from the ceiling. Our hero would then spin the basket around while she was securely positioned on top of his penis.

These movies were all English subtitled, but I was, more often than not, the only Caucasian in the theater. After the movie, I'd have yaki udon and saki in a small restaurant around the corner. Enjoying my Japanese hosts' absolute respect for privacy, I'd sit for hours, reading or composing lyrics.

One evening, I'd been engaged in approximately the above routine, when I ran into Mickey Hart, drummer for The Grateful Dead, on the street. Unlike Yours Truly, the perpetual dilettante, Mickey is a black belt in karate, and I was asking him about various moves while we were walking along. But when we began to try some of them out on each other, a group of Oriental boys pulled up to see if I was all right. Thinking Mickey was inflicting the deadly martial art on me, they were about to do a community service by showing him what four teenage boys could do to an "old man" of thirty, whom they'd decided was clearly a threat to an innocent "lady." I smiled and waved so they'd know everything was okay. Japantown was sometimes safer than I wanted it to be; Mickey was one of the men I would like to have "joined," had the opportunity presented itself. It never did.

I purchased several samurai swords, which I used in theatrical scenarios, both on- and offstage. During one of our tours, I dressed head to toe in an aikido Kabuki outfit, which had very little to do with the lyrics of our songs. It was just my fascination with all things Eastern that prompted the particular getup. Peter Kaukonen, who was then our lead guitar player, was wearing lots of flamboyant makeup that night, so the audiences might have thought we'd raided the David Bowie closets for our wardrobe. But then, having seen me in LAPD shirts, Girl Scout dresses, Indian caftans, Adolf Hitler mustaches, bath towels, and at one point, no shirt at all (it rained at an outdoor concert in a park in New York, so not wanting to get the silk blouse spotted, I simply took it off), they were probably not surprised by the samurai princess suit.

36

Jefferson Starship

Paul was in the process of putting the "new" band together. John Barbata, a drummer for The Turtles, replaced Joey Covington, and we had Pete Sears on keyboards, David Freiberg on bass, Grace on Blue Nun wine, Paul on twelve-string guitar, the occasional hot licks violin from Papa John Creach, and Marty Balin came back into the fold, crooning. Marty was in top romantic form right then, and produced several hits ("Miracles," "Caroline," and "With Your Love" among them), putting us back into No. 1 position on the charts.

On that first Jefferson Starship tour, a positive turn of events happened that would affect my life forever. Coming back to the hotel after one of our concerts, an incredibly beautiful dark-haired woman asked if she could chat with Paul and me for a while. She came up to our room to hang out, stayed for about a half hour, and then decided to leave. I knew the rest of the crew and the band would be milling around in the hall and I peeked out the door, waiting to see who'd be cool enough to entice this gorgeous woman into his room. As she walked down the length of the hallway we all occupied, the clever remarks and invitations came flying at her from all directions, but it wasn't until the end of the rock-and-roll gauntlet that she stopped and turned into somebody's room. A man whom I'd never seen before, Skip Johnson, our new lighting director, apparently had said just the right phrase or made the winning move that drew the woman into his one-man party.

When we all converged the next morning for the ride to the airport, I made sure to see what this hustle master looked like up close. It was easy to figure out what it was about him that won him the previous evening's prize over all the other drooling competitors. Skip stood six feet tall with long black hair and green eyes surrounded by thick black eyelashes. Add to that his laid-back, cocky attitude, and I felt like I was once again at a Judy Levitas pool party, having my heartstrings tugged by Alan McKenna. Skip was twenty-two; I was thirty-four. Another good-looking dark Irish Catholic boy had overwhelmed me with nonchalance and young man enthusiasm.

The next day in Phoenix, Arizona, the entire group, including the crew, took over the hotel's outdoor area, filling most of the tables with loud rock banter and lousy margaritas. Everyone except Paul, that is, who'd flown to L.A. on our day off to talk to the RCA suits. Some of the guys were sitting down by the diving board, discussing the best way to make moves on several ladies seated across from us at the pool's other side, when suddenly Skip stood up, waved, and shouted, "Girls—could you come over here, please? You wanna fuck?"

The other hotel guests were shocked, we were cracking up, but damned if those girls didn't smile, get up, and come over to sit with this cute goofball with the foul mouth.

I decided to join them.

Later in the afternoon, Craig Chaquico, our new lead guitar player, and I had several interviews to do, so Skip offered to drive us around the city to the various radio stations. By the time the three of us got back to the hotel, I was determined to spend the night with this young man, who was friendly but seriously unimpressed with my fame. He'd worked for The Who and a lot of other top groups, so this Starship job was just one more entry on his rock-and-roll resumé. He was *so* unimpressed, in fact, that he actually said to me once for no particular reason, "You're too old, too fat, and too drunk. But I love you." The best backhanded remark I'd ever heard.

Okay, so now what? I was living with Paul, I had a beautiful daughter, and the band was pulling in the crowds again. But I was lost in romance land with this bright troublemaker who had no ties, no restrictions, and no regrets. Speaking of regrets, there's an old maxim that says, "It's not what you *did* that you regret, it's what you *didn't* do." So go for it.

I did. As everybody watched the seduction escalate, it became clear that the Grace/Paul duo was in for some trouble. And since Paul thought Skip was gay, it was easy for me to hang out with Skip pretty much whenever I wanted to, without creating concern. *Why* did Paul think Skip was gay? Probably because of the short red dress Skip wore to his own twenty-third birthday party in a sedate hotel bar on April 28, 1975. With the dress (borrowed from Yours Truly) he'd decided to wear sweat socks, high-tops, his mustache, and his hairy legs.

Knowing how much midwesterners love the big-city drag queen look, we all took advantage of their hospitality and celebrated as if there were nothing unusual about a member of our entourage sporting West Hollywood chic.

Paul didn't think any heterosexual man would do that. But my father used to do it once a year, when the San Francisco bankers had a men-only party. Everybody not only dressed like women, they actually rehearsed for the shindig and put on an entire musical, each showing up in his own version of a RuPaul chorus girl. So much for gay-only cross-dressing, but the humor was lost on Paul. As it probably was on most of the local crowd at the bar that night.

At the time, rock and roll was predominately a world of heterosexual male musicians. The loose morality of the times made experimentation an option, but gender differences were generally not the favorite topic of conversation or behavior. With one exception on my part. My friend Sally and I were goofing around getting loaded one night when Paul was out of the house. After we'd played some David Bowie records, we began talking about David's bisexuality and how cool it would be to go to a party and have one hundred percent of the room at your disposal. We decided to give it a go in the spirit of widening our possibilities. If it worked, that would be cool. If not, no harm done. We drank a little more champagne, we kissed a little, we touched each other's breasts, and then we burst out laughing.

"Let's get serious," we said, trying to keep in mind how expanded our dating world would be if this worked out. But in five minutes, we were laughing again. We finally gave it up as a lost cause and resigned ourselves to forty or fifty percent of the room. I never tried it again, figuring that Sally was cool, bright, and beautiful, and there was nothing wrong with her that I could determine, so if I couldn't get it on with her, I couldn't get it on with anyone. At least not a woman.

The truth is that I'm just not into vaginas. Because they're pretty much a mucous membrane, gushy and hot, and they can develop an awful lot of strange bacteria, my idea of hell is putting my face in somebody's pussy. If it's nice and clean, of course that's better, but I'm still not into it. That's not to say that I'm judgmental about lesbianism or that I think pussies are bad. I just happen to love the way men are built, that you can *see* when they're aroused and that everything is on the outside. With women, it's all inside and men have to figure out whether we're pretending to be aroused or not. We have to let them know what we want or just enjoy whatever's going on.

So much for Grace's lesbian possibilities. Skip was a far more realistic fantasy for me and a lot more dangerous. After the tour was over, and we settled back into San Francisco, Paul hired a publicist for Starship named Cynthia Bowman. Every man has his own distinctive expression of pleasure when he sees a woman who appeals to him, and I remember the look on Paul's face when he met Cynthia. I figured it wouldn't take long for the tall blonde ex-model to engender more than silly facial expressions—at least, that's how I rationalized my own faithless behavior with Skip. But Paul is a guy who can take his time; it wasn't until about five years later that Cynthia gave birth to China's little half brother, Alexander. That made two children out of wedlock for Paul (that he knows of)—one by Cynthia, one by me.

I'm still friends with Cynthia to this day, and we engage in some of our best sarcasm tournaments with Paul and the kids on Thanksgiving or Christmas. I also call Sally Mann in Texas and hang out with Darlene Ermacoff in Malibu. One of the strongest bonds you can have with a person is love of the same man. Jealousy is useless. The attraction both of you have for the same individual means you have a strong interest *in common,* so why not create a friendship instead of sucking on old resentments?

37

The Brandy Twins

In 1974, about a year before I met Skip, I'd announced through my lyrics (the same prescient way Jorma had in "Chelsea") that I needed to be figuratively unshackled. The words *escapar* (escape) and *libertad* (freedom) kept appearing in the Spanish section of the theme song on my solo album, *Manhole*.

> *Look up—the roof is gone*
> *And the long hand moves right on by the hour.*
> *Look up—the roof is gone.*
> *La música de España es para mí como la libertad . . .*
> *Convenir resueña para escapar.*

That title, *Manhole*, was meant to shock the women's libbers, and the lyrics—half-Spanish, half-English—were meant to please *me*. It was recorded, in part, at Olympic Studios in London with a symphony orchestra and a group of bagpipers in kilts—the real thing. The head bagpiper, a

249

quintessential Scotsman, healthy, robust, and bearded, pulled a small bottle of Scotch out of his high socks, which he sipped a little bit at a time, from sunrise to sunset, without getting soused. It was good fun; the album was a heteromorphic success and a commercial flop.

It was a year later, when I was still thrashing around, wondering where to aim myself, that I allowed Paul to steer me and some other loose-cannon musicians into Jefferson Starship—a veritable gold-record machine, as it turned out. The drug-fueled, anomalous lyrics of Jefferson Airplane smoothly shifted into the more languid boy/girl laments that made up the critical mass of popular songs in the post-hippie decades. Now it was Marty's turn to be the focus of attention, while I turned my passion toward our young lighting director.

For some reason, John Barbata felt it necessary to tell Paul that not only was Skip heterosexual, he was inter-acting with Yours Truly in more than a "touring bar pal" sort of way. I suppose Paul had been in denial of the obvious, but with John's sobering words, he understandably lost it and fired Skip. While he did his best to replace Skip (it's not that easy to find a lighting director who knows your songs well enough to cue a hundred lights exactly in time with the music), I was on the move. I'd stay in Detroit one night to perform, then fly to Chicago the next day to be where Skip was doing lights for someone else. Then I'd fly immediately back to New York to sing with the band again. After that, I was off to Washington to fit myself into Skip's tour schedule. Basically I was throwing a lot of money at the commercial airlines for about three months.

In one of the hotel rooms along the way, I sat down on the bed to think. How long could I keep the game going, I wondered, without creating the inevitable confrontation?

When Jefferson Starship got back home to San Francisco, Skip was on the road with Stephen Stills's group, and Sally and I decided to go to Alaska where they were playing. Good ole Sally, it turned out, was interested in Stephen *and* his keyboard player, Jerry Aiello, so we told Paul that we were going to stay for a while at the Boar's Head Inn, a quaint establishment in Carmel owned by Clint Eastwood. Neither one of us knew Clint, so I don't know why we thought that sounded plausible. But it worked. The problem—or fun, depending on how you look at it—was an airline strike. We had to take four different flights on five different airlines (I don't know, you figure it out) to get to Anchorage. Each time we boarded a different airplane, Sally and I cleaned out their liquor supply, so by the time we finally got to the hotel, we were plastered.

When we checked in and called Skip, our crocked condition didn't seem to bother him at all. He arrived at our room and leaned casually on the door frame, wearing a fireman's helmet with a swirling red police car light on top. Even though Sally and I could be formidable jerks when we were liquored-up, Skip was a veteran, having worked with some of the champs at overindulgence.

When he'd first come on board as production manager for The Who, they all got ripped one night and decided to initiate him into the fold by asking him to get the fire extinguisher and move the couch from the hotel room out into the hall—using nothing but the spray from the hose. Skip had taken up the challenge and had actually started the redecorating, but when he broke the glass on the hose box, an alarm went off and Hyatt security was on the scene before the couch could be adequately relocated.

Sally and I were ready to trash the tundra when we arrived in Alaska, but Skip *did* have to work. While he was at the concert hall doing the setup, Stephen's drummer, Joey Lala, Sally, and I went out in the twenty-below blizzard to check out the *Call of the Wild* territory. As we were walking along one of the snow-covered streets, a large man came flying out of a bar, landing facedown in the gutter. The even larger bouncer stood at the door looking like he'd just tossed out a small bag of rat turds. I made a remark like, "What if the guy freezes to death?" But Joey reminded me that this was still frontier land as far as the tough guys were concerned. Besides, the alcohol would probably keep him from turning blue until he came to and found another saloon to inhabit.

Skip more than proved his ability to handle almost anything on that tour by taking care of three difficult situations at once. The first was looking after the Brandy Twins (Sally and Grace); the second was taking on the job of road manager after the first guy suddenly freaked out and quit. The third was in Seattle, on the way back down the coast, when Skip saved one of the boys in the band from committing suicide, by tackling him when he tried to drown himself by diving off the hotel balcony into the Puget Sound. All that and lighting director, too—I was getting more impressed by the minute.

Sally and I made it back home on Christmas Eve, just in time for us to flip into mother mode for Jesse (Sally's son by Spencer) and China. Jesse was about the same age as my daughter, and Sally and I were about the same age as Beavis and Butt-head. We loved our kids, but we hadn't quite finished being children yet ourselves.

For a while, the sneaking around was exciting, but I finally had to admit that it wasn't fair to anybody. After making a decision to put an end to it, I got out the want ads and found an apartment in Sausalito. I then called Jefferson Starship's trucker, Mike Fisher, and asked him to meet me at the Seacliff house with the truck. Finally, I talked to Paul. I told him I couldn't pretend anymore, and I moved

"No rghuofmr!" (Roger Ressmeyer/© Corbis)

out and into the new apartment—all within a period of about twenty-four hours.

Sadness, yes. Regrets, no.

Although it was an unpleasant time for Paul, I'm sure he felt relief as well; it takes two people to ensure the failure of a relationship. Certain pop psychologists disagree, but I believe that staying together "for the child" creates a hideous atmosphere of daily bullshit in which the kid is surrounded by mixed messages at best and, at worst, chronic battles that make so-called family life a sham. I'm grateful there were never any custody fights over China. Paul and I shared her without written agreements or arguments.

During that time, Sally and I took up residence in the new apartment, which she referred to as "the combination palace." Skip stayed there off and on when he was between tours, and the three of us—sometimes accompanied by the "real" children—stayed in that *Three's Company* configuration until Skip was hired back by Jefferson Starship on a full-time basis. It was inevitable—he was the best, and there's just no substitute for adept professionalism. Now, living together as a bona fide "couple," Skip and I resumed touring with the band and tried to maintain a social environment as free of open hostility as possible. I roomed alone on that tour as I always had, savoring my privacy and indulging whims as various as shouting at the moon and, literally, walking on the edge.

An affinity for near-death experiences doesn't necessarily indicate that a person is miserable and wants to deanimate the body. That devalues what may be really going on. Perhaps the person is just attempting, in a primitive way, to join the cosmos, or bump into his or her original DNA, or flush out his or her adrenaline. Bungee-jumping, race car driving, astronautics, working on an art project until you drop, taking psychedelics, swimming the English Channel—these are all extreme activities pursued by people who're trying to "push the envelope," trying to test so-called limits. That urge to know why and why not has resulted in incredible discoveries that have changed the face of our culture forever. And sometimes it has just boiled down to an individual yearning to be part of the greater picture.

To wit:

It happened in the Midwest, where the elements regularly put on a spectacular thunder and lightning show, the likes of which I'd never seen. One such storm was in full swing that night and the entire sky was alive in fast-frame time. Undulating colors moved in and out of gray, white, blue, and black exploding clouds, which were sliced down the center of their fat, rolling surface by spears of bristling electric white light. And beneath their high-voltage crackle was the crashing bass of thunder.

I wanted to be a part of it—it was an instantaneous reaction. I opened the window, took off all my clothes, climbed out on the ledge, and cheered like a rabid sports fan for the clashing natural Titans. I could feel the rain and the wind on my naked body and I could sense the sound of the thunder in my chest. My hair was thrown and whipped around my face. My own shouting voice moved in circles up through the percussion of thunder claps. For just a few minutes, I was embraced by the *original* choreographer.

Fantastic—until I heard the flat voice of caution.

"Grace, this is your drummer, John Barbata, speaking to you. Get back into your room!" He was using that pseudo-authoritarian crowd-control tone that security employs when large groups of people are threatening to become unruly. I don't know if he thought I was going to jump, or if he was just worried about the group's having to come up with a quick replacement for a vocalist, but he was clearly confused about my intentions. That was understandable;

I'm not an athlete, so I suppose he was justified in questioning my ability to maintain balance under the circumstances.

The short of it is that I eventually stepped back through the window and lived to tell the tale. I'm not ordinarily a nature girl, but there are some weather opportunities that can't be refused.

38

All-Access Pass

In 1976, I was back in the place of my birth, Chicago, for another offer that couldn't be refused. Skip and I were on tour, enjoying an evening of room service and lovemaking, when he suddenly asked me to marry him. My marriage to Jerry Slick had been nothing more than assumed theory sliding into practice, and Paul and I never tried to formalize things, so no one had ever *actually* proposed to me before. I was honored and delighted. But since Skip was so young and we were both high at the time, I said, "I love you, too, but it's late, we're loaded, and maybe you're just reacting to the moment. If you still feel this way in the morning, ask me again. And if you don't, I'll understand that it was just temporary enthusiasm."

Since Skip had to get up early for work the next morning, he was gone when I awakened, but there was a note on his pillow that said, "Will you marry me?" The guy was serious.

YES, I wanted to be his partner; there was no question about it. And I knew that China adored him, which also helped me make my decision. Skip was young and energetic enough to offer her more than the usual "I'll watch while you play" togetherness that often passed for adult/child bonding. Both mother and daughter found his antics pretty irresistible.

The group always tried to book Hawaii as the last job on our tours so we could stay a while afterward and enjoy the islands. One afternoon in Oahu, Pat Dugan, China, and I were hanging out in Pat's hotel room on the ninth floor, when she looked over at the window and let out a yell. There was Skip, who had climbed up the outside of the building. Casually swinging one of his legs over the ninth-floor balcony railing, he smiled and said, "Good afternoon, ladies." China did a hand-clapping giggle, I decided Skip was Robin fucking Hood, and Pat wanted to strangle him for almost giving her a heart attack.

That same night, the band and crew had dinner at Michelle's, a fantastic restaurant right on the beach. The open room included long, wide windows facing the beach, close enough to the ground for a child to climb out and run off for some fun in the sand. Skip and China took advantage of the situation. While the two of them headed off in a random dance toward the water, the reddish pink sunset and bright blue ocean surrounded their silhouettes—a clear memory that I call up from time to time when I want to remind myself how lucky I am to still have both of them in my life.

Skip is from Philadelphia, and as a lighting director, he literally shines his lights on me, so this old Elton John song still makes me get out the Kleenex:

Shine a light,
Shine a light,
Philadelphia freedom,
I love you.

Another wedding party: Cynthia Bowman, the bride, China Kantner, Skip Johnson, and Billy Johnson. (Ivan Wing)

From cleaning toilets at the Spectrum in Philadelphia to production manager for The Who in the space of three years, Skip was one of the lucky kids, like myself, who saw it, wanted it, and got it.

The all-access pass.

Drugs, groupies, limos, five-star hotels—we lived the all-expenses-paid life that everyone dreams about while they're wiping off the countertops at Burger King. A lot of people will tell you, quite sanctimoniously, that money won't buy you happiness, but as David Lee Roth said, "Maybe not, but it'll buy you a big fucking yacht that cruises right up next to it."

Sure, there've been times when I've been miserable over one thing or the other, but I'd rather not have the burdens

259

of back rent, no job, and an overdrawn bank statement to pile on top of whatever the base misery may be. Bucks grease the hassles; a good attitude drives the whole car. But maybe it's a matter of personality types, because I've noticed that some people are unhappy no matter what's going on. I remember feeling pretty good, even in my rats-in-the-basement, shit-hole apartment in Potrero Hill in San Francisco, so I guess I've managed to live my entire life in a kind of splendid Disney denial. Whether I'm ecstatic or furious, my life seems part of some colorful fairy tale that just rolls out in front of the 130-decibel soundtrack with endless production credits.

Skip and I were married by a Japanese justice of the peace in the outdoor pavilion of the LaHaina Hotel in Maui in November 1976. Right up to the last minute before the ceremony, my mother was helping me sew organdy flowers onto my wedding dress. Nervous and afraid we wouldn't finish in time, I snorted some cocaine to zip through the sewing process, then popped a quaalude to get "serene" for the wedding. Everything came off as planned, but, in hindsight, I would have preferred to be a totally sober bride—no chemicals at all, not even food.

Some kind of belated desire for purity.

China was the flower girl at the ceremony on the beach, where we both stood by Skip in front of a spectacular Hawaiian sunset. Cynthia Bowman was my maid of honor; Skip's brother, Billy, was best man, and I brought the entire band and their families over for the occasion. Everyone seemed genuinely happy for us, and the party afterward took place in various parts of the hotel until people were *wearing* the champagne and confusing some chips of fallen white ceiling plaster for lines of cocaine, trying to snort up the rugs. Paul wasn't there for obvious reasons, but neither was Marty. Why? Who knows. The man remains a mystery to me. Everybody else in the group brought their girlfriends, wives, and children, but I guess Marty had his own illusion to attend.

39

Firing Myself

Sometimes I'll be driving on the Pacific Coast Highway in Malibu, watching the ocean roll in and out under a sun-blasted sky, and I get so happy, tears run down my face. That happens about once a week these days—the feeling of things being exactly perfect—no drugs, no reason, just some spontaneous reaction to beauty. But in the late seventies, it was hard for me to see that much beauty in anything.

In 1978, Jefferson Starship was bound for a European tour. Let's bring wives! Mothers! Children! Oh boy!

Arghh. My idea of hell.

By that time, everybody was competent enough with whatever instrument they played to pull off the shows without a hitch, but the disparities in personalities were not as easily mastered. The comedy of errors and irritations escalated until they became nearly unbearable for Yours Truly, and while everybody else seemed to think this Jefferson Starship tour was a great family-fun adventure, a big rock-and-roll party atmosphere all the time, it made me very uncomfortable.

Imagine the confusion of fifty people showing up for a train ride, someone's kid kicking someone else's kid, and the parents, of course, sticking up for their own kid. Somebody's girlfriend forgetting her hair dryer and the entire pack of us waiting for her to retrieve it. And since China was with us, we brought along Pat Dugan to watch her because Paul and Skip and I were all working. I ask you, how many insurance companies, banks, publishing houses, etc., bring a circus to work? Since I was the kind of person who prefers to do one thing at a time, my biggest problem was dividing my attention between the ex-boyfriend, current husband, daughter, and entourage. Not to mention travel considerations and attention to performance.

It literally made me sick.

When I went to Europe with my parents back in 1957, about every three days I remember coming down with a vomit/diarrhea combination, resulting from exposure to various water bacteria. When the Starship family-fun entourage got to Lorelei in Germany, my body started shooting out reminders of 1957. Trips to the toilet ranged in frequency from between three to five minutes, making it difficult, if not impossible, to perform even one song without having to excuse myself to fill up the latrine.

When I told the band—with a doctor in agreement— that I couldn't go on that night for obvious reasons, Paul decided they shouldn't play without me.

"Why not?" I asked him between toilet runs.

"Would The Rolling Stones play without Mick Jagger?" he asked.

"No, of course not," I answered, "but The Rolling Stones only have *one* lead singer. We have *two*, and Marty can carry it off quite nicely."

In fact, the international hits we had at that time were mostly Marty's anyway. But Paul was adamant. While arguments continued whether to play or not to play, word leaked to our audience that we were considering canceling. The timing was unfortunate. By the time Paul was about to come around, the American soldiers based around the area were so pissed off that we were considering canceling, they made the decision for us by completely trashing the stage. Now the performance *had* to be canceled. But the guys got new equipment, the camaraderie in the group was ostensibly patched together, and I was well enough to press on to the next show.

Frankfurt.

At the airport, I stopped in at one of the tourist shops and purchased a quaint, Heidi-cute, German dirndl skirt and a felt vest with puffy white sleeves—an Aryan costume that I thought would be a nice contrast to my opinion of the Germans' unbelievably stupid WWII performance. I took the outfit back to the hotel, but after imbibing some alcohol, I decided that cute was not the way to go. On went the black shirt, black pants, and the black jack boots. I'd decided to *become* the remembered enemy, with the encouragement of a well-stocked minibar.

It was time for the fingers-up-the-nose-of-the-guy-in-the-front-row trick. I know *exactly* what came over me; instead of it being an act of God where my insides were spilling out totally beyond my control, this time, I created the unpleasantness all by myself. Hammered to the tits, well into the first song, I was inexorably attracted to a pair of nostrils in the front row. They were attached to a German guy who had no idea what was about to happen when I staggered toward him with the intention of picking his nose. He didn't seem to mind too much, or at least he was so shocked, he didn't do anything.

But even as I pulled that stunt, it was clear to me that I'd developed a major attitude problem. I didn't like pandering to Nazi offspring, I didn't like the "reconstituted Airplane" situation, and I didn't like *me* for taking part in it. I wanted the Germans to see a mirror of repulsive self-loathing, I wanted the band to see an uncontrollable mutant, and I wanted to be so out of line that when I fired myself the next day *nobody* would object.

The ultimate American punk.

The truth is, I'd had it with everything and everybody except Skip and China. Since Skip had been on my side of the argument with Paul over whether or not I could actually sing and shit at the same time, he was ready to leave as well. Skip and I were both out of there the next day, and the tour continued without us, Marty singing solo lead for the group's remaining appearances.

40

TUIs

After that fateful tour, Marty left the group again, Grace was already gone, and Starship began the search for a new lead singer. While they were regrouping, I'd settled (?) back home and was alternately working on a solo album titled *Dreams* and driving the highway patrol nuts.

Some drunks sit around and cry or watch infomercials, but when I was high, I just *had* to drive a car. It is a great bit of good fortune that I never hit any living beings, because an automobile is definitely a weapon in the hands of chemically altered individuals. I *was* arrested during the seventies on three separate occasions for drunk driving, but I wasn't actually in the car for any of the three arrests.

How did that work? It's called a DUI—"driving under the influence." But in my case, it should have been called a TUI—for "talking under the influence."

When my first arrest occurred, I'd had a couple glasses of white wine (Vanessi's restaurant in San Francisco had *enormous* glasses), Paul and I were arguing in the car on the way home, and I was driving. When he got tired of the debate, he reached over, pulled the keys out of the ignition, and heaved them out the window onto somebody's front lawn. Completely disgusted, he got out of the car and started walking home, while *I* also got out of the car and started rooting around in the grass on my hands and knees, searching for the keys. After about ten minutes of unsuccessful close-to-the-ground ferreting, I heard the delicate footsteps of someone approaching me on my right side. Turning my head to view the inquisitor, I came face to feet with a pair of black boots. Lo and behold—it was a member of the SFPD. He stood there in full regalia: navy blue outfit, badge, hands on hips, and an expression that asked, "What's going on here?"

When I heard him actually utter the words, I started laughing because I had a good idea where I was going next—the Bryant Street police station. I stood up to face him and he repeated the question, "What's going on here?" Now I *knew* where I was going next because instead of answering him, I kept on laughing. Cops don't like it when you laugh instead of answering; they get highly offended when you show them you don't give a shit. They also don't like it when you're down on all fours, rooting around in some strange person's lawn. I already had several strikes against me.

At the jail my cellmate was puking all over the place, so I started practicing karate, knowing that if they thought I might be violent, they'd give me a single-person cell. I was transferred to alternate accommodations, but unfortunately, I was accompanied by a girl, high on speed, who sang Paul McCartney's "Band on the Run" *all night long.*

After three forms of gray food for breakfast, bail was posted, I was let out, and my name appeared in the newspaper for my parents and friends to enjoy with *their* breakfast.

The second TUI was a result of not checking the oil gauge in the car. At 150 mph, racing uphill on Waldo Grade in Marin County, a car without oil is bound to give the driver some strong objections to that oversight. On the way back down the hill, when my Aston Martin started belching and throwing flames out from under the hood, I pulled over to the side of the freeway and got the hell *out* of the potentially exploding car. As I waited (it was 3:00 A.M., so there wasn't much traffic) for someone to flag down, a guy in a Volkswagen pulled over. "Do you want me to call the highway patrol for you?" he asked.

"Yes!" I said.

In about five minutes, the black-and-white pulled up. I was ready to do the female in distress thing, but the officer, six feet, four inches, with thumbs hooked in his belt under a beer gut, said, "Okay, what's going on here?" His mistake. My problem.

"I'm having a goddamned party at three A.M. all by myself on the fucking freeway," I heard myself answer. "That's what's going on here."

We took an instant dislike to each other: I didn't like his helpful tone of voice and he didn't like my snappy rejoinder. I was booked for a DUI masquerading as a TUI and spent the night at the Frank Lloyd Wright Marin County Jail.

The last TUI happened when I played Omar Khayyam in a black pickup truck. I thought it would be romantic to take a loaf of bread, a jug of wine, and a book of poetry, and go out among the woodsy back roads of Mill Valley. I was already out of the truck, sitting against a tree trunk, reading, eating, and drinking, when, in sharp contrast to the lovely green foliage, the old black-and-white swung around a curve in the road. The uniformed driver got out, stood there, and watched me for a moment. I was clearly enjoying myself, but he decided to inquire about why I happened to be there. The fatal sentence escaped his mouth.

"What's going on here?" he asked. (Don't they know any other words?)

"Is it really any of your fucking business?" I answered.

That was the wrong answer. I could have been pleasant and said, "Just having a peaceful meal in the woods," but badges, liquor, and those four little words turn me into a smaller version of Roseanne at best, or a larger version of a wolverine at worst.

So Officer Krupke says, "I'm arresting you for being drunk in public!"

"Public!? You call pine trees, squirrels, and you PUBLIC?!!"

Back to lovely Marin Civic and my old room in the female lockup for the evening. Skip and a lawyer friend rescued me in the morning.

My glib recounting of these events comes off like I didn't give a shit about anything or anybody. But really, I've always felt a kind of contrition when I cause pain to people who've done nothing to deserve it. Lawyers get paid to post bail or show up in court, it's their *job*. But I *do* care about my friends whose days are interrupted by calls informing them that "the nut is at it again, trying to bad-mouth the police" or "we need to get Grace out of the slammer again." I know these unfortunates all have better things to do than come to the aid of Yours Truly. Unfortunately, there's this hard-to-squelch part of me that comes off like some ninety-year-old Ozark ruffian determined to guard her illegal gin mills to the death.

Is it genetics? Environment? Or just plain irresponsi-

"Gun Mouth Grace" (Grace Slick)

bility? Probably all of the above, and too much pepper in the bouillabaisse. But I don't blame the Master Chef in the sky; there's a slippery rascal down here spicing her own soup.

271

41

Immoderation

The CHP finally got tired of seeing my face at the registration desk. When I was informed that unless I went to six months of AA meetings I'd lose my driver's license, I was confused. I didn't want to lose my freedom to drive, but I imagined that AA was one of those sermon-and-a-free-meal Christian deals where they try to convert the penniless.

I told the judge, "You don't understand, I can pay for my dinner. How about community service?"

"No, *you* don't understand," she said. "Alcoholics Anonymous isn't a charity. It's an organization of people who help each other stay sober."

Oh.

I began attending daily AA meetings, and to my surprise, I immediately loved the concept. There were no overseers with funny outfits, no cultural, racial, or gender exclusions, no Bible, Talmud, or Koran thumping, and no "You're going to hell unless you . . ." threats. It was just a simple premise based on spiritual progress. While I went to the meetings and stayed "sober" for as long as it took to quiet the authorities and placate my family, I learned to listen and appreciate the affecting personal stories of people from dissimilar backgrounds. I also learned to burn "this too shall pass" into my repertoire of clichés. And I made new friends.

But the idea of never again using chemicals didn't register as a lifelong pursuit. Since I was fascinated by collective self-examination and the power of group energy, I continued to go to meetings long after the CHP had lost interest in my behavior or my whereabouts. But as far as drugging was concerned, I made up my own rules. I figured it was a good idea to stay out of the driver's seat while chemicals were still altering my motor skills, but for me, that didn't necessarily mean sobriety.

In the meantime, there was some turmoil erupting between Skip and me. With my preference for liquor and Skip's affinity for opiates, we'd begun to exist on different planets of altered lack of consciousness. But because my loaded behavior was usually acted out publicly, while Skip's was private, *I* was the one who obviously needed restraining. People like my father and Skip, who spent most of their time quietly ripped, managed to enjoy their excesses without bringing down the wrath of the community.

It was decided that I should go to Duffy's, a rehab unit that was located smack in the middle of California's wine country.

Ironic.

Someone dragged me, the offending drunk, up to the facility in the middle of the night, and I woke up in heaven—nothing but grapes bulging with potential everywhere I looked. Some of the other guests apparently had convulsions and died before they could appreciate the satire, but the humor of the situation and the location of this particular "Fidget Farm" were not lost on Gene Duffy, the sarcastic bullhorn of a man who owned the place. The first words I ever heard him say were, "Good morning, assholes!" With that opening comment, I liked him right away. He was correct, of course. No one got to Duffy's by exemplary conduct.

I wasn't there for long before I noticed some fellow drunks who were a bit further along in the game than I was. One man was shaking so badly he had to grab a towel, wrap it around his neck, and hold it steady with one hand like a pulley, in order to bring his orange juice up to his mouth without spilling it in his lap. Others just sat in chairs, reviewing their lives with a kind of unearthly stare. Those of us under the age of forty who were still able to sweat out the hangover took solace in the delusion of immortality that buttresses young souls.

After a couple of weeks at the Fidget Farm, if you seemed to be making "progress," they allowed you to go on a walk by yourself to the center of the town, which happened to be Calistoga. I took advantage of the freedom by visiting the various wine-tasting concessions that dotted the area, and, when I returned, no one seemed to notice my infraction of the rules. At that time Duffy's did no drug testing, so at the end of the required three-week residency, I was permitted to leave with the customary reminder to continue going to AA meetings.

My story is and has always been that I enjoy being sober and I enjoy being drunk. I just wish it didn't unhinge my family and friends as much as it does.

Some reasons (not excuses) for my incurable immoderation concerning food and drugs:

At five feet, seven inches, 140 pounds, I consider myself

about three inches too short and about ten pounds over-weight. I maintain that slightly hefty appearance because about once a week I like to stuff myself on foods that I *love*. If I don't like the added weight, I take it off. If *someone else* doesn't like the extra ten pounds, they can go right ahead and not like the remaining 130 pounds right along with it—that's their problem. The main reason for dieting is that I'm lazy and I don't like lugging the blubber around. But, ah, the taste of a fine meal.

Concerning my intermittent drug use, people have asked me, "Aren't you happy in your natural state?"

Yes. I like the "natural state" (Montana?). I also like spaghetti, but not three meals a day, every day, all year. I like variations, both for my taste buds and for my forty-odd neural/chemical receptors. During my life, I've used drugs for a number of different reasons: to experience other levels of consciousness, to remain wakeful, to try to induce hallu-cinations (which I've never really had), to quiet my nerves, to lower my cholesterol levels, to shut up the committee in my head, to get silly, to reduce inflammation, and on and on.

The list of pharmaceuticals and street drugs I've availed myself of is endless, but the worst drug reaction I've had was caused by a prescription pill called Zomax. It was touted as a minor anti-inflammatory chemical mix that worked fine on rats—but unfortunately didn't agree very well with humans. I took Zomax to relieve a pulled back muscle. But when I swallowed one of these harmless-looking little cylinders that a doctor had prescribed for Skip, within a half hour, I was on my way to the hos-pital—cramping, throwing up, emitting diarrhea, and breaking out in a head-to-toe rash. The paramedics were forced to shove wet towels down my throat so I could breathe (my throat was so dry, it stuck together, blocking the air passages). When I told my doctor what I'd taken, he said, "Oh, they took that off the market—it was killing people."

What a waste—it didn't even get me high.

42

Working Solo

While I was being cautioned about my drug and alcohol problems by authorities, associates, and friends, I was working on one of my solo albums, *Dreams*, which incorporated the sensibilities of the AA twelve-step programs. Although for many years I loved being a part of a rock-and-roll group, traveling and singing with the various versions of Airplane and Starship, I've always preferred *writing* solo, focusing on whatever inspired me. By contrast, Paul Kantner has always liked collaborating, so he was overly generous in sharing credit for songs that were mainly his creations. Sometimes we'd be hanging out talking, he'd hear a line from me that he liked, he'd use it in a song, and then my name would appear on the album as cowriter.

But I like writing my own thoughts in my own time. I have a theory that my preference for writing solo is a result of playing by myself so much when I was a child. As I grew up and continued to work at my own pace with my own ideas and my own tools, *sole authorship* became a habit that was hard to break. I respect collaboration; when two or more people *do* manage to produce a successful joint venture, it's like a brief marriage of souls, an accomplishment that's very satisfying. But in my case, collaboration has always been an awkward effort; I really find no pleasure in marching to someone else's drum, and it can be uncomfortable trying to force my input into another's vision.

With Airplane's Jorma Kaukonen, I enjoyed writing lyrics to music he'd already written (we did that a couple of times), but that wasn't so much a collaboration as it was a result of independent efforts. One person wrote the music, the other the lyrics. That's a common division of labor for songwriting teams—Rogers and Hammerstein, George and Ira Gershwin, Elton John and Bernie Taupin, Lerner and Loewe, Rodgers and Hart. I was about to add Lennon and McCartney, but they may be the exception to the rule, since they often interacted on both the words and the music.

Paul McCartney came over to a rehearsal at the Fillmore once, just to hang out and compare bass guitar notes with Jack. I remember feeling like we'd been blessed with an appearance by the Dalai Lama. Even though our album *Surrealistic Pillow* had stayed in one position or another on the *Billboard* Top Ten for fifty-six weeks, in comparison to The Beatles, we were still just part of the congregation. Paul was in the pulpit.

But even with the esteemed Lennon/McCartney collaboration as a role model, I always preferred writing alone, which I got to do when I was recording *Dreams*. I'd just blown off the group in a rage against what I perceived to be our collective animosity and mediocrity, and I didn't even know whether I could continue to make records. How? Solo? With studio musicians? What did I really have to say in the lyrics? Did I care enough to do all the organization, the contracts, the interviews, hire new musicians, write the songs, go on the road "alone"? For what? Applause? Money? Habit?

Since I was a kid, I've always written songs, stories, poems, and free verse. I had no thought of *doing* anything with them. I just wrote for fun—to see if what I created fell into the realm of acceptable communication. Sometimes I'd show my stuff to my parents or friends, but "professional output" never even occurred to me. After I quit Starship in disgust with both myself and the music business in general, I continued to write as I always had, generating bits and pieces of thoughts in rhyming patterns. I never stopped writing, and since I had a collection of about six or seven song lyrics when I left Starship, Skip suggested I *do* something with them. "You've got almost enough songs for an album, why not make one?" he suggested.

Why not?

Of course, there was a downside to going the solo route. For me, doing solo albums felt like being in a plastic bubble. Sure, I was protected by the label and the status I had as the top-billed musician on the record, but my isolation was constant. If things weren't right, it was *my* fault. If ideas were discussed, people would usually accept *my* call, even if it was mediocre. If *I* wasn't up to par on a given day, no one could step in and do *their* song instead. It was at the recording stage that the feeling of separateness weighed most heavily. I preferred writing the songs alone, but when it came to bringing them to life, the input of people who had equal status made the effort so much more intriguing and unified.

That said, meeting whole new groups of musicians and producers for each successive record brought a fresh sound to the music that was both exciting and gratifying. It taught me a lot, too. So with Skip managing me and pulling together the various and demanding elements, we hired Ron Frangipane as producer, combined some lyrics I already had with some new ones, and made *Dreams* for RCA. Since I was working solo, this album contained my most personal grouping of lyrics up to that time. Instead of pointing my finger at "you" like I'd done in the past, very often "I" was the subject of these new songs. Although I was still distancing myself by using the pronoun "she," it was obvious that the concerns expressed in the lyrics were mine. Take, for example, one of the album's songs, "Do It the Hard Way":

She said I've got to make 'em all think I'm winning so I'll
   just tell 'em lies
That way I can make sure no one ever knows just exactly
   what I mean
Then I can beat the drums and yell it to the skies
I'm the queen of the nuthouse, I'm the queen
     And I can justify myself—say I've been cheated
     I'm the only one in this game who knows how to play
     And if it weren't for time—I'd never be defeated
     But people, places and things—they get in my way
       And I don't like what they say.
She's gonna keep on doing it till she proves that they're all
   wrong
She's got to let 'em know she's the exception to the rule
She's got no friends 'cause she thinks she's so damn strong
But she's the only one who doesn't know that she's the fool

Talking about hurt, pain, and fear has always been diffi- cult for me. I've viewed that type of "victim's" lament as pathetic inertia, so when it came to expressing my feelings in lyric writing, I usually tried to shuffle the linguistics so that no one would see the pathos card whining at the bottom of the deck. I was more comfortable being perceived as irritating rather than brooding. Empathy, yes. Sympathy, no. But with *Dreams*, the boundaries were getting thin.

Did my solo albums sell? No. If I'd been willing to go on the road to promote them, they might have fared better. What wasn't fully clear to me then is abundantly clear now: no one in his or her right mind puts out an album without tour support. Steely Dan is the only outfit I can think of that managed to stay alive without doing concerts, and I think even *they* finally caved in and hit some clubs later in their career. To add to my self-created promotional difficulties, I had this grandiose idea that onstage every song on my album should have a completely different set to fully complement the lyrics. That was not only physically impossible, it was financially unrealistic. But I was unwilling to go out and do a half-assed Airplane set in order to sell records.

To be honest, doing solo albums scared the shit out of me; making music was no longer fun, it was nerve-racking pressure. For someone who couldn't handle a quarter cup of coffee without wondering where the quaaludes were, working solo was just a couple of steps short of flinging myself off a 150-foot diving board. I much preferred to write the songs and give them to a group of friends to help me make the music in a band format.

Only a handful of people have been able to sustain solo careers after leaving a popular band. Sting, Peter Gabriel, Diana Ross, Phil Collins, and Michael Jackson come to mind. Most egos can't wait to get their hands full of their own importance, and when they do, they realize it's not as easy as they thought.

Of my four attempts, *Dreams* was probably the best and *Manhole* the most unique. But if you don't or can't give all of yourself to a project, it's easy for listeners to recognize a lack of inspiration. In the case of my solo albums, every detail was not attended to, every aspect was not evaluated by the person responsible—me. For instance, when I needed to have my English lyrics translated into Spanish for *Manhole*, instead of taking them to a professional Berlitz kind of guy, I used an easier method. I honked up a bunch of cocaine and stayed up till about five in the morning, waiting for the Mexican janitor to come into the recording studio to clean up. He and I swilled some wine together and I had him translate my lyrics. We traded languages the best we could, which resulted in "Celtic Taco" grammar, so if you don't understand Spanish, the lyrics in *Manhole* sound okay. But if any Latinos heard it, they probably wondered who put the WASP in the tequila. It was fun hanging out with a fellow wino, but rough on album continuity.

My solo albums were each like a half-finished puzzle; they represented only the beginning of a full picture. Simply put, they were inadequate and incomplete. Skip did everything he could to manage the productions and make things run as smoothly as possible, but even the finest Ferrari goes nowhere without the juice. All the people who worked with me were tireless, talented, and accommodating, but it took me four albums to realize that, in my case, true passion required the presence of an ongoing band of musicians rather than a linear autonomous framework. Give me the wolf pack and I come alive. Segregate me and I suck my thumb. Masturbation is fabulous, but nothing beats the old tango.

Even though I was working and putting out music during the time I made *Dreams*, my erratic emotional behavior was affecting Skip and China. I knew it, but I didn't have a grip on who or what was going to inspire me to change it. Tripping over my own unanswerable questions, I felt like I was walking a tightrope without the pole; I was losing it and I couldn't see the net. I was too cynical to keep on with the "we can be together" flowers in the park stuff, and too old to pull off the angry young drunk punk, although at least it would have been more honest. I saw myself as Queen of the Nuthouse then, imagining people thinking, "Hey, let's go over and watch Grace rattle the bars and yell for room service."

Coinciding with my own maudlin "dark night of the soul" was Skip's painful physical illness, which increased his need for prescription narcotics. His body *couldn't* work and my spirit didn't *want* to work. But sometimes, fate, karma, or just plain dumb luck coaxes the phoenix out of the ashes, or at least out of the wine vats.

43

An Easy Ride

In 1979, while Skip and I were still waging our silent (and sometimes not so silent) battles with chemicals, Paul organized another version of Jefferson Starship. Minus me. The group was composed of Aynsley Dunbar on drums, Craig Chaquico on lead guitar, Pete Sears on keyboards, David Freiberg on bass, Paul on rhythm guitar, and a new lead singer, Mickey Thomas (who'd sung the hit "Fooled Around and Fell in Love"). The new group produced a successful album, *Freedom at Point Zero*.

While Jefferson Starship was working on a second LP, the producer, Ron Nevison, in conjunction with Kantner, called to ask me if I'd like to come in and put down harmonies on one of the songs. The group was recording in Sausalito, just five minutes away from the house Skip and I had bought in Mill Valley, so it seemed relatively uncomplicated. No pressure: just hang out, sing a little bit, see old buddies, and get friendly with the local recording studio operation.

As we entered the eighties, long songs about revolution and chaos were mostly in the past, now the property of the Brit punks, so rather than rely on group-written material, Starship reached out to outside writers. Of course, because most of us considered ourselves songwriters, we would have preferred to have our own songs on the records. But when an outside writer provided the producers with what they thought was an excellent song, or possibly a hit, we swallowed our pride and deferred to consensus.

To give you a sense of how commercial considerations had—and *have*—taken over, consider a song I wrote in 1989, the year of the Jefferson Airplane reunion album, called "Harbor in Hong Kong," about the initiation and success of the opium/tea trade and the eventual turnover to Communist China. It was a good song, not simple enough to be a single, however, and too anachronistic to rate as an album cut. So it wasn't used. Back in 1968, though, I would have recorded it, objections be damned, and the fact that it was quirky would have been even *more* reason to include it in the final product. But times had changed.

"You want to make strange albums with no single possibilities in the eighties? Use your own money, Grace."

I didn't.

Eventually, the group's commercial pandering got to Paul, starting with the pimple cream sponsorship to which we'd all agreed. By that time, mounting a rock-and-roll tour took a ton of money: the trucks, lights, sets, and transportation all required big bucks. So sponsorship was necessary. I didn't really object to it, but you had to be careful who your sponsor was. Integrity nags, so I certainly wouldn't have wanted to advertise Exxon. On the other hand, Tom's of Maine toothpaste just didn't have the bucks behind it to mount a tour. So the alternatives we were left with were few. Result: this way-over-thirty band accepted pimple cream money to support touring expenses.

Adding to Paul's misery were songs of the "Baby, why don't you love me?" ilk. He just couldn't handle it, and he also resented the time limits set for the length of songs. There could be no more eleven-minute songs because Top 40 radio wouldn't play them, and the rest of the group wanted hit singles to help sell the albums and pull in the bucks.

Also driving Paul batty was the overreliance on the same formulaic song structure: verse-verse-chorus-verse-chorus-bridge-verse-chorus-out. It simply wasn't Paul's style. His personal integrity was crashing into the desire of the rest of the group to go with the current trends.

Was he right? Sure. From where he was standing. And we thought we were busy being sensible and modern. As usual, somewhere in the middle was the truth. But Paul knew his *own* truth. He left the band in disgust, and Jefferson Starship continued as simply Starship.

The record company, on the other hand, couldn't have cared less who wrote the songs as long as they sold, so the new Starship wound up soliciting Top 40 hits from "pros" and "up-and-comers." The multitalented Peter Wolf (no, not Faye Dunaway's ex) wrote "Sara" with Ina Wolf, Diane Warren wrote "Nothing's Gonna Stop Us Now," and Bernie Taupin, collaborating with Peter Wolf, Dennis Lambert, and Martin Page, contributed "We Built This City." All three songs quickly went to No. 1 and ensured the group a consistent string of successful records and tours during the mid-eighties.

As fate would have it, my participation in the latter two songs with Starship led to a continuing role. Between *Welcome to the Wrecking Ball* and *Software*, two forgettable solo

Left to right: David Freiberg, Mickey Thomas, Grace Slick, Paul Kantner, and Pete Sears, smiling, sober, and selling out. (Roger Ressmeyer/© Corbis)

albums I managed to squeeze out, I was bumped up to singing duets with Starship's Mickey Thomas. That was fine with me, but Mickey had envisioned himself as commanding the spotlight (by himself) at the front of the band—until I arrived to ruin his vision. Since two of Starship's monster singles were our duets, it became increasingly difficult for him to make a case against pairing up with me. He was never vocal about it, but it was easy to tell that singing with the old broad clearly wasn't his idea of the ultimate rock-band lineup.

I thought Mickey would recognize that singing duets wasn't a lifelong sentence, and that if he could put up with me for a few more albums, he'd gain the commercial clout to go out on his own and pull in the stadium crowds. But he didn't see it that way. As it turned out, neither of us mentioned our discomfort to each other, and polite acceptance lingered until 1986.

Another problem arose: Aynsley Dunbar, our new drummer, was fired, and that's how Donny Baldwin, one of my all-time favorite people, became the drummer for the rest of the Starship records.

After Paul left, I remained the last shred of the original Airplane lineup, and I was enjoying an easy ride. Skip, having recovered from the worst part of his illness, once again took on the lighting director job. With him, Donny Baldwin, Pete Sears, producer Ron Nevison, and Peter Wolf all part of the mix, I was surrounded by friends and good traveling companions. The congenial atmosphere made our pop MOR (middle of the road) music tolerable, and the three chart-toppers supported our various families of children, dogs, grandmothers, and mortgages.

Life had become more stable—with the exception of a few unavoidable incidents that were related to celebrity. One night, I was lying awake beside a sleeping Skip, letting my mind wander, when I saw a figure appear in the darkness of our bedroom doorway. For some reason, I thought it was one of the band or crew members screwing around, so I tapped Skip on the shoulder and asked him, "Do you know who that is?"

Since my eyesight isn't as good as Skip's, I didn't see the gun in the man's hand. Skip did, however, and let out a wordless yell that was so loud and excruciating, the guy ran out of the room, down the stairs, and right through a plate-glass door, his plans thwarted by sheer decibel volume. Good old rock and roll. Caught by the police after we lodged a complaint, the screwball said that an extraterrestrial had sent him to Maria Muldaur's house to make contact. (With a gun?) The poor fool had apparently confused me with Maria Muldaur, another dark-haired singer who also lived in Mill Valley. I never did call her to find out if he'd honored *her* with his unraveled presence.

China was an easy child to love and care for, and Skip was, and still is, my "rock" and my "brother." There were few intrusions into our much needed respite from the more exciting but ultimately ravaging celebrations of full-on drug rock. Sober, smiling, and selling out, I realized I was becoming my mother—not a bad role model, but not *me*. And yet, playing Virginia Wing was better than playing the deadly games I'd favored previously.

Unfortunately, Paul, now gone from the group, was beginning to exhibit some of his own peculiarities by compiling a collection of bad Starship reviews and jokes made at the group's expense. When Starship checked into the various hotels where it was booked, our cubbyholes would be full of these bad reviews. They arrived before we did; Paul had individually addressed them, wanting us to have something negative to think about while we were enjoying our commercial grand slam. Although some of the jokes he sent were actually funny, we recognized the gesture for what it was: an indication of how much pain he was feeling.

For me, the eighties incarnation of Starship that Paul had left felt entirely opposite from the 1969 version of Airplane. It was almost like having two different occupations. The two bands had different focuses, purposes, and conduct; one was a circus, the other a musical shopping mall. Starship was a *working* band: do the albums, do the videos, do the road trips. No drugs, no alcohol, no wild parties, and no fooling around with anyone but my husband. I drove China to and from school when I was home, did the grocery shopping, and conducted myself with uncharacteristic reserve.

Going for the glam. (Roger Ressmeyer/© Corbis)

Left to right: Grace Slick, Jane Fonda, and Mickey Thomas: two seconds with a hotshot. (© Steve Schapiro)

Any hanging out with hotshots during the eighties happened incidentally in uneventful moments during awards ceremonies or talk shows. For instance, I met Meg Ryan in the ladies' room before an appearance on *Good Morning America*, traded snide comments about cocaine with Chevy Chase on *The Merv Griffin Show*, did a couple of Letterman stints, had my picture taken with Joe Montana at the Bay Area Music Awards, went to drug-abuse counseling with Jerry Garcia, listened to Gene Simmons of Kiss talk about his post-coital Polaroid collection, met Sting, met Phil Collins. I'd love to be able to relate something profound—

A middle-aged person on a rock-n-roll stage. (AP/Wide World Photos)

or even titillating—that I took away from these encounters, but they were all of the five-minute variety without either substance or glaring impropriety.

During that time, although I *felt* pretty much okay, I was keenly aware of how strange it was to be a middle-aged person on a rock-and-roll stage.

> *I never thought there were corners in time till I was told to stand in one.*
>
> —GRACE SLICK, FROM *HYPERDRIVE*

I wore the fashion of the moment, whatever it was—no let's-be-freaky outfits. I cut my hair, smiled for the cameras, answered press questions, watched the charts, made the records, and kept my ass out of jail. I didn't even mind the restrictive lifestyle because it was unique for me—a new link in a chain of shifting priorities that served to remind me of who I was, who I could be, and who I wanted to be. But conformity is never more than a temporary diversion for me. Inevitably, I revert back to my true nature.

In any situation, I ask myself, "Does this particular way of being resonate with *my* being?" Yes? Then I grab an extra-large helping. No? Then fuck it. I take what I can use and leave the rest.

44

Exits

It was 1984, the year George Orwell made famous, when my mother died of a heart ailment. I was at the Hyatt in Los Angeles, getting ready to do the TV show *Solid Gold*, when I received the call from my father. In the saddest voice I'd ever heard, he told me that everything possible had been done to help her, but it just hadn't worked.

I received the information and then I turned into a machine. Automatic pilot. I didn't tell the band that my mother had died until after we'd performed, and I have no idea how the performance went or what songs we played. I just knew I had to keep moving, because if I stopped, I'd have to think about an incomprehensible loss. The days following my mother's death were a gray vacuum. I remember Skip being gentle, not at all melodramatic, just close and concerned for my feelings. He'd have to be that strong again a few years later when my father died while we were on the road.

For several months before his death, my father had a private nurse attending to his needs. I'd call him from the road or write silly postcards trying to cheer him up, but I don't think there's any substitute for the physical companionship of someone you love when you feel sick and lonely. I've often wondered why I'm never *there* when people die. I'd like to have held both of my parents and shared some of their thoughts on the process of dying. I'm not sure I could have said no to touring without causing major problems to Starship, but the more I think about it now, I see that I should have been with my father. Even with the nurse there, family might have made him a bit more at ease with what he knew were his final days.

"Now *you're* the matriarch," Paul reminded me of the natural but bewildering reality.

Some whiny little part of my mourning was anger—"How could you leave me?" No matter how old a person is, it feels like it's too soon for them to go. I talk to my father and mother sometimes, hoping their spirits can hear, about my love, my mistakes, and my gratitude for their peaceful parenting.

The older I get, the more I see the striking similarities between a parent's and a child's genetic makeup. In my case, I got my mother's personality, or at least the showtime aspects of it, and from my father, I got an almost exact duplicate of his body (minus the critical gender specifications). But there's an added element that distinguishes each of us, one from the other. It's the individual's specific way of perceiving the world that swings the whole game in a different direction.

The way I see it, that missing number in the DNA soup

is the soul, our unique spirit that puts a seemingly new spin on the predetermined template. But sometimes the inherited parts are so similar, it's astounding. Everything about my body structure, hair texture, and the shape of my hands, feet, legs, and nose corresponds with my father's. It goes so far that when the dentist made a mold of both the top and bottom rows of my teeth for braces, and I placed them beside my father's molds, each tooth was in exactly the same place. Not just similar—exact. When I looked at him then, I thought I was seeing myself thirty-five years in the future, doing some conservative banker cross-dressing. But his shy, retiring personality was not part of the genetic hand-me-down.

That's where my mother stepped in. She and I could make the same remark at the same time about the same person, without any of it having been part of the context of the previous sentence. And she gave me my only paranormal experience. Several months after she died, I was lying in bed reading an unrelated spy novel, and I heard *her* voice say, "Grace?"

All right! I thought. *I'm going to talk to a spook, and it's my mom.* I said, "Yes?"

But that was it, no comment, no advice, no warnings, no bad jokes, just a query in the form of my name. I kept at her for a while, talking out loud, saying, "It's okay. I'm not afraid, you can chat—say anything. I can hear you. What do you want to talk about?" But she didn't feel it necessary to say anything more. She just made the brief connection—then silence. I still don't know exactly what I was supposed to understand from that, maybe just that she does indeed live without form. Is it something my mind did for the comforting aspect? No, I'm already open to intangible phenomena, so I wasn't looking for proof. It was the shortest gabfest I've ever had.

I know my parents live in me, with or without aural remarks. They are not missing, but their forms are missed.

45

Panda

In 1985, somewhere on the road, I was watching TV and saw this fat little black-and-white ball of fur sitting on a weighing scale in the middle of a roomful of popping flash bulbs, shuffling cameramen, yelling reporters, squirming children, and white-coated veterinarians. It was a baby panda at the Ueno Zoo in Japan, and they were all closing in on him like he was a sack of diamonds. When I noticed that he was watching the chaos with a certain dignified composure, I was intrigued. I knew he must be feeling some fear, and I could relate to that. After all, I'd been in the rock-and-roll press pit, in the midst of a frightening pack of agitated, overadrenalized Homo sapiens shouting out my name, ignoring whatever civilized behavior had been attributed to their species.

The panda just sat there. He could have tried to lurch off the table, but he seemed to be enjoying the stupid human tricks, and I learned an important lesson from him: it's all just a passing show. When I got back home from the tour and was sorting through my mail, an envelope with a picture of a panda in the upper left-hand corner caught my eye. I hadn't cared one way or the other about animals before; I'd always thought they were just a part of the scenery. But that little guy in Tokyo had shown me something I'd never noticed in anything but humans—a *soul*.

I suddenly realized that all these creatures were running around with fur and feather outfits on, just like our skin suits, and for the first time, I saw that inside all the different forms were individual personalities. These "animals" were, in fact, sentient beings who wanted the same things we wanted—food, shelter, peace, entertainment, health, and all the rest of it. Some of them could fly, swim, run, and sleep better than we could, and some of them could swat your head off in one fast move—like a panda bear. I'd discovered a whole new set of friends to hang out with. For a "city girl" like me to come around to this perspective was akin to landing on another planet. Except I hadn't landed on another planet so much as I'd taken a good hard look at the one I was on.

I'd love to *have* a panda, I thought. So I wrote to the outfit with the panda logo and asked them how to go about acquiring one.

They were nice enough *not* to say, "Wow, are you dumb!" Instead, they sent me a load of information, which included the fact that pandas couldn't be owned by anyone but the Chinese government, which, if it felt like it, occasionally gave one or two to another country as a diplomatic gesture. But that was it. Pandas were almost extinct; there were one thousand or so left in the entire world. Their land had been taken by man, and bamboo, their main source of food (each panda eats forty pounds of it per day), routinely dies off en masse every sixty years or so. Without land or bamboo, the pandas were in big trouble.

So, no, apparently I couldn't have a panda. But I could write a song about them:

He can feel the night, the last sunset is in his eyes
They will carry him away, take his beauty for their prize
Ah, but hunger would have come when the bamboo
forest died . . .

Oh Panda Bear—my gentle friend
I don't want to say goodbye
Oh Panda Bear—when will the killing end
When will we get it right?
Panda

Once I'd gained this new awareness of the animal kingdom, I remembered that Skip, on Christmas or Thanksgiving, used to take a large plate of leftovers "out to the backyard for the animals."

"What animals?" I'd asked him.

"Oh, you know, possums, squirrels, foxes, raccoons . . ."

Raccoons? They're related to pandas—cousins with the same heavy eye makeup.

I started putting food out at night (raccoons are nocturnal animals) and looking out the window to see if any masked bandits wanted to dine at our house. Yup. Several bellied up for dinner, and several more of their fellow critters followed: foxes, possums, vultures, squirrels, deer, even the occasional neighborhood cat or dog. In fact, it got to be such a spectacle that some humans with cameras from the local TV stations arrived to film the menagerie.

My favorite visitors, though, were the raccoons—they were smart, tough, and surprisingly peaceful. They brought their babies and they'd hang out with each other and play under the solar panel where I burned the words *Raccoon Saloon* into the supporting horizontal wooden beam. I was hooked. Every night they'd come and eat two large bags of dry cat food, two dozen raw eggs, four bags of Oreo cookies, and assorted grapes, watermelon, leftovers, and anything else lying around in the grass, creating a scene that looked like one of those anthropomorphic paintings of animals doing human activities. They would lie around on the lounge chairs, swim with each other in the pool, eat grapes, and have sex on the lawn—a regular Roman orgy.

Among the tribe who lived part-time around the south end of our property in Marin were a mother and baby raccoon who arrived every evening for about a month. One particular night, when they reached the top of the hill near the solar panel, I noticed they were moving at a pace that was far slower than usual. Then I saw that the little one had dragged himself up the hill by his front paws with both of his hind legs splayed flat and immobile on the ground.

I called a wildlife organization to ask how best to trap the young raccoon and bring him in to be treated, but they said it wouldn't be a good idea, that his mother might not take him back after he was returned. I had to just leave it alone and see what happened. Skip dubbed the baby Sore-foot, a sweet sort of Native American–sounding nickname, and night after night, I watched this amazing scene of a patient mother climbing the hill from wherever they called home during the day, guiding her baby to the food at the top of the hill. I called the mother Torn Back, because she had four gashes about an inch and a half apart down the side of her hindquarters. The deep scratches looked to be the result of a fight with some kind of large wildcat or puma, wounds she probably had received while protecting Sorefoot from becoming a meal for the feline predator.

After about a month and a half, I noticed that Torn Back's oozing scratches and Sorefoot's seemingly dead rear feet were starting to heal. Eventually, thick soft fur covered the mother's scars and the baby began to run and play with the other young raccoons as if nothing had happened. Did they know about some herbal healing root? Did they just wait it out, dealing with what *is*, rather than succumbing, as humans often do, to what *should be?* Maybe mom rubbed his hind legs, or baby licked his own wounds and hers—I'll never know. But I'll always honor the courage and compassion these raccoons had for each other, and their inner knowledge of how to exist, no matter what the circumstances. Torn Back and Sorefoot—teachers come in all shapes, sizes, and strange given names.

May they all continue to ravage your garbage cans. And mine.

After I wrote to the panda people, my name was added to the universal master list of "Suckers for Animal Causes." The mail poured in. From PETA (People for the Ethical Treatment of Animals) I received, among other distressing photos, an image of a white rabbit torn open to his ribs for the purpose of cosmetic testing. That one really hit home, and I began to seriously investigate the phenomenon of animal testing and biomedical research (fraud).

After several years (1987 to 1992) of reading American

Medical Association "white papers," along with hundreds of books and reports on the practice of vivisection, I started to get offers from radio stations, TV programs, and magazines to give my views on the subject of biomedical research. I even found myself on the same side of a debate once with G. Gordon Liddy (the mind boggles), who from a scientific rather than an ethical stance was objecting to extrapolating from animal studies. In the end, our strange combination of personalities probably did more to undermine our point than prove it. After all, if Grace Slick and G. Gordon Liddy, coming from extreme left and right politics, actually agree on something, isn't that a demonstration of solidarity that both sides ought to stay away from? But it also demonstrated that, when it was necessary, political adversaries could drop their differences for a universal interest.

Since the rest of this chapter has nothing to do with prurient sex in the sixties, you may decide to skip over it, but for what it's worth, here are three solid reasons to be wary of pharmaceutical drugs (yeah, the ones that are endorsed by "the suits"):

1. More people experience incapacities or death from pharmaceuticals than from all street drugs combined.
2. Pharmaceuticals are *all* tested on animals.
3. We have more illnesses now than before the advent of mass animal testing.

What part of the above don't you understand?

If you want scientific (not ethical) information on the subject, my esteemed editor, Rick Horgan, will *not* supply you with further instruction because he doesn't have either an M.D. or the paperwork. But there *are* some medical professionals (not "animal rights" groups but people with a great deal of impressive initials in front of and behind their names) who *do* have relevant facts about the matter, *won't* blow smoke up your ass, *won't* try to sell you gut-wrenching chemicals, and *will* send informative material. Specifically:

Physicians Committee for Responsible Medicine
5100 Wisconsin Avenue NW, Suite 404
Washington, D.C. 20016
or
P.O. Box 6322
Washington, D.C. 20015

Medical Research Modernization Committee
P.O. Box 6036 Grand Central Station
New York, NY 10163-6018

A final word on this extensive topic:

I'm selling out on this one, because what I'd really like is for half of this book to focus on my life and music, and the other half to be about biomedical research fraud. But when I submitted twenty pages of views on the latter, I was told they were too preachy. In deference to the people who're paying me for this tome (here comes the selling-out part), I edited the stuff down, going from twenty pages of preachiness, which even at that length is too condensed, to three pages of being overbearingly adamant.

46

The Political Pie

I came away from the sixties with a presumptive trust in the ability of people *in general* to act in a way that makes sense. But by the eighties, my disenchantment with political *individuals* had reached an all-time high. What with cowboy/actor presidents and Bush wars, I figured the whole thing was turning into a farce. On a good day, it was funny, but most of the time, it looked like a slow disintegration into some kind of mindless corporate board game.

The political system I'm in favor of has no name. It's based—not in a lip-service way but in a *real* way—on the concept of "government of the people, by the people, for the people." Remember that old slogan? In my perfect world, the government would send each of us a book filled with all the possible things that can be facilitated by our tax dollars and we'd choose our favorites.

Here's a theoretical list:

1. Anything military
2. Anything peaceful
3. Eco-manipulation
4. Shoe lifts for short senators
5. National parks
6. Free medical attention for carnivorous plants
7. Antibiotics for giraffe feed
8. Free education
9. Free Dr Pepper for hundred-year-old athletes
10. I. M. Pei–designed slum areas

And so forth.

Then the government would give us a list of funding needs for each, and we'd come up with an equitable distribution of tax money. In other words, after deciding what's most important to us as individuals, we'd prioritize allocations using a simple pie format.

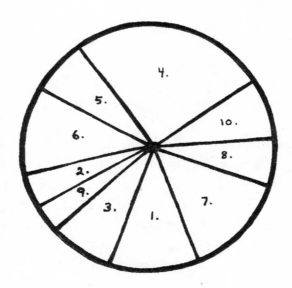

"Political Pie" (Grace Slick)

Once the computer finished its number crunching, we'd know exactly what the majority wanted. In the above figure, representing the current political setup, shoe lifts get top priority while old people get the shaft. My suggestion is, why not simplify the tax forms and find out what U.S. citizens *really* want? Surely we've learned by now that the democratic process is thwarted by representatives' questionable motives and by a lack of trust on the part of citizens themselves.

Now you may ask: Has any large-scale "government"—U.S.A. or other—ever given this much autonomy to its constituents? No. Which is why this pie-in-the-face routine would need the overwhelming support of the people to be implemented.

Whether or not Washington types decide to adopt my particular suggestion for a new form of taxation, I still think the existing system needs an overhaul. Voting now boils down to do-you-want-a-punch-in-the-arm-or-a-kick-in-the-leg? There just isn't much choice between the parties anymore and not enough access to the "fine print" of a given issue to vote with conviction. So why bother? On the other hand, if Texas's Ann Richards runs for president, I'll be right out there with a red-white-and-blue table, sitting in front of a supermarket, begging people to register.

After I'd come up with my pie drawing while writing this book, I saw a *Newsweek* cover story (October 3, 1997) titled "Inside the IRS. Lawless, Abusive and Out of Control."

What a fucking surprise! Tell us all something we don't already know. Then I read journalist Hunter S. Thompson's book *Better Than Sex*, his marvelously skewed look at addiction to politics and the decline and fall of our "nation of dreams." I agree with him that nothing seems to change, the costumes just get sillier as time goes on. And since the

311

average citizen doesn't have a clue what's happening, the test of a given administration becomes the fullness of our pocketbooks. When the U.S. of A. is through strutting, Japan (or some other country with the cash and arrogance) will crown itself, and we'll take our place beside Italy, Spain, and the U.K. among the other old warriors who've been out-muscled in the world power game.

Benjamin Disraeli once said, "In politics, there is no honor," but that didn't keep him from helping Queen Victoria annex most of the known world for the glory of the British Empire. I don't have anything against cutthroat capitalism—*after* basic medical, educational, and housing benefits for all citizens have been secured. Then everyone gets a shot at playing Donald Trump if they choose to invest their energy in that particular crapshoot.

The sad part is that we *do* have the resources to give the basics to our citizens, but the lobbyists tend to swat down high-minded funding proposals with their special-interest baseball bats. More often than not, the trade-offs they concoct turn into banana peels beneath their feet.

Whether it's a simple marriage or the merger of international conglomerates, successful human interaction depends on how separate the participants choose to view themselves in the evolutionary process. Too often it becomes *us* and *them*. How about just WE?

That's a question I asked in the sixties, seventies, and eighties. And in the nineties I'm still asking it.

47

The Cold Shoulder

By 1987, I'd rejected most political concerns, and my life was divided between my interest in biomedical research and recording with Starship. As it turned out, though, my career was about to come to an abrupt close.

It happened like this: one of the songs on the last Grace-included Starship album was scheduled to be a duet between Mickey Thomas and myself. At least, we'd practiced it that way in rehearsal. But when I went to the studio to put down my harmony part, Mickey had already done it as a solo piece. He felt that because his wife was having a baby and the lyrics alluded to children, he had a personal connection to the song. Seemed reasonable. It also seemed like a convenient way to skirt the duet process.

I didn't resist. Understanding both Mickey's desire to be sovereign and feeling a growing urge to get more involved in protecting the rights of my four-footed—and feathered—friends, I'd already decided to leave the group when the contract was finished. Then, unfortunately, a case of bilateral capsulitis, better known as frozen shoulder, stopped me one job short of my final scheduled gig with Starship. The concert was to be in Southern California, but several weeks before the date, while we were still in Marin, my left shoulder had begun to give me trouble. Over a period of a couple of weeks, I'd lost so much movement, I only had a ten-inch range of motion. Since I didn't have maids, hair-dressers, wardrobe people, or any other cosmetic assistance, it would have been impossible for me to pack, do my hair, lift suitcases, etc. So once again (this time for "legitimate" reasons), I pulled out before the completion of a tour.

I underwent six months of physical therapy, which involved having my arm shoved around in painful posi-tions. It was unnecessary torture; it turns out they could have used the MRI (magnetic resonance imaging) machine to pinpoint the problem at the onset. When I finally had the MRI done, it became clear that I needed a serious shoulder manipulation. "Put her under anesthesia and *jam* the damn arm up over her head to break the adhesions" was more or less what the docs said.

It worked.

For a period of several months I was stationary, healing my shoulder, making dolls out of clay, reading biomedical reports, and staying home in our Mill Valley house. Skip was often on the road with various bands, doing lights or production. When he came home, we went to alcohol-abuse counseling together.

When I picked him up at the airport after he'd com-pleted his rock-and-roll tours, we usually hugged and greeted each other in the normal friendly way, but this one particular day, he held on to me longer and harder than ever before. I dismissed it, thinking he was just especially delighted to be home this time, but I was wrong. It was the clinging of sadness because he had a secret. A friend had told him that to confess would bring a kick in the head from Yours Truly, but Skip felt he should tell me the truth and accept the consequences.

The "other woman" was twenty-three years old and looked like a prom-queen poster child. I remembered that when I'd first met her some time before, I figured she was going to be trouble for some poor woman whose man had tired of his existing relationship. I just didn't know that woman would be *me*.

Skip confessed he'd been "seeing" her off and on for about six months, but that it was over now and he wanted to try to make our union work. Our circle of friends was almost exclusively made up of people in the twelve-step programs, and since this young woman was also a part of AA, I figured everybody knew about the affair but me. Shit, here comes the inner AA drama routine of people taking sides, sponsors shooting advice all over the place, and unctuous sympathy games for poor old Grace. I felt hurt and defeated, but I had to nip the melodramatic gossip show in the bud.

As soon as Skip had finished his confession, I went to a very large AA meeting where I knew I'd find her. I also knew I could address her there, in a scene that I could use to my advantage. Accustomed to being in front of large crowds, I placed myself in a standing position below the podium and beckoned her to join me there, in front of the four hundred or so seated individuals who were waiting for the meeting to start. She looked dubious as she walked to the front of the room; Skip hadn't filled her in that he was going to tell me about their trysts.

I gave her a short embrace to let everyone know there'd be no fireworks display and calmly told her I didn't want any animosity. After all, I'd done the same thing to Paul. The rock-and-roll lifestyle was full of interchanging couples, I conceded, and even though it made me sad, I understood the predicament. The lack of hair-pulling excitement was exactly what I wanted—no fun for the "audience." They now knew that I knew, and that I wasn't going to lose it all over the "other woman" and she wasn't going to go off into the sunset with Prince Not-So-Charming.

Skip suggested couple's therapy, to which I agreed, but it only served to reveal he'd had several other one-nighters on the road. Then, one afternoon in L.A., when I was having some coffee in a hotel room, reading magazines and feeling pretty peaceful, my heart started beating as if I'd just run a four-minute mile. I generally don't sit around and freak out for no reason. I knew it was out of character, so I was paralyzed with fear. I just couldn't figure out what was going on or what to do about it.

"Grace," I said, "get yourself into the car and go to Cedars Sinai ER. It's only a mile away, you can do it, *just get up out of the chair.*" I was absolutely terrified, but I made it to the hospital and asked them what was wrong.

"You're having a panic attack," they told me.

Panic? Over what?

"Maybe you should see a psychiatrist."

Sometimes I do what I'm told.

After several visits at $250 an hour, the shrink said, "You have a broken heart."

Aww.

He was referring to the Skip/mistress thing. So tell me something I don't already know. The doctor was speaking figuratively, but I wasn't *figuratively* sick. I thought the *actual* heart might be a cause for concern, and after getting an echocardiogram, I confirmed that, indeed, I had a problem—a common enough condition called mitral valve prolapse, which manifests itself in symptoms similar to a panic attack. So the shrink got a thousand bucks for his

melodramatic call on something that was, in fact, a physical impairment the doctors could literally see on a monitor.

"Careful of the stimulants," was the admonition from
the cardiac specialist. Like the coffee I'd been drinking in
the hotel. So it wasn't *all* Skip's fault. From a childhood
diagnosis that I had a heart murmur, I'd simply graduated to
mitral valve prolapse. Pomp and circumstance.

Skip and I continued to live together in a brother-sister
configuration for another six years; it was hard for me to let
go of a basically good man even if it was obvious we'd eventually separate. And I knew we'd separate as soon as I
admitted to myself that the passion had disappeared. I've
always been attached to the initial feelings of passion in a
relationship. It's an energy that I still find so captivating, I
can't imagine living without it. In fact, at the onset of a
romance, I think about sex so much, it's surprising I can get
my socks on. But as soon as my partner shows too much
interest in a hardware store or a computer game, I turn off.

Unfortunately, when I'm without the absolute focus of
passion that drives the human spirit, I'm pretty much just a
bunch of functioning body parts. Without a particular man
to occupy my attention, I can channel romantic energy
into other areas, and I *do* channel it—into things as various
as drawing, music, sewing, talking, writing, or studying biomedical research.

The idea that a relationship can survive based solely on
respect and common interests is still beyond me. I can get
respect from a Saint Bernard and common interest from a
museum curator, so without passion, I'd rather live alone
and be able to come and go whenever I feel like it.

Some people never grow up.

Just when I'm close to believing I'm a determined and
focused type, I have to remind myself that most of the

direction-shifting events in my life have come about when I was shuffling along without a road map.

I didn't grow up with an intense dream of being a singer; I just happened to see Jefferson Airplane at a nightclub and it looked like a good way to make a living and goof off at the same time.

I didn't take political science in college and think, "I'm going to work for liberal agendas." The liberal view of social organization just *happened* to coincide with my own sensibilities.

I didn't think, "Okay, now is the right time to write an autobiography." A friend of mine, Brian Rohan, and my agent, Maureen Regan, almost bodily forced me to talk to publishers, and I just *happened* to enjoy the process once I got started.

So many things have seemed to crawl into my lap at the right (and sometimes wrong) time, I get the impression that predetermination and an implacable genetic scorecard are running the puppet show. I'm enjoying the performance, but I often wonder how much control we *do* have over the seemingly open banquet of choices. Sometimes the best strategy seems to be to keep shuffling and hope for the best. Surprises —both bad and good—turn up in the most unlikely places.

An example. Long before the mitral valve prolapse episode—in 1973, to be exact—I had a pain in the chest on the left side, and when I consulted the docs they suggested I go to a shrink.

Funny how often that suggestion keeps popping up in my case, isn't it?

Anyway, I went to the head shrink at the University of California. After four sessions that included the standard queries regarding family, emotional stress, sexual habits, etc., he glanced down at the floor where my purse was bulging.

"How much does that weigh?" he asked.

I picked it up and handed it to him.

"About twenty pounds," he said, hefting it, "and if you're right-handed, you probably wear this hanging off your left shoulder. Right?"

I nodded.

"Try taking some of the stuff out of it, or wear it on your right shoulder for a while. You're not nuts, you're just over-loaded."

I followed his instructions and the pain stopped immediately. So sometimes, if you have a sore throat, a helpful podiatrist might tell you to take your foot out of your mouth.

48

The Gamut

As I've negotiated the twists and turns of my own life, watching China run the gamut of social and educational extremes has been both fascinating and irritating. But always, she shows a rebounding ability that brings her back to her own center. Apart from being my daughter, she is also one of my favorite characters—animated, self-willed, talented, dramatic, and never boring. I love her, and, fortunately, I also *like* her. Sometimes, those feelings are not necessarily in sync, but on the whole, I couldn't have dreamed up a better child or a better friend. When we fight, it's an even match, and when we're close, it's an even love. Our styles may be different, but the absolute focus is the same. We can each be aggressively obnoxious or persistently entertaining. When China jumps into a "role" with both feet, its the same steamroller that Mama drives—rampant.

While she was attending Marin County Day School, China conducted herself in the proper beige manner expected of private-school girls. When I arrived to pick her up after school in my gullwing DeLorean, it seemed that between the outrageous car with doors that swung out and upward, my black knee-high leather boots, and my short skirts, I stuck out as true rock-and-roll sleaze next to the other moms who drove up in their BMWs in tastefully blended afternoon matron attire. Result: China was embarrassed—her mom was a freak.

Then a shift occurred.

When China's hormones and the boom box took her in the opposite direction, Mom's unusual employment and deportment were suddenly okay. Thirteen-year-old China no longer wanted to hide the fact that her mother might have sprung, claws bared, out of a boiling counterculture. She was now proud of her musician parents, and had even gone a few steps ahead of us by sporting the new punk look—asymmetrical short spiky multicolored hair, a line of pierced rings all the way up one ear, four inches of silver bracelets, and ripped shirts, jeans, genes, and friends.

Then the balance.

At age fifteen, the two extremes blended into a Duran Duran–loving, long-blonde-haired California girl appearance. Her summer job as MTV's youngest VJ was a high school kid's dream—she got to hang out in New York, meet and interview the bands, get her face on TV, and put some money in her pocket. During the punk stage, China's grades had been predictably rotten, but when she graduated from high school, her report cards contained primarily A's and B's. She'd tried on the polarities and settled into a balance that fell in line with her own disposition. Always quicker than Mom to recognize potentially destructive patterns of behavior (either right or left), she now alternates between being *my* parent and friend and being part of her *own* somewhat disenchanted generation.

Not that she's turned into a doormat. Sometimes more

Grace and China, *Evening Star* premiere: different styles, same focus. (Fred Prouser/Reuters/Archive Photos)

of a pit bull than I *ever* was, she's able to do what I generally couldn't: express *sober* rage. Skip's ex-mistress (remember the AA prom queen?) was still carrying a torch after some length of time, and China, more of a mail ferret than I, sniffed some perfume on a letter addressed to him. Matching up the envelope to previous pieces of Miss X, seventeen-year-old China telephoned her and left this little reminder on her answering machine:

"If you ever interfere with my family again, I'm going to send Mafia wise guys over to break your whoring ass."

So much for becoming friends with all my boyfriends' lovers.

49

On the Road Again

I know it's holy rock and roll, but I spike it.

—ANONYMOUS

In 1988, Paul called together all the original members of
Jefferson Airplane and suggested a short (one album, one
tour) reunion. After some brief discussion about logistics,
we all agreed to the adventure.

Fantastic, I thought. This time Airplane will be assisted
by one of those professional management teams in L.A. (as
opposed to well-meaning hippies from San Francisco) who
really know how to put a rock-and-roll package together.
Now that we're all old enough to prefer seamless negotiations, it'll be a snap.

Sure, Grace, and polar bears use toilets.

The old Grace and Paul versus Jack and Jorma game
resumed immediately. Skip, in alignment with my tight
organizational vision, recommended Trudy Green from
H.K. Management. After meeting her, I was delighted with

both her easy manner and sharklike business sensitivities. She was my unequivocal choice—a smart blonde Jew from L.A. who knew how to laugh and bark at the same time.

But Jack and Jorma wanted to have a fan/friend/lawyer type call the shots. This man was already managing their blues band, Hot Tuna, and he was afraid that if the West Coast (e.g., Trudy Green from H.K. Management) ran things, his two meal tickets would split for sunnier pastures. He didn't know Jack and Jorma well enough; they'd always chosen the more intimate club scene, and that wasn't about to change. The Airplane tour would only magnify their visibility, and when they returned to their smaller, more down-home jobs, which they actually preferred, they'd have benefited from the high-profile management coming out of Trudy's office.

The lawyer's reservations may not have been the only factor, however. The truth is, the unfamiliar, high-profile L.A. business scene probably made Jack and Jorma nervous.

There was no way, though, that I was letting Trudy Green disappear because of the other guys' fears of the West Coast entertainment monolith. Skip acted as arbiter, Paul was satisfied with Trudy's competence, Marty didn't care, and the guys eventually agreed; we signed with Sony for the record and gave responsibility for the tour to Trudy at H.K. The only deviation from the original group was the absence of Spencer Dryden due to an illness. He was replaced by Kenny Aronoff on drums, but the rest of the original line-up, including a yoga-healthy, blond Marty Balin, was finally ready to hit the boards.

We rented a bus, Jorma brought his wonderful dog, Marlow, and we got back into the old rock-and-roll tour mode—minus the narcotics and alcohol. I can't ever remember enjoying singing with Marty as much as I did on that tour. We'd both grown up, and in the process, we'd lost whatever competitiveness had been present in the earlier phases of Airplane.

Did we have groupies or group grope? No. Everybody was married and temporarily or permanently faithful.

Did we get ripped to the tits on large amounts of "medication"? Nope. Too old. The livers would explode and the AAs would converge. Besides some pot for the native San Francisco boy, Paul, it was a fairly clearheaded journey.

Did we tell cops to eat shit and die? Not at all. Several "lawmen" were in the paying audience, and they were half our age.

Did we scream about government stupidity? No. Too lazy? Too old? Too numb? Or just defeated? Who knows? We were a nifty little rehash that reminded boomers of how it sounded when they didn't have to take Metamucil to get it out and get it on.

Depressing? Sure, if you're looking at it through the imposed radical chic of rock-and-roll parameters. But when a group of people come together to enjoy music, it can be a polka or a slam dance. When it's viewed from a nontrendy position, it really doesn't matter.

So apart from ten extra pounds on each of our middle-aged bodies, the quality of life enjoyed by members of the 1989 Jefferson Airplane was far tighter than the 1969 version. We were treated to higher-tech equipment, better venues, relatively sober audiences, good management, no incidents with law enforcement, egos tempered by age, and a tour's worth of relatively successful concerts. And because there was no lifelong commitment among the group members, we were more like a caravan of old friends who happened to be musicians than musicians involved in a "business deal."

Album sales? I don't know the figures, but nobody went out and bought a Lear jet. Maybe some of us paid off tuition for offspring or Jorma got another goat for his farm—simple acquisitions for a graying crowd of musical gypsies. Did we care? If I said it didn't matter, you'd know right away that I was so cool, I was beyond social pressure. We've all read the Buddhist books, telling us that attachment leads to suffering, and we berate ourselves for our attachments to material things. But that's not what the wise men intend for us. Be more gentle with and tolerant of your humanity.

Following that line of thought, I can say that, although the tour was not a financial gold mine, it was a good thing. By the time it was over, we'd traded a lot of energy, renewed our friendships, and had closed some uncompleted circles.

Nice.

PART

Four

50

Rising with the Sun

It was 1990, the Airplane tour was over, and I felt a mixture of peace and resignation. I was relieved that I could look, act, and think like a "real" person. I eliminated the goofy outfits—just took a shower in the mornings and put on some sweats. Like a "normal" human being, I went to the grocery store, did the laundry, fed the raccoons, and hung out with my equally casual friend, Pat Monahan. A small, determined Native American/Irish woman, Pat was both courageous and shy, blunt but self-effacing, spiritual and profane, funny and serious—the "five of one, half a dozen of the other" qualities that demonstrate the fascinating yin and yang of human behavior.

I found then (and I still find) extraordinary beauty in following a simple way of life. Those of you looking for "action" may not understand, but I was finished with my previous lifestyle. I enjoyed rising early with the sun, silently preparing my body and my surroundings for the day, studying a subject (biomedical research) that engaged both my intellect and compassion, trading love and lies with open-minded friends, and closing the night in a warm feeding ritual that coincided with the sunset.

Basic regeneration.

Although Skip and I were still married, we spent very little time together. He was located near Minneapolis, living in an apartment that was close to the large entertainment compound owned by "The Former Artist Usually Known as Prince." Skip was doing production for the Purple One's projects, so although we spoke on the phone each day, I hardly ever saw him. Essentially, I was living alone, with his occasional visits on holidays. Neither of us could make the final break.

I didn't mind living alone, but it's sort of strange to see gas station attendants and grocery clerks more than you see your own husband.

My new boyfriend went by the name of Buckminister Ratcliff Esquire III. Every day, I'd drive to Tiburon and change his sheets, make his breakfast, straighten up his lodgings, and play with his fat, furry body.

He was a gentle, overweight lab rat.

"Bucky," who'd been silently and carefully liberated from the University of California's research facility, was now living a pampered life, being looked after and loved by Pat Monahan and myself. Located on Main Street in Tiburon, Pat's animal store was one in a string of beautifully maintained turn-of-the-century shops along the San Francisco Bay. Early each day, before the customers started to fill up the area known as Arc Row, Pat and I would invite Bucky to have chocolate brownies with us in the store's center, which was filled with stuffed animals and various items for cats and dogs.

Like a little Buddha endowed with the ability to be charismatic without doing anything other than just being

himself, he made converts of visitors who'd previously considered rats vicious, plague-ridden consorts of the devil. His
girth gave him the friendly fat-boy appearance that is cute
in animals and babies but gross in the adult human species.
An excellent representative of his species, he lived as he
eventually died—in peace.

So in the morning, it was the rat, and at night, the raccoons. Quite a shift from making "strawberry jam" with Jim
Morrison, eh?

I often spent the middle of my days attending Marin
Humane Society functions or participating in meetings on
how to stop construction of the huge biomedical research
complex called the Buck Center. After Beryl Buck left several million dollars in her will "to benefit the aging population," local lawyers, business people, the University of
California Research System, contractors, and a host of
other opportunists saw a potential gold mine. But today,
twenty-five years of objections later and with half the
money now lining the pockets of the center's supporters,
the facility still exists only on the drawing board. Architect
I. M. Pei collected a million dollars just to draw the structure.

The Buck Center's proposed site, atop Mount Burdell in
Novato, California, is located directly above an earthquake
fault—a nifty location for a bunch of toxic chemicals. And,
of course, many facilities already exist that do exactly the
same sort of research. A better way to have spent Beryl
Buck's money might have been to create the Buck Center
for Research on Human Stupidity. We all suffer from that
ailment to varying degrees, and if they ever figure out a cure
for it by rat testing, I'll have to rethink my position on the
subject.

But there *are* no cures for the hardball game of living;
there are only processes that manipulate the symptoms.

Meanwhile, we continue to mutilate everything in our path, trying, perhaps, to distract ourselves from the constant fear of death.

Which brings me to the ultimate topic of distraction: talk shows. Distract yourself from the living/dying process, sell your product, publicize your lifestyle by appearing on talk shows—it's the national pastime. Even when I was living my quiet life in Marin, I revved up a little excitement by playing "Butt Bongo" on *The Howard Stern Show*. I didn't even have a product to sell. I just like Howard and thought it would be an amusing experience.

When I was performing with Airplane and Starship and the records were climbing the charts, our publicist got on the horn and we were booked on all of the talk shows. Way back in the beginning, there was Jack Paar, but I was too young for him. Instead, I caught the polite boys: Mike Douglas and Merv Griffin; Dinah Shore's down-home chat; *The Smothers Brothers Comedy Hour*, where goofy was okay; Dick Cavett, the reigning intellect; Geraldo "Hard Copy" Rivera; early irascible Tom Snyder; easygoing Larry King; and smart and smirky Letterman.

All of that was prelude, of course, to doing Butt Bongo on *Stern*.

My daughter, her then boyfriend Kelly, and I played look-out-here-comes-the-fast-ball with "The King of All Media." Howard decided that China's beau looked liked the devil and told him so. Then he decided I should play Butt Bongo with him, which I did. I positioned himself across his lap and he did Ringo on my fully clothed butt cheeks. It could have been worse, and it probably will be when I do the promo tour for this book. Nobody is exempt from that fun-loving freak Howard Stern—especially not fifty-eight-year-old granny rock stars.

To liven up the usual chat format, I might bring along

some of my own games to play with the Chin, Harpo, Worldwide Pants crowd (for a jargon translation, see back issues of *Entertainment Weekly*). Maybe I'll come on as my father, or be escorted by the police, or bring the current celebrity "in recovery" with me to see which of us unsuccessfully took more drugs.

As long as it's something tasteful.

Maybe I'll get everybody to streak into the bookstores, looking for an immediate upgrade in their spiritual condition by buying several copies of Grace Slick's autobiography.

51

Fire and Passion

It was toward the end of 1993, Skip was vacationing in Hawaii, China was living in L.A. pursuing an acting career, and I was close to accepting a monastic life of simple endeavors, when violent surprises started rearranging the tableau. My quiet world of Marin County living was split wide open by two formidable elements: fire and passion.

I returned home one afternoon after doing some errands in San Francisco, and when I drove up the hill that led to my house, I noticed two parked white cars. Nothing unusual in that, except that they were completely covered with orange stuff.

What the hell was it and what was going on?

A little farther up the road, I encountered the chaos. The entrance to my street was blocked by police cars, men were running around talking on cell phones, gesturing to each other as if something unpleasant was going on beyond the barriers. Something was. They stopped me and suggested that I turn around and go back down the hill.

"But I live up there," I told them.

"Which house?" they asked.

"Eighteen Escalon . . . what's going on?" I demanded.

A man paused and slowly said, "One of the houses up there burned down."

"Which one?" I asked. Somehow I already knew.

"I don't know. Let me call the fire marshall to get the address." He fiddled with his handset and finally said, "Eighteen Escalon."

I went numb. They took me up to the property, which was crawling with newspeople ready to interview me. "Miss Slick, Miss Slick, what do you think about it? What are you going to do? What happened? Who, what, where?"

"I don't know anything," I said. "I haven't even seen it yet."

A host of photographers followed me as I walked up to the front door to see what, if anything, was left of Skip's and my seventeen-year stay in that home. Something inside of me felt cold and sunken, like I was watching a bunch of vultures hover over a dying friend. My beloved house, that once sturdy protector that just hours before had been full of familiar possessions and memories, was now reduced to charred beams and ash.

Fortunately, as devastated as I felt, I was also immediately convinced of the accuracy and timing of the universal process. No matter how it *seemed* on the surface, I knew the event was somehow providential.

The house was almost totally gutted, so where were my two cats? Someone had seen them take off into the forest area behind the house. Good. The raccoons never showed up till after dark, so they were all right, too. I had a sense of relief, however small, that no beings were hurt. Now I had to move on to the depressing business of sorting through the ashes for leftovers.

I got a hotel room at Howard Johnson's in Sausalito and sat there, watching my house burn on the evening news while I tried to find Skip. Apparently, he'd left the hotel in Maui where he'd been staying, bound for an unknown destination. I called Los Angeles, trying to get hold of China, but she'd already gotten the news and was on her way to the airport to come see me. Someone finally reached Skip—I don't know who—but by the time he arrived, six or seven hours later, I was full of red wine and mad as hell at him for *always* being away. I blamed the dark side of my own isolation on him, when in fact, I'd done it to myself.

China and a couple of her friends eventually arrived at the hotel to be with me, whatever condition I was in, and they watched me convert my sense of loss to anger and direct it at Skip. He'd seen it before—Grace's misdirected fury posing as righteous indignation. The next morning I apologized, but if Skip was already gone in spirit, I'd certainly done a good job of driving the rest of him away.

The insurance company showed us several temporary homes we could use during the time that it took to either rebuild the old house or buy a new one. The short-term dwelling we selected was a beauty, but because our marriage was reaching its end point and our home had been trashed, it was hard to enjoy the new, albeit temporary, Tiburon house that was perched on top of Raccoon Straits overlooking the entire Bay Area.

Ironically, we later learned that the Escalon fire had been started by careless county welders who were putting up a sign that read DANGER/FIRE AREA. Somehow, they'd forgotten to watch where the sparks were flying. Eventually, Skip and I received enough money to allow us to purchase homes in Pennsylvania and L.A., respectively.

While all this was playing out, into an already confused atmosphere came the explosive element, passion, in the form of Len Calder, an old friend I'd met in San Francisco when I was about eighteen years old. Len was living in South America and we'd been corresponding sporadically over the years. Sporadic became frequent as his relationship with his common-law wife of twenty years disintegrated and my own marriage did the same. Both of us were greatly in need of comfort, and we toyed with the illusion that we could help each other.

It all came to a head when Len found herpes cream in his wife's medicine chest. Since *he* didn't have the virus, where did *she* pick it up? Incited to finally take action, he boarded a plane with nothing but a checkbook and a passport. Within twenty-four hours, he'd made it to San Francisco, and the game was on.

By the time Len arrived, Skip and I had officially separated; I was staying in the house on Raccoon Straits and Skip had moved into a small apartment in Mill Valley. There was no chance of rebuilding either the house or the marriage—not at *that* point anyway—so I was glad Len had come. But the fact that he'd arrived with more problems than just an unfaithful wife was something I wouldn't figure out for several months.

In the meantime, I took him around to visit his old haunts—UC Berkeley, where he'd gone to school, a rose garden that he loved in the East Bay, some restaurants he remembered from when he'd lived in San Francisco before, and a pier on Fisherman's Wharf where we'd ripped off our clothes and partied till dawn when we were in our early twenties. Len said he felt like Rip Van Winkle waking up after a long sleep, and it was good to see an old friend experiencing the delight of being "home" again.

Whether we were driving up the coast, shopping in Monterey, or walking through Muir Woods, I never saw anyone exhibit such enthusiasm for anything and everything. I bought him a computer, hooked it up to an electric piano, and he sat for hours every day, creating some of the best instrumental music I'd ever heard. And that *mind* of his—the information, the comic slant on the news, the ability to comprehend everything but his own debilitating problem.

Early in 1994, we took an afternoon walk on the beach and climbed around like children on a huge construction machine that was parked near the shoreline. That night, after having dinner and lots of drinks, and chatting with "Bear," a wonderful bartender at the Cliff House, we came back to Tiburon and decided to do some target practice on empty bottles we'd lined up in the backyard. After a while, I decided to stop shooting because I was afraid the neighbors would call the cops about the noise. Len didn't want to stop, though. He was annoyed with me and started in with, "You just do whatever pleases you at the time, you don't care what someone else wants to do. You think because you're famous, you can just drop everything and ignore people."

We started arguing and he lost it. He began shoving me around, breaking handles off the screen doors, knocking lamps off tables, and yelling about what a brat I was. He finally gave up when I wouldn't react, and he went to the back of the house. To sulk? To go to sleep? I didn't know what he was doing back there and I was afraid to find out.

At 2:00 or 3:00 A.M., the doorbell rang. Len went down the hall to answer it, while I headed for the bedroom in search of the shotgun. I'd been robbed three times in Mill Valley, so I thought that this might be another shitty late-night episode of some sort. But what idiot thief rings the doorbell? By the time I'd arrived at the front door, shotgun in hand, there were four cops standing around Len, who was on his knees, handcuffed and yelling "Shoot me!" at the top of his lungs.

"Jesus, what's going on here?" It was my turn to ask that insidious question. What I didn't know was that when he'd been in the back room, Len had called the cops, telling them *I* was crazy and he needed a ride out of Tiburon. But apparently, he'd made some other remarks that made the police think *he* was disoriented, so ironically, they'd come to protect *me*.

When they saw me standing there holding a gun, they said, "Put the shotgun down, Grace."

"Not until you tell me what's going on here," I repeated.

They weren't forthcoming and I wasn't giving in. Finally, in a fabulous move (for which he later received an award), one of the Marin County blues did a football block from the side, knocking me down, ending the standoff. On went the handcuffs. They took Len to the local psych ward and me to the drunk tank. When they let me out the next day, I got Len out, too.

We arrived home before the media trucks showed up. But show up they did. There they were, guys waiting, ringing the doorbell, walking around the house, calling on the phone—the usual. We closed the blinds and responded to no one for about forty-eight hours, until my lawyer made his appearance. I thought that when I eventually ventured out to the grocery store or the gas station, just running my daily errands, people who'd heard about my middle-of-the-night altercation with Marin County's Finest would see me and quietly turn away or be rude about the matter. But when I showed my face, the response was shocking. Guys with thumbs up said, "Right on!" And women were saying things like, "If the cops showed up at my house with no search warrant, I hope I'd have the guts to tell 'em off, too."

I couldn't believe it. These polite Marin County types,

apparently "normal" people, were harboring the Don't-fuck-with-me, old-Western-movie attitudes I thought were uniquely mine. But the gun-totin' image of Granny Yoakum from Li'l Abner comics is usually only entertaining when it's not a member of your family. Skip and China weren't the least bit amused.

In retrospect, when I checked Len out of the local nut ward of Marin General Hospital, I should have driven him straight to the San Francisco airport and put him on a plane back to South America, but I thought the alcohol was to blame; he was the worst drinker I ever saw besides myself. He promised never to use alcohol again while he was with me. I was satisfied that that would solve the "loony" problem.

The joke (?) was on me.

Since China was living in L.A. and I was no longer the proper Marin matron, I decided to get a house in Laurel Canyon. This was a place where I knew the screwballs of the rock industry were at least accepted, if not welcomed. Old Psycho, my affectionate but all too accurate nickname for Len, came with me and started a series of episodes that helped him live up to his name. His "disease" was beginning to define itself.

We were at a supermarket, about to pull into an empty parking space, when a woman yelled, "You took my spot!" I pointed out that she was *entering* where the street arrows pointed *exit*, but she kept on screaming and began throwing banana peels at my car. After I walked over to her and told her to "shut the fuck up," and then walked back to my car, she launched some kind of fluid at us and Len lost it again. But this time he was sober. He went over to her car and started wildly and methodically opening and closing her driver's side door while she yelled and cringed from his peculiar assault. Three supermarket secu-

rity guys had to tackle him to make him stop the odd display of anger.

Okay, so Len's problem wasn't alcohol. I was still
charmed by his intellect, though, so I made up excuses
about his weird antics. He was just hot-tempered, I rea-
soned, and since he was six feet, two hundred pounds, I figured I'd better watch my sarcastic tongue. I just didn't want
to admit to myself that the guy needed more help than I
could offer.

A short time later, on the way back from a trip to Death
Valley, Len pissed in my car, angry that I wouldn't spend
the next year or so crawling around in 120-degree weather
looking for his lost wallet in the sand dunes. "I'm not getting out of the car, you'd take off without me," was his
reason for using the front seat as a toilet. When we got back
to Laurel Canyon and called the hotel where we'd stayed in
Death Valley, the wallet was right there where he'd left it.

The next episode took the form of a sudden bolt from
the house during the O.J. double-murder trial. After
denouncing lawyer Robert Shapiro in an extremely personal way and flying out the door with no further explana-
tion, Len returned eight hours later, out of breath and
red-faced from walking up the long grade from Sunset. He
lurched through the front door, saying, "Where are they?
Who's here? Somebody is here."

"No, there's nobody here," I told him.

Except maybe his nine other personalities.

The last straw came when I'd gone to bed after an argument to let him cool off with the computer. In the darkness
of the bedroom, I heard his footsteps entering. Pretending
to be asleep, I was curled up facing the wall and couldn't see
what he was doing, but I heard a crackling noise like
someone bunching up paper. After a minute or so of the
strange sounds, he said, "Well, look what we have here."

I turned over to face his self-satisfied grin. The other side of the bed was on fire and I rushed out to get a bucket of water while he just stood there. After I'd doused the psycho bonfire, I walked back into the kitchen, put away the bucket, and called 911. When the cops arrived, they asked me if I'd accidentally left a cigarette burning in the ashtray.

"No, I've never burned anything with a cigarette," I told them, "and why the hell would I call 911 for *that?*" They asked me if I wanted to press charges. It was a tempting idea, but Len swiftly reminded me that since I was still on probation for the shotgun incident, it probably wouldn't be a wise idea to get my name on the books and in the paper again.

Clever.

Then I remembered a day, sometime before, when he'd said, "I don't know, I think I might be manic-depressive." I hadn't paid much attention to him at the time, but now I decided I should check it out. Since I didn't know what being manic-depressive actually involved, I went out and bought a book on the subject. Yup, the extreme highs and hideous lows were there, the highs being so high that taking medicine to *flatten* the mood swings was something many manic-depressive people tried to avoid. I called Len's common-law wife south of the border, and speaking through a phone translator, she told me her therapist thought Len was not only manic-depressive but psychotic as well.

Oh, great, just what I needed: to be audience of one while Len offered his personal rendition of *One Flew over the Cuckoo's Nest.*

Nice as I could be, using a soft voice so as not to disturb my housemate's errant synapses, I said to him, "Maybe we aren't right together. Your daughter needs you, and your wife is lonely. It would probably be best if you went back to Rio."

345

As soon as you can get your fractured brain out of here.

I loved the man dearly, but I also knew from my own experience that when you have a condition or personality trait that continuously drops tacks in everybody's path, you have to at least *consider* other options.

Len was the last live-in relationship I've had to date. Now I live alone, I'm unintentionally celibate, and I'm also a fag hag. I love male energy, but I don't want the melodrama that goes with the male-female hetero dance. My buddies, Vinnie Marino, Ron Neiman, and Justin Davis, have kept me out of trouble and made me laugh until my face hurts. Next to musicians and comedians, I think gay men have the best sense of humor of any group of individuals I've met. And they're also more understanding of fringe behavior than most of the "straight" people I know.

By the way, celibacy doesn't necessarily suck. If the mind-numbing illusion of falling in love comes around again, I'll probably drift into its short-term cloud, but right now, I'm enjoying the solo existence that is allowing me to do whatever I want, whenever I want to do it. Turning all the lights on at 3:00 A.M., coming home at any hour, blasting music at any time of night or day—it can be fun.

Looking like a slob puts a damper on the sexual fires, though, so if I ever decide to redo the romance dance, my wardrobe of sweatpants will have to be discarded in favor of fancier duds. If I pair up, there'll also be morning breath to contend with (my own and his), deciding who takes out the garbage, and such questions as, "What time will you be home?" . . . "Why won't he *talk* to me?" . . . "Why won't she let me hang out with the guys?" . . . ad nauseam. Is it worth the trouble? I say no right now, but I'll probably change my mind and pile back into the nesting frazzle whenever it seems like life would be better as a shared experience.

346

But I do have a lot of reservations, and *often* is a pivotal word in my book.

How *often* can I offer my understanding to someone who's demonstrating his confusion by being a total shit? Once a week? Once a month? Never? I can do anything for a while, but those *whiles* add up and then I'm dealing with *too* often. The statistics speak for themselves. If fifty-two percent of marriages collapse, maybe that means we're not arranging our time in the optimum manner for our particular species. Constant togetherness might just turn out to be *too* often. Would inserting some specific time/space restrictions into the conjugal format ease the friction? Or is it inevitable that other people's imperfections will just drive us nuts after a period of time, and we're doomed to repeat the same illusory pattern over and over again?

None of these questions I have seem to lend themselves to pat answers. But if you have a lock on how to realistically and permanently socialize human couples, Rick Horgan, my esteemed editor, would be more than delighted to hear from you. Just send it to that address again, the same one for sending information on the whereabouts of the plaster dicks.

52

Rock and Roll and Aging

People sometimes ask me, "How come you don't sing any-more?" Huh? I sing all the time. At the moment, it's just not an organized effort. I sang for my parents. I sing for myself. I'll sing to the kitchen sink, the rabbits, my car, the bedroom walls. It doesn't matter. It's sort of like intermittent breathing; I sing because I'm alive. I just don't feel like repeating myself anymore by doing the same material every night onstage. Performing again wouldn't be fair to an audience, because most of them want to hear the old favorites, which I don't want to sing, and I'd be saying, "I don't do any of that stuff, you only get new material."

Oh *really*, you selfish ASSHOLE.

When they decided to repeat Woodstock a few years ago, I was asked to participate. I refused, because I believe some things, although they may have worked beautifully the first time, simply can't and shouldn't be redone. As far as I'm concerned, that was the trouble with Altamont, but

Cher on tile. (Justin Davis)

I didn't watch the latest Woodstock, so I can't venture an opinion about whether or not it was any good. I just know that even in your prime, when you go onstage every night to perform, you have to repeat yourself, anyway. After twenty-five years of performing, the idea of not only singing the same old songs, but actually trying to do that in the context of the same concert, is not all that appealing. But that doesn't mean my love of music has changed.

My adhesion to music goes from a Band-Aid all the way through the complete body cast—from the scrape or gash that propels the shout, to the iodine and sutures of putting it down on paper, to the physical therapy of getting the kinks out onstage. And somewhere in there is my favorite part of the artistic healing process: the recording studio. This is the place where I get to build the idea and the sound, using the machinery to balance the original expression.

Even without the reward of distribution, just *making* a song is something I've always loved. And in the studio, I cherished the luxury of being able to keep doing it until it was right. The input of musicians, producers, and engineers was like having professional ears attached to personal friends who knew how to translate my sometimes sketchy ideas. I'd walk in with a piece of paper that had some words and chord changes written on it, and a few or several hours later, I'd emerge with a full cast of musical characters who'd come together in the desire to "say" something aural and let it be heard by millions (hopefully) of people.

Today, I'm in love with what I can create outside myself—something that doesn't involve my appearance—like painting, drawing, sketching, sewing, interior design, writing, playing piano for my own amusement, good con-versation, philosophy, spirituality, just lying around, thinking. And since professional recording is presently a thing of my past, instead of music, I now use color in the form of pastels to show how I think and feel.

Because I only do a drawing once, each piece is an expression of how I am at that point in time. Kinko's can take care of repetition if it's needed or warranted. Anyway, I consider performing rock and roll to be a young person's game. Old farts leaping around, trying to hang on to their flapping skin, is not an uplifting experience for me, either to watch or perform. There are certain kinds of performances that simply don't lend themselves to wrinkles. Like hard rock.

With classical music, it doesn't matter how old you are. The formal, sit-down attire combined with the music itself makes it appropriate for an aging ensemble. But hard rock? Picture spandex on Ted Koppel, or Newt Gingrich behind a drum set. Hideous, right?

That doesn't mean I think everybody over the age of thirty ought to give up; it's just *my* take on the situation. If you don't mind geriatric rock, that's fabulous. It'll buy Grace Slick a home in Saint-Tropez if you continue to show up at concerts in throngs of thousands and give up your forty dollars a head to listen to a fifty-eight-year-old woman say, "Up against the wall, motherfucker."

That was okay in 1969. But would you buy that *now?* Maybe I could be the first rocker to have a bedpan roadie, an oxygen unit onstage between songs, a change of Depends, and a Count the Liver Spots contest, or . . .

Give rock and roll back to the kids, and make sound-track instrumentals like a good old rascal.

That's my opinion of geriatric guys making music. So what about listening to it? At first, in 1990, when I stopped the business end of rock and roll, it was hard to turn on the radio without being heavily judgmental: "If only the bass were louder, the harmony is off, put echo on that screechy voice, turn down the top end," and on and on.

I couldn't seem to just *listen*. But after a while, I was able to enjoy music without getting my "professional opinion" all over it. Today, I like listening to the radio because they play things I'd never hear unless someone else was making up the playlist. If I solely listened to my own tapes, it would be Gipsy Kings over and over. Radio gets me out of my own rut. But if I had Bill Gates's cash, I'd hire a guy to wander around beside me, playing flamenco music on a daily basis. It wouldn't just be a rut, it would be Iberian overkill—*España locura me* ("Spain crazy I am").

I won't say a final no to ever making music again. I have trouble saying no to anything, but if I decided to perform again, it wouldn't be in the same context as I've done for the last thirty years. Maybe a hellish little set at the Shady Pines nursing home would be in order. Me and Martha Stewart on cocaine doing a Sid Vicious lullaby. Vocals without music, spoons beating on bedpans.

It *could* happen.

Let me clarify my point. If you're a woman who's over fifty and have had no plastic surgery, put a mirror flat on the floor beneath you, take off all your clothes, and try getting down on all fours. One quick glance at the mirror will show you how the woman-on-top position looks to your partner. Gravity has pulled your sagging skin into the terrible folds of a Shar-Pei dog, your features are distorted by the inevitable droop, and your ego accurately tells you, "That's not who I am!" In the spiritual sense, all that floppy meat is *not* you, but in a physical sense, we *do* have eyes, and that reflection in the mirror is hard to dismiss with a load of cosmic platitudes.

Black comedy: the wiser you get on the inside, the uglier you get on the outside. People who're trying to be polite, or simply displaying a lot of denial about aging, will say, "Yes, but she has that glow that makes her lovely." True, a happy gramma looks slightly better than a morose old woman, but ugly is ugly.

Not good or bad, just flat-out ugly.

Some of the world's great gurus have beautiful things to say about living, but they generally look like shit. You may have seen them, the toothless degenerating fat old monks with acceptance written all over them. Do we love them? Sure. Are their bodies attractive? No.

And another thing—why is it that Cher and I are the only nonpracticing comediennes who've admitted to thoroughly disliking the physical aspect of aging? It's not going to make me do any cliff-diving, but I'd prefer to look as good as I feel. I'm not going to don the flowered chiffon dresses that are considered appropriate for a woman my age, but I'm not piercing my body parts to be au courant, either.

The trouble is that the Ruth Gordon–type character is much beloved if she's seventy-five or eighty, but fifty to sixty is a midrange, with no discernible margin for eccentricity (without looking like a nut case). Think of any fifty-five-year-old woman you know. Is she exhibiting outlandish attire or behavior? This age group that I'm now a part of is a peculiarly conservative group, unwilling or unable to jump out of its own self-inflicted rigidity. We run companies, dress acceptably, and pander to our children's concepts of who they want us to be. We're chattel who've

"Return to Sender" (Grace Slick)

crawled back into the brittle dialectic handed down by our parents.

Myself, until I figure out a personal, creative alternative to body piercing, I'll continue to persist in the anonymity and comfort of sweatpants, and I'll be just another slob at the supermarket, picking up a six-pack of V8. The Joan

Collins getups take too much time, and unless there's a point or a reward, I'm not interested in spending hours every day at a makeup table or in my closet, choosing the right outfits. It isn't worth it; the best response Joan can hope for is, "My, she looks good *for her age*." That's not enough of a reaction to get me rooting around at Neiman Marcus. However, if men suddenly got seriously enamored of old broads, that might be enough of an incentive for me to play with my credit cards. Since that probably won't happen, who cares? Dressing for other women (my Chanel is better than your Donna Karan) is what's left for the old-timers. Men could care less what a sixty-year-old woman is wearing.

All that said, it may be that there's a method to the madness—a *point* to aging and the deterioration that comes with it. The Buddhists have proposed a loose block of time frames and the appropriate conduct to be carried out in each stage of life:

The first—from birth to the age of twenty—
is the learning time, when we're taught by elders about
the social and intellectual ways of our own particular
culture.

The second—between the ages of twenty and forty—
is the time of action. We have our babies and make our
way in the world, caring for the very young and very
old, making "right livelihood."

The third—between the ages of forty and sixty—
is a shift into study and inquiry. We amass information
and prepare for the next phase.

The fourth—from the age of sixty on—
is a gentle time of going inside, learning to laugh at the
poignant struggle of everything in form, and listening
for the call to transition.

Ram Dass, a spiritual teacher whom I greatly admire,
took care of his father in the final stages of his life. Relatives would come to visit in the hospital, put on a happy
face for the old man, then go out in the hall and say, "He's
not like he used to be. He's so quiet—he just sits there
looking out the window." They were used to the gruff,
driven, aggressive tycoon he *used* to be. But Ram Dass said,
"I've never felt so close to my father. I take care of his needs
and we just sit there quietly, appreciating the scenery and
enjoying each other in a way we were never able to do
when our goals were so polarized." His father was turning
inward, becoming reflective, and waiting, with no particular attitude, to die.

The opportunity to "go out" by closing down peacefully
is almost as good as just going to sleep one night and not
waking up. (Although "waking up" on a spiritual level is
exactly what we might be doing at that point, according to
some theologians.) I'm not interested in leaving the Earth
just yet, but there are compelling reasons for working *with*
the loss of the senses rather than against it.

For starters, when your hearing and sight fail, that's the
perfect time for meditation. There are no distractions and
mobility is limited—it's a good time to sit in meditation
practice, slowly getting used to being spirit without form.
Sounds like a hard thing to do if you're busy hanging on to
who you *used* to be. But we *do* have choices. We can go nuts
over not being able to go bowling any more, swallow some

Drano and get it over with, or relax into the silence and touch places we missed when we were so busy yelling "Strike!" the other realms of being simply escaped our attention. I like to think I'll take the latter path. The high road, so to speak.

Then again, when the time comes, I might freak out and demand to be hooked up to every prosthetic device known to man: industrial-strength hearing aids, synthetic corneas, a plastic gall bladder, morphine and vitamin IV drips, a Mae West jacket, a Maserati wheelchair, a colon bypass uplink—the whole robot kit strapped onto my rotting frame.

It's not a pretty picture, but the entertainment value has enormous possibilities.

53

Dropping the Body

Weight loss? Yup, the bodiless person can pretty much certify his diet has been one hundred percent successful. Westerners generally call it "passing on" or "passing over" or "deceased" or "he's history" or "he's dust." There are endless euphemisms for that four-letter word, DEAD.

Maybe all the linguistic contortions aimed at denying the reality of death are rooted in disbelief that some people who have particularly powerful and charismatic personalities can actually cease to exist.

Bill Graham, who "owned" a hundred yards of whatever space he was in, was one of those people. He was an animated fifty-foot action figure, a mammoth supertoy who was able to consolidate, cajole, entertain, listen, roar, and make mistakes with a larger-than-life burst of energy. At his funeral in 1993, at Temple Emmanuel in San Francisco, a sad but familial spirit permeated the huge temple. The place was filled with people who, along with their grief, were also feeling grateful to have known such a wonderful character who could expand himself for charity, for friends, and for raging anger—all in equal proportions. Ordinarily, I don't like funerals, but the atmosphere at his was unusually harmonious. It featured none of the embarrassingly morbid formalities that turn most funerals into acts of showy bathos.

When someone dies, many of us feel bad that the person's opportunity to enjoy more of life's pleasures has been cut off. But many of us are also sharply reminded of our own mortality, and *that* is the biggest fear—and the biggest mystery of all. All the religions have a story link about the "hereafter." Atheists consider you stupid if you think of death as anything other than *the end,* and most people don't know exactly what to think except that they don't like it. We're programmed to seek survival, and the medical profession considers death a failure.

The French have a phrase, *petit mort,* which means "little death." It's most often used in conjunction with post-orgasmic malaise. The ennui or resolution of passion after sex is kind of relaxing and pleasant to me, so I'm not sure why they call it *petit mort.* But I do like the phrase as a way to describe other events or emotions that don't involve actually stepping up to the spirit world. When people lie to you, it's a little death—the death of trust. When you fail to reach a goal, you feel *petit mort.* When a lover cheats, when a business folds, when a home is destroyed, when a friendship is ruined by anger or resentment—these are all little deaths, little pieces of your being slowly falling away into a grave of sadness. The loss either teaches you to persist in the face of suffering, or hardens you into a bitter cynic. Sometimes, it does a little of both.

I'm not thrilled by the idea of dying, but since I've had several strong experiences of déjà vu, I'm inclined to embrace the "theory" of reincarnation. I have such an affinity for all things Spanish, I feel I must have spent many lives in that country, as well as in California when it was under Spanish rule. Flamenco guitars, the Gipsy Kings— they move me in a way no other music has. I find it's not even a choice. It's not that I think things Spanish are better or worse than things derived from other cultures. It's just part of me somehow, and it's so powerful I can't ignore it.

One example of this mysterious Spanish connection at work occurred when I was watching a movie scene where they cut to a shot of the ocean. When they pulled back into an old church, I started crying because I knew, even before the narrator said where it was, that it was San Juan Capistrano. And I'd never been there. My tears were not about sadness; I believe they were in response to an overwhelming recognition of some previous experience I had while living on the once-Spanish coast of Southern California.

I'm not inclined to join cults or weird groups (other than rock-and-roll groups), so it's not in my nature to buy into goofy, Hale-Bopp comet stuff. But I do pay attention to things that have repeatedly reinforced their presence in my life. I don't care if other people believe what I'm experiencing. I'm not proselytizing for anything; it's simply a fact that supernatural phenomena—or at least, the hint of such phenomena—have played a strong part in my own life.

Agnosticism is probably the safest position from the point of spiritual debate. The universe is a metasystem, and we are a subsystem that can never completely know the full operation of the more complex metasystem. So when people tell me they know "how it is," I tend to view it as hubris. I have strong ideas about certain phenomena, but can they be proved? Of course not. How can I possibly know what incredible form of energy organized this cosmos, or exactly why the universe evolves as it does? But I can be pretty sure of one thing:

> *"It's all going the way it's supposed to be going.*
> *Otherwise, it would be going some other way."*
> —SANDY HARPER, 1978

Sandy is a normal guy I once met, who made that statement just before giving me several tapes by Ram Dass. Both men are gentle, searching individuals who seem to be as comfortable as the animals with "the way it is."

When I look carefully, the physical *pain* of dying is what I fear more than the actual death itself. And then, pride enters into it, too. I don't want the mailman to show up one day and discover a bloated, gassy mess with a rictus grimace. The poised sleeping beauty pose would be nifty, but since it's too late for that, a more artistic alternative has occurred to me. The following is in no way a death wish. I like life just fine, but when the time comes, my favorite way of dying would be by . . .

EXPLOSION—all over white walls!

I would initially swallow a tiny pill—unfortunately they haven't invented it yet, but imagine it's on a timer. Maybe the duration would be fifteen seconds, just so there's not too much time to think about it. When the thing explodes, I'll be pulverized into so many millions of tiny pieces, nobody will be able to identify me. I'll simply be all over the place, splattered on the walls, the ceiling, the floor, the furniture. And the fragments will be so minuscule, the effect won't be the slightest bit disgusting. You won't be able to identify my brains from my liver from my heart from my fingernails. There'll just be reddish, bluish, yellowish colors all over the place. Body colors. Then you can cover the whole thing with Verathane to preserve it as a one-room art piece. The ultimate art piece. Too bad Andy Warhol is gone; I know he could have gotten into it.

My last idiotic contribution to humankind.

My only stumbling block is the pill. Somebody needs to invent it. If a medical scientist reads this and is interested in getting involved, you know who to contact. Good old Rick.

Until then, concentration on living in balance seems to be the ticket, so I intend to continue my artistic pursuits by drawing and writing because it makes me feel at peace and alive. During this year, 1997, as Andrea and I are writing this book, so many people who've contributed to the happiness of the world have died in just the two months of August and September. It's a grouping of losses that seems to ask all of us to rethink our own priorities, to appreciate rather than deprecate, to enjoy, to laugh, to help, and to try to get to our own truth. A spiritual teacher, Stephen Levine, reminds us: "Live like it's your last year of life."

54

A Few Closing Words

I see this life as a portrait that is mine to manifest in my own way, a universe of pictures we trade with each other as kids trade baseball cards. And on the other hand, if information comes through that renders that concept ineffective, I'm going to have to swallow either my pride or a bowl of battery acid and get over myself.

Do I contradict myself? Of course. When the evidence comes in that I've constructed yet another house of cards that's about to fall (unless I start over and construct a different foundation), what am I going to do—stand under all that crumbling plastic-covered paper and try to hold it up?

So what are *you* doing with *your* empty canvas? Here's what *I've* done with mine, and I'll continue to change it as the opportunity arises.

Looking backward or forward is easier than looking in the mirror *right now* to determine who I am. The image is crowded with past perceptions and tantalized by future possibilities. All I can say for sure is that at the moment, I'm living in a house in Malibu, painting life and wondering about death, being enchanted by the beauty of this land by the ocean, watching time carve lines in my face and hands, running up long-distance phone bills to my friends spread across the country, turning up the heat in the pool for my thin-skinned friends here in L.A., getting to know and love my cowriter, wishing my mom and dad could come and stay in my peaceful house, hoping my daughter enjoys the "trip," and waiting for the next curveball to come sliding out of the Master Pitcher's mysterious south paw.

Will I get back into the music business? Not unless Mark Isham calls up and says he has a title track that requires a singer with the vocal range of a four-ton frog.

Will I get married again? No, I still feel married to Skip Johnson, and besides, Timothy Leary's dead.

I love that the changes keep surprising me, that we're given the palette of colors at birth and the majority of images are ours to create.

Life, the constantly mutating funeral party.

Do I have anything I'd like to say in closing?

YES.

DISCOGRAPHY 1966–1995

JEFFERSON AIRPLANE

Jefferson Airplane Takes Off (RCA, 1966)
Surrealistic Pillow (RCA, 1967)
After Bathing at Baxter's (RCA, 1967)
Crown of Creation (RCA, 1968)
Volunteers (RCA, 1969)
Bark (Grunt, 1971)
Long John Silver (Grunt, 1972)
Early Flight (Grunt, 1974)
Jefferson Airplane (Epic, 1989)

Live Albums

Bless Its Pointed Little Head (RCA, 1969)
Woodstock (Cotillion, 1970)
Woodstock Two (Cotillion, 1971)
Thirty Seconds over Winterland (Grunt, 1973)
Live at the Monterey Festival (Thunderbolt, 1990)
Monterey International Pop Festival Volume 3 (Rhino, 1992)
Woodstock—25th Anniversary Collection (Atlantic, 1994)

367

Compilations

The Worst of Jefferson Airplane (RCA, 1970)
Flight Log (Grunt, 1977)
2400 Fulton Street (RCA, 1987)
White Rabbit and Other Hits (RCA, 1990)
Jefferson Airplane Loves You (RCA, 1992)
Best Of (RCA, 1993)

JEFFERSON STARSHIP

Dragon Fly (RCA, 1974)
Red Octopus (Grunt, 1975)
Spitfire (Grunt, 1976)
Earth (Grunt, 1978)
Freedom at Point Zero (Grunt, 1979)
Modern Times (RCA, 1981)
Winds of Change (Grunt, 1982)
Nuclear Furniture (RCA, 1984)

Live Albums

Deep Space/Virgin Sky (Intersound, 1995)

Compilations

Gold (Grunt, 1979)
At Their Best (RCA, 1992)

STARSHIP

Knee Deep in the Hoopla (RCA, 1985)
No Protection (RCA, 1987)
Love among the Cannibals (RCA, 1989)

Compilations

Greatest Hits (Ten Years and Change, 1979–1991)
   (RCA, 1991)

PAUL KANTNER & JEFFERSON STARSHIP

Blows against the Empire (RCA, 1970)

PAUL KANTNER & GRACE SLICK

Sunfighter (Grunt, 1971)

PAUL KANTNER, GRACE SLICK, & DAVID FREIBERG

Baron Von Tollbooth and the Chrome Nun (Grunt, 1973)

GRACE SLICK

Manhole (Grunt, 1973)
Dreams (RCA, 1980)
Welcome to the Wrecking Ball (RCA, 1981)
Software (RCA, 1984)